HARPER FORUM BOOKS

Martin E. Marty, *General Editor*

SOCIAL ETHICS

Issues in Ethics and Society

HARPER FORUM BOOKS

Martin E. Marty, *General Editor*

Published:

IAN G. BARBOUR
SCIENCE AND RELIGION: New Perspectives on the Dialogue

A. ROY ECKARDT
THE THEOLOGIAN AT WORK: A Common Search for Understanding

JOHN MACQUARRIE
CONTEMPORARY RELIGIOUS THINKERS: From Idealist Metaphysicans to Existential Theologians

GIBSON WINTER
SOCIAL ETHICS: Issues in Ethics and Society

Forthcoming: 1968

JAMES M. GUSTAFSON & JAMES LANEY
ON BEING RESPONSIBLE: Issues in Personal Ethics

EDWIN SCOTT GAUSTAD
RELIGIOUS ISSUES IN AMERICAN HISTORY

SAMUEL SANDMEL
OLD TESTAMENT ISSUES

SOCIAL
ETHICS:

Issues in Ethics and Society

edited by

Gibson Winter

1817

HARPER & ROW, PUBLISHERS

NEW YORK, EVANSTON, AND LONDON

Published as a Harper Forum Book, 1968, by Harper & Row, Publishers, Incorporated, New York, Evanston, and London.

LIBRARY OF CONGRESS CATALOG CARD NUMBER: 68-11746

With appreciation to

ROBERT W. TERRY

ARTHUR PRY

BARBARA STUHR

CONTENTS

HARPER FORUM BOOKS

Often dismissed with a shrug or accepted with thoughtless piety in the past, religion today belongs in the forum of study and discussion. In our society, this is particularly evident in both public and private colleges and universities. Scholars are exploring the claims of theology, the religious roots of culture, and the relation between beliefs and the various areas or disciplines of life. Students have not until now had a series of books which could serve as reliable resources for class or private study in a time when inquiry into religion is undertaken with new freedom and a sense of urgency. *Harper Forum Books* are intended for these purposes. Eminent scholars have selected and introduced the readings. Respectful of the spirit of religion as they are, they do not shun controversy. With these books a new generation can confront religion through exposure to significant minds in theology and related humanistic fields.

MARTIN E. MARTY, GENERAL EDITOR
The Divinity School
The University of Chicago

INTRODUCTION

Religion, Ethics, and Society

IT is difficult to represent the field of social ethics with a few readings. The alternative is to collect many short readings and miss the substantial issues. This volume opts for a few complete essays on crucial issues. If the reader can get a clear grasp of the nature of the field and a method for coping with problems of social order, the volume will have served its purpose.

No attempt has been made to sample the range of issues and perspectives in social ethics, and with a few exceptions even classical essays in the field have been scanted. The essays in the volume were selected for their adequacy in dealing with facts pertaining to the issues, clarity about relevant norms of evaluation, and explicitness of the religious perspective. Thus, three elements—factual descriptions, evaluative norms, and religious perspectives (interpreting religion in the broadest sense)—formed the criteria for selection of essays. Various religious and philosophical perspectives are represented. Different views of the relationship between religion and morality are included. A plurality of views of social ethics are to be found in the volume. The unifying focus is the problem of social order.

THE ORIGINS OF SOCIAL ETHICS

Social ethics is a very old discipline.[1] Man is a social being whose existence is organized in communities. Reflections on the rightness of these communal arrangements, however rudimen-

3

tary, are social ethics in embryo. However, social organization has been relatively stable through most of human history (allowing for periods of revolution and upheaval); that is, societies assumed that their social order had existed from time immemorial; they applied the rules rather than questioning them. Changes did, in fact, occur, but change was usually interpreted as proper application of tradition. This traditional mind prevailed much less, of course, in the high period of Greek culture, although even in that era a relatively stable patterning of life was taken for granted. In stable societies, social ethics clarified the given order and explicated the principles on which that order rested.[2]

If we are careful not to overstate this stability in earlier social orders (all societies have gone through changes, however gradual), we can argue that complex, high-technology societies have accelerated the rate of change in social organization, bringing into question many social patterns which had been relatively stable over centuries, and stimulating basic ethical considerations. Concern over a "new" sexual morality, reconsideration of grounds for divorce, proposals for a guaranteed income, to mention only a few issues, give some sense of the changes occurring in our society. Hence, social ethics attains a qualitatively new significance in contemporary society. In fact, the emergence of the sciences of man can be attributed to the changes experienced in the nineteenth century under the impact of science, industry, and emerging technology. The sciences of man developed in close association with reflections on problems of moral order. We now take the social sciences for granted, but the idea that man would subject himself and his society to objective, scientific scrutiny is unusual, only gaining widespread acceptance with the emergence of technological society. (There were, of course, precedents for these developments in classical Greek culture.)

Although social ethics and social science emerged in the nineteenth century as integrally related inquiries, the sciences of man sought scientific status and gradually alienated their work from ethics. Ethics became an implicit element in social science.

There are signs that this long dissociation is open to reconsideration; however, the relative neutrality of scientific description has to be protected if a new integration of interests is to be achieved. The century has thus produced gains, since religious ethics is becoming clearer about the distinctions between religious, ethical, and scientific judgments, while the sciences of man have clarified and refined their methods. In brief, the time is ripe for new advances in the field of social ethics.

How are these disparate disciplines related in a single field of inquiry? Can scientific and evaluative concerns ever come together without destroying the objectivity of science and subverting the moral imperatives which are clarified by ethics? The essays in this volume furnish an interdisciplinary approach to problems of social order, integrating science, ethics, and theology with varying degress of success. We could, of course, let the essays speak for themselves. However, some reflections on basic questions of method may help to clarify the criteria of successful integration of the disciplines in resolving problems of social order. The following considerations should bring to light the major issues in social ethics: (1) the subject matter or problems of social ethics; (2) the practitioners of social ethics; (3) social ethics and social science; (4) religion and morality; (5) ethics and science in the formation of public policy.

PROBLEMS IN SOCIAL ETHICS

Most of us feel that we can identify moral problems. We think of such issues as keeping promises, telling the truth, respecting the rights and property of others, etc. However difficult it may be to work out the logic of such moral judgments (the language philosophers have helped considerably in trying to unravel these difficulties), the problems of a social ethic seem more complicated and obscure.[3] Why speak of social ethics at all, since ethics is always social—involving public standards and the interests of others. The word social is, to be sure, somewhat equivocal in this field of religion, ethics, and society. The term should really be societal, since it is the evaluation of societal organization and public policy in the shaping of society with which social ethics is concerned. If societal were not such an awkward term, we could more properly be considering problems in a societal ethic. In general, then, social ethics deals with issues of social order—good, right, and ought in the organization of human communities and the shaping of social policies. Hence the subject matter of social ethics is moral rightness and goodness in the shaping of human society.

The study of prejudice illustrates this view of social ethics. For some decades social scientists and ethicists have been concerned with problems of prejudice in American society, particularly anti-Semitism in the 1930's and 1940's and racial prejudice in the period after World War II. The problem of prejudice was approached for a long time in terms of attitudes.[4] There was an assumption that the ideal American was "unprejudiced," so that there was a protracted search for causes of the prejudiced personality. It became apparent after much research that personal attitudes were dependent upon status differences in the relationship between groups; meeting one group only in an inferior position would create or increase prejudice; hence, attitude and institutionalized relationships were interdependent. Generally, those who experienced relationships with members of other groups in relatively equal status situations came to see that group with less negative prejudice. Studies of public housing, for example, indicated that segregated public housing was associated with continuing, high levels of prejudice and mixed housing was associated with reductions in levels of prejudice. Studies of this type formed a backdrop for the Supreme Court decision in 1954 on the unconstitutionality of "separate but equal" in education—it was decided that "separate" entailed "unequal."

The nature of social ethics is exemplified in the problem of prejudice and the institutionalized relationships within a society; for one thing, the organization of the social relationships between groups can create, aggravate, or diminish feelings of prejudice; moreover, policy on a national or local level can aggravate or reduce prejudices which are damaging to persons and to the community at large. Personality is shaped by the communal relationships which it helps to create. This interdependence of person and community, personal good and societal order, is the subject matter for social ethical reflection. The studies of prejudice led to the recognition that the "unprejudiced person" does not exist. We all have prejudices. Some of them are damaging. These prejudices are constituted not only by personal needs and psychological difficulties but also by the communal contexts in which our values and expectations are shaped. Prejudice is a moral problem on the personal level; we *should* treat people according to their actions and not by our prejudice. But these problems cannot be separated from the occupational, educational, residential, and other communities in which men, women, and children experience their world. Our immorality is often the reflection of "the immoral society," and so with our morality. Concern with prejudice as a personal moral problem led to the recognition that it was first and foremost a problem of societal disorder.

Problems of moral order become conscious and explicit where difficulties are experienced. Our moral principles and rules are mostly hidden in the culture; we would be hard put to give an account of many of these principles. We take them for granted. They are the moral recipes for daily existence, as Alfred Schutz often noted. Our social existence is patterned by typical modes of acting and anticipating. Some expectations bear the moral weight of imperatives—reflected in value terms such as good, ought, should, must, and right. "We ought to repay loans." These imperatives, most of the time, constitute a taken-for-granted order in our social life.[5] In periods of rapid change and/or at points of difficulty and uncertainty (for example, when a group protests discrimination) they come up for reconsideration. These moments of evaluative consideration characterize moral reflection. They constitute ethical evaluation of social organization when the norms of personal community, educational process, economic production, international relationships, etc. are reconsidered.

Problems of social ethics are historical in that issues arise with social changes and cultural innovation. There is no once-and-for-all formulation of ethical imperatives in the organization of society. Certain ethical norms may have a long and continuing authority (individual liberty in the American experience), but the meaning changes with the developing character of man's social existence, especially in times of rapid social change. Even the most traditional societies change in social organization and in the order of social life, although that change may be barely perceptible and the sanctions for change are understood as an application of an unchanging tradition. Hence, social ethics is historically relative, dealing with issues which are appropriate to a time and situation, concerned with universal imperatives but as they bear on particular issues. This fact about social ethics makes the simple application of historical examples to contemporary problems relatively meaningless, even when those examples are drawn from holy texts. Certain norms and principles may be embedded in a sacred tradition, but the meaning of these principles will be radically altered in new contexts. This historical relativity of issues in social ethics and the shifting relevance of norms can be seen in this volume. A few decades ago such a source book would have included problems of labor and management and even further back a serious consideration of the justification of slavery. Now, if there had been available space and suitable materials, essays on the internationalization of space, the substitution of guaranteed income for earning, and the limitation of national sovereignty in a nuclear age would be appropriate. (At a time when new nations are following a nationalistic path, the high technology nations are demonstrating the limited value of the nation-state.) Social ethics is, thus, the continuing and daily business of man in his social existence; it seeks universals but works with the relativities of an historically conditioned situation.

THE SOCIAL ETHICISTS

The question arises as to who carries on social ethics, especially in a complex, high-technology society like our own. Social ethics, as we have described it, is the business of every reflective citizen, since problems of social order form the backdrop of our everyday existence and we all have responsibility for that order in a democratic society. On a practical level, we are all engaged in social ethics, though such considerations are more explicitly the work of legislators, judges, public officials and others who are responsible for public policy. Where issues of social order and public policy come to explicit attention, we are dealing with social ethics in the everyday world of common sense. Indeed, maintaining a democratic way of life in a complex society requires the broadening of knowledge and sensitivity to problems of social order among the citizenry. Media of communication should now make possible such a consciousness of choices confronting the society and the evaluative principles which are at stake, but the sheer complexity of massive organizations leads to the delegation of much of this consideration to administrators and managers who are not publicly accountable. In both instances, however, social ethical consideration is the stuff of daily life.

The essays in this volume are the products of social ethical consideration by religious and philosophical specialists who are at one remove from the practical involvement of well-informed citizens and political representatives. These ethicists are also engaged in society and concerned with moral outcomes to which they themselves are committed, but their stance is more theoretical, systematic, and generalized. Thus, the systematic social ethicist is doing the same kind of thing as the citizen or legislator; he is considering problems of practice and organization from an ethical perspective, but he has a commitment to clarity of concepts, to testing the logical consistency of evaluative statements and to developing the systematic unity of the discipline. (We shall speak from this point on about social ethicists in this systematic sense, recognizing the continuity of their practical involvement in a moral community with all members of that community). Systematic social ethics should be a resource for an informed citizenry and its public representatives, although a market for their products has yet to be developed. Social ethicists do not create the society's ethic. They bring it to light, pressing for consistency and evaluative warrants. They may innovate, of course, by reshaping evaluative meanings, but their reflection is embedded in the societal struggle for a human order. For example, much of the writing on problems of poverty and race relations has simply brought to light the inconsistency between our professed ideal of equal opportunity and the inequalities which various groups encounter.

The social ethicists in this volume represent various strands of religious tradition in the West. Their essays include descriptions of the situation, norms for evaluation, and interpretations of human fulfillment. They arrange these elements in different ways and develop them with varying degrees of explicitness. However, these three elements should be present, since an evaluation of social organization or policy implies some standard or norm; it also involves some account of the actual situation; it also involves a view of man and his fulfillment. These elements of social ethical consideration can be illustrated by further consideration of the studies of prejudice.

SOCIAL ETHICS AND SOCIAL SCIENCE

The social ethicist and the social scientist may both be interested in the problem of prejudice; however, the social ethicist considers the justice or injustice of prejudice and its effects, whereas the scientist investigates the social and cultural causes which create and perpetuate prejudice. If several problems of equal relevance are available to the social scientist, he may well choose the one which has more immediate ethical relevance, but he studies it in terms of social conditioning. The *evaluative* problem is decisive for the social ethicist and also determines his selection of problems.

Furthermore, in social ethics the evaluative concern is the leading consideration in the development of the factual inquiry. In taking up the problem of segregated education, for example, the social ethicist is concerned with the justice of the educational process—its embodiment or subversion of values such as freedom, social equality, and personal dignity; the ethicist is also concerned with the effects of educational experiences on human aspirations and on participation in the total cultural enterprise of man. Hence, he evaluates education within the total meaning of societal fulfillment. To be sure, the social scientist is concerned with all of these things as citizen and as man, possibly more deeply concerned than the ethicist, but *as scientist* these evaluative concerns are not decisive. The theoretical problems of his field lead the social scientist to inquire into such matters as the effects of segregated educational schemes on personal attitudes, sense of self-worth, motivation to achieve, success and failure in educational attainments, etc. He is likewise concerned with the impact of economic, social and political arrangements on human communities. In each case he clarifies the ways in which particular social patterns shape the possibilities of human fulfillment. To him *as* scientist the evaluative issue is secondary but his studies of social conditioning and its consequences are indispensable to the evaluative task.

Although the ethicist is guided in defining his problem by an evaluative concern, he is dependent upon knowledge of the factual situation; he too needs to know what is the case. The ethicist has the problem of clarifying and grounding the imperatives which are relevant to the particular issue; he also has to delineate characteristics that mark the embodiment or subversion of these imperatives in particular social arrangements. The social ethicist may feel that he has completed his task by asserting that education should be carried on under conditions of equality, since equality is an accepted moral principle. However, the conditions of equality have to be made clear before an effective social policy can be developed. Does equality include housing or only classroom time, etc.? Hence, the social ethicist has to develop criteria to designate the presence of a value and investigate the actual state of affairs where studies are not available.

The specification of conditions to be met for the realization of an imperative may be carried through by the ethicist or the policy-maker; however, the descriptive task of social ethics is indispensable. In most cases, the ethicist discovers the imperative in exploring ethical issues, clarifying it as he comes to understand the situation and devising appropriate policies in the course of his inquiry. Hence our distinctions are logical; we find both ethicists and scientists exploring social conditions and making evaluations.

The social ethicist is first an ethicist but inescapably a social scientist or consumer of social science. During this long period of alienation between social science and social ethics, ethicists have been dependent upon scientific studies—many of them peripheral to the basic issues with which ethicists were concerned, studies pursued with methods which sometimes obscured evaluative concerns. A rapprochement of ethics and social science will make available scientific research on issues where the ethical concern is paramount. The objective, scientific considerations are in no way slighted when the evaluative concern is primary; the descriptive generalizations of science are needed by the ethicist in discerning the problems of moral order. In turn, many of the implicit evaluations and ethical concerns of the social scientists can be clarified and enriched through collaborative research.

RELIGION AND MORALITY

The relationship between religious concerns and ethical evaluation is even more troubling than that between social science and ethics. The transformed world view of our society has unsettled many dogmatic positions 'which undergirded religious ethics in the past; we still encounter theories of natural law, but they seem alien. Moreover, the changes in social organization which created our urgent ethical problems have brought into question the ethical positions which were fused with our religious heritage. Even as the society gropes for moral foundations, the religious heritage itself is in question. This was the moral dilemma of Europe in the nineteenth century. It is now confronting the ethicists on the American scene. They are asking what, if anything, religion has to do with ethics.

Recent philosophic discussion has clarified the relative autonomy of moral discourse, elucidating the difference between moral justifications and statements of fact, whether the latter be statements about nature or supernature. A moral imperative cannot be generated from an indicative statement, whether that statement be about matters of fact or about a transcendent order. This is one set of problems besetting the essays in this volume. Religious ethics has often justified ethical norms by making assertions about a transcendent order or divine will. Actually, religious ethics has scanted the whole question of ethical warrant; certain traditional value terms such as freedom, equality, and participation have been assumed or a general principle of love was asserted. These values and/or the ethic of love are ingredients of the Western tradition; they furnish imperatives for the evaluation of social policies. Where religious ethics follows this line, little or no attention is given to problems of justifying the ethical imperatives. Where religious statements about ultimate reality are introduced to justify such imperatives, some serious category problems need to be worked out.

To recognize the distinction between religious and moral modes of reflection and discourse is a first step toward clarifying the relationship between religion and morality. The distinction affirms that a moral argument requires an ethical premise or it is not a moral argument. When we grant the autonomy of ethical argument, we may still place the problem of social order within a more inclusive order of ultimate reality. The religious ethicist, as we interpret his work, takes this view; he treats the claims of justice and benevolence as imperatives, but he sets these imperatives within an ultimate order which is antecedent to the human enterprise and lures that enterprise beyond any achieved goods. Symbols such as the Kingdom of God would thus "qualify" the moral order by relativizing its absolute claims and summoning men to more inclusive human communities.

The religious traditions of the West have usually founded man's commitments to the moral order in one of three ways: (1) they have affirmed the ultimate nature of the moral order as divine law; or (2) they have stressed a transcendent will in history, pointing to a highest moral principle such as love; or (3) they have conceived the social order as a restraint on human sin, finding forgiveness in divine grace and real hope in transhistorical salvation. There are, of course, varieties of natural law, divine will, and salvationist views, as is evident in the essays, but, in each case, the religious symbols point to the ultimate seriousness of man's moral struggle. Thus, religion confirms man's moral struggle.

"Religion also copes with problems which are internal to morality. Morality always points beyond itself, although moral questions may be pursued without engaging in reflection on ultimates. Freedom, self-awareness, and self-transcendence are presupposed by morality and point beyond morality. In positing the question of the good, man also posits his power to doubt the good and the obligations in which he has been reared. He can even extend his doubt to the meaning of the moral enterprise itself, coming to see his freedom as absurdity. In every case, the foreclosure of doubt with a commitment to a moral community or the rational grounding of a moral imperative means that the ethical enterprise has founded itself in an ultimate commitment which it cannot justify. (We have noted the ultimate concern which religion brings to morality.) Moreover, the inconsistency between our moral intentions and our conduct leaves us with guilt which no moral order can redeem. Further, the consequences of social immorality are felt by victims who are innocent, littering our history with tragedies which discredit the moral enterprise. Such problems form the "religious" backdrop of the existential question in social ethics. Interpreting religion in the broadest sense as man's ultimate concern, we can affirm that morality raises questions of guilt and tragedy which it cannot contain.

No argument is made here that anyone *has* to make a religious commitment in order to be moral. Much of our moral action is habitual—grounded in our early family experience. Radical reflection in social ethics, nevertheless, reaches beyond the moral to ultimate questions—pressing the problem of faith or doubt. In this respect, the religious dimension of experience (however understood) constitutes the ultimate horizon of our ethical considerations, shaping our moral commitment and understanding through ultimate trust or skepticism. Thus, religion qualifies the moral imperative with its ultimate vision, while sustaining the relative autonomy of the moral order. Man's moral possibilities and problems are founded in his freedom. They cease to be moral if they are grounded elsewhere than in this freedom. However, freedom points man to problems of reality in which both freedom and morality are disclosed as absurd or ultimately significant. At this point of intersection, the moral question of meaning presses toward a religious answer. By the same token, man's moral awareness, challenges his religious symbols and his views of divine goodness in an evil world. These spheres are not isolated.

Social Ethics and Policy

Moral reflection seeks to illumine our choices on moral problems. Reflection in social ethics has a similar function in the development of public policy. Thus, decision-making and policy give focus to the various elements of moral consideration. The social ethicist has a limited but useful task in this total picture; he cultivates the practical integrity of the society by challenging its inequities and bringing moral considerations to bear on its policies. Practice in the society is the material of his reflections, even as practice is the aim of his work. Social ethics is a practical discipline.

Different perspectives on social ethics organize social ethical consideration in different ways. Three elements have been identified in social ethics: the factual situation (which could be called societal conditions[6]); the evaluative norms (which could be called the ethical order); and the ultimate or comprehensive order (which could be called the religious vision). Different perspectives on social ethics are ways of organizing these three elements—social conditions, evaluative norms, and religious vision. Each perspective makes one of these elements decisive in its view of man.

One approach to ethics stresses the survival of the society—

its conditions of existence. For such an ethic, policy is good when it conduces to the survival and development of the society; ethical norms are regulative, reflecting the stage of development of the society in coping with problems. This is what Max Weber called an ethic of responsibility, meaning by this an ethic of effects or consequences; in his view, the role of science was to increase the society's grasp of the consequences of action and thus its accountability to social consequences.[7] Man is the evolving problem-solver. The ethic of self-interest which Reinhold Niebuhr developed has affinities with this approach, although he qualified the ethic of survival through his notion of reason and general interest. Religious ethicists are usually unsympathetic with such an ethic of social adaptation, whereas most social scientists embody in their social theories an ethic of adaptation or equilibrium. These implicit views of human fulfillment become explicit in the development of policy, since policy projects a social order into the future with an implicit view that it is the best or most practical course of action.

An ethic of absolute values or natural law organizes the three major elements around the ethical order. The conditions of societal survival are treated as limiting conditions, but the normative order is violated when survival takes precedence over rightness and goodness. Man is understood as the moral being. The American perspective has been too pragmatic to entertain such a categorical ethic. This view has its roots in a Kantian tradition and finds its way into our theological texts through the influence of European theology. We also find a modified expression of such an ethic in the natural law tradition of Roman Catholic ethics (see the encyclicals in this volume) and in some of the work of Paul Ramsey (included in this volume). In addition to these religious expressions of the priority of ethical order in social policy, pacifists and sectarians have stressed a legalistic ethic as the organizing principle of morality and society (not represented in this volume). Whereas the pragmatic perspective treats survival of the society as the fulfillment of man, the ethical formalists see conforming to moral order as the expression of man's nature and fulfillment; in religious terms. God creates through ordering whether in universal laws or particular edicts, and man finds fulfillment in obedience to that order.

A third way of organizing the elements of social ethics lifts up the relationship to Being or ultimate reality, seeing man as ultimate concern for Being. This perspective relativizes the ethical order. Man's fulfillment has usually been expressed in the West by a principle of love. The ethical order of justice then becomes regulative, limiting man's waywardness with ethical boundaries. However, true ethics flows from Being, as in "Love and then what you will, do."[8] Societal survival sets limiting conditions for the realization of the vision but is not decisive. This Augustinian tradition in religious ethics has had increasing vogue in the radical writing on contextual ethics.[9] By contrast, Reinhold Niebuhr and Paul Tillich (in this volume) demonstrate the centrality of religious vision in a *systematic* relation to ethical order and conditions of survival.

These basic perspectives on man are evident in the shaping of policy; here the priorities have to be stated. Each perspective organizes all three elements around its view of man. In prescriptions for policy, we see the constitutive principles of an ethic —what counts in man's fulfillment—survival, moral conformity or ultimate loyalty. These elements have to be organized in policy; hence, there can be no neutral or value-free analysis of public policy. Policy leads to action, and action involves commitment. To this extent, the sciences of man, the ethical systems, and the religious perspectives disclose evaluative commitments as they move from reflection to recommendations for policy. Social ethics is, thus, the expression of ultimate commitments in the shaping of man's future, embodying a view of man and his fulfillment in concrete recommendations for public policy.

I

Associational Community

THE following essays are grouped by communities of interest and power—associational, economic, political, and global. These are major communities which develop in high-technology societies. Several other communities could have been included, such as scientific, legal, artistic, and religious communities, but for the limited task of this volume the simpler grouping should be sufficient. From associational to global is a movement from more private to more public, from more voluntary to more compulsory, from more personal to more objective communities.

In the perspective which informs this volume, every social experience has a public character. However, the distance between private and public increases as one moves from associational to global communities, with the consequent tendency for stereotypes of other persons and groups to become more pervasive and controlling in the larger communal contexts. Personal encounters may always cut through these typifications, as in student exchange programs between countries, but the stereotype goes almost unchecked beyond the limited context of associational communities.

The transition from more private to more public requires an increase of objective specification of rights, duties and sanctions. Where personal sanctions cannot control actions either because personal encounters are too rare or because the relationships

21

are too indirect, as in political representation, the limitations on force and fraud have to be explicit and legally enforceable. The global community barely exists as a community with common cultural expectations, even though technology is creating such a community. On this global level, men have experienced disastrous conflicts and annihilations which become possible when stereotypes dehumanize and limits on force are lacking. The press toward global community and world order thus becomes part of the unfinished business of human organization.

The first section deals with more personal and voluntary relationships. The social ethic of these associational communities is rather well developed. Only two issues were selected for this volume; however, these are crucial questions in a changing society. The selections from *Towards a Quaker View of Sex* give the thesis of the group, but the whole booklet should be read to catch the sense of freedom which informs this work. The Quaker essay could well have been titled, "Toward a *Human* View of Sex," where human means moral in the true sense. Paul Ramsey's critique of this Quaker view is included because Ramsey brings out the problems which arise in Christian ethics which stress decision and action without reference to the rules that can guide conduct. This distinction is clarified at the end of Ramsey's essay (the concluding section could well be read first in order to clarify the point he is making). Ideals and rules on sexuality are seriously in question today. Sexuality is a more private affair. In tribal society it is political as well as communal. This shift toward the private involves a new ethic which is only in the making. The Quaker Group sees this. Perhaps Paul Ramsey sees it. Both Ramsey and the Quaker Group look for help in an ethic of responsibility; for Ramsey, responsibility means taking the rules seriously in the sphere of sex; for the Quakers, responsibility is first taking one's relationship to the other person seriously. (Note that Paul Ramsey's references are drawn from the original and not the Revised Edition; however, the Friends come down on the quality of the personal relationship and Ramsey is insisting that this quality, which he also affirms, has to be specified in rules.)

"Segregation and the Right to Being" by Kyle Haselden is in some ways an unusual selection in view of the massive literature emerging on race and civil rights. Nevertheless, this brief statement identifies the moral question that is at the root of the long struggle over segregation—the right to belong. This is the right which segregation violates according to Haselden. It is a right which is mediated in society and founded in divine order. Clinton Gardner's essay has similar theological roots, but Gardner brings out the problems of integrating the Christian principle of love and the ethical order of justice. Salvationist views have appealed to the principle of love as an alternative to justice, thus rejecting the kind of moral right to which Haselden appeals in his critique of segregation. The ethic of love suffers such ambiguity because it is transmoral as well as moral, reaching sacrificially beyond the just due of moral order. Gardner tries to guard against the disjunction of love and justice by stressing the *more than moral* rather than *less than moral* quality of love.

by a Group of Friends

A NEW MORALITY NEEDED

from *Towards a Quaker View of Sex*

THE CHURCH AND SEXUALITY

IT will be relevant at this point to refer to the history of the Church's attitude to sexuality throughout the centuries, and to elements in that attitude that seem inconsistent with some of the deepest insights in the Bible.

Throughout nearly all its history and in some sections of the Church today, the myth of Adam and Eve (called without justification the Fall of Man)[1] is treated as though it were historical fact on which logical arguments can be built. In this way, sexuality came to be regarded as necessarily polluted with sin in that event. Even when rejected as historical fact, this myth still has its effect upon the attitude of some Christians to sexuality; it will therefore be wise to think more about it. First, this, like other myths, had an earlier Babylonian origin and was used for religious purposes by the Jewish teachers. Further, like all myths, it is a poetic and symbolic representation of the condi-

Reprinted from *Towards a Quaker View of Sex,* Alastair Heron, ed. (rev. ed.; London: Friends Home Service Committee, Friends House, 1964), excerpt comprising Chaps. IV and V (pp. 43-56). By permission. The GROUP OF FRIENDS who carried on the discussions resulting in this volume are: Kenneth C. Barnes, Anna M. Bidder, Richard Fox, G. Joyce James, Kenneth Nicholson, Mervyn Parry, Lotte Rosenberg, Alfred Torrie, Keith B. Wedmore.

tion and predicament of man. It is not exclusively or even primarily concerned with sexuality. It is a myth representing the transition of man, either in his racial history (phylogenesis) or his development from babyhood (ontogenesis) from an unreflective obedience to instinct to a condition in which he is responsible for his actions, in which he can reflect on them and make judgments and moral choices, weighing up possible courses of action in the light of a concept of good and evil.

It is a story, not of man's fall, but of man's growing up, and of the pain that growing up involves. It is significant that God is recorded as saying (*Gen.* 3, v. 22): "Behold, the man is become as *one of us,* to know good and evil." To recognize and love what is good is to know also what is evil, to fear it and to be tempted by it. To know the good is to know joy, but it is also to experience pain, to be tempted to pride and presumption.

It is unfortunate that sexual intercourse takes place between Adam and Eve only after the expulsion from the Garden; this perhaps provides an excuse for thinking that sexual intimacy is associated with a sinful and disobedient state. But this is not given in the text nor is it a necessary implication. Indeed Eve claims the help of God in the matter. The shame associated with nakedness immediately after the eating of the fruit of the tree of knowledge need not imply that sex became tainted there and then with sin: it may imply a recognition that our sexuality more than anything else in us can lift us to the heights of self-realization or plunge us into degradation; it is the focus of our self-awareness. The awareness of nakedness may further be a symbol of the awareness of vulnerability, of exposure to pain that must come with self-consciousness.

No doubt from the earliest days of Christianity there have been men and women for whom the sexual relationship was illumined and deepened by the Christian message of love, for whom it expressed a true equality, an equal-sided valuation and respect, for whom coitus was an expression of tenderness and unity, not merely the gratification of animal urges. But it is one of the great tragedies of history that not until recent times has this implication of Christianity found public expression.

Dr. Sherwin Bailey, a leading Anglican authority on this subject, can find no evidence of this expression in any theological writing before the appearance in the seventeenth century of *Holy Living,* by Jeremy Taylor, a married bishop of the English Church who owed much to the support and companionship of his wife. In that book coitus is for the first time referred to as an act that relates two people in togetherness. It was an experience "to lighten the cares and sadness of household affairs, and to endear each other." Dr. Bailey writes, "Taylor maintains that marriage is the queen of friendships, and husband and wife the best of all friends; the love that binds them together is a 'union of all things excellent': it contains in it proportion and satisfaction and rest and confidence." (Bailey, 1959.)

In contrast to this, for the previous fifteen hundred years almost every writer and leader in the Church, both Catholic and Reformed, regarded sexuality as unavoidably tainted with sin, and the sex-relationship in marriage (apart from procreation) as a licensed outlet for the bestial impulses in man. This latter concept of marriage is overwhelmingly repulsive to many of us now, yet it is no exaggeration to say that it has lingered in the Church almost to the present day, and only recently has it become possible to be married in church without hearing an echo of it in the marriage service.

Dr. Sherwin Bailey, writing of earlier centuries, says: ". . . the general impression left by the Church's teaching upon simple and unlearned people can only have been that the physical relationship of the sexes was regarded by religion as unworthy, if not as shameless and obscene. The effect of such teaching must necessarily have been grave; it caused a distortion of principles and values which has left an indelible mark upon Christian sexual thought and we can only guess at the psychological disturbances and conflicts which it has produced in the lives of individuals." (Bailey, 1959.)

Only in the present century have Christians dared in any general way to follow in the steps of Jeremy Taylor and to accept that, irrespective of any other purpose, coitus can be justified and dignified as the expression of a deep relation between two persons. We do not blame Christianity and Christians of earlier centuries; we can seek the origin of misconceived attitudes in the compromise between pagan and Christian thought and in the social conditions of the Dark Ages.

We have then to reject the idea that there is anything necessarily sinful about sexual activity. A better understanding of the nature and value of myth, and a more scientific approach to problems of human behaviour, have delivered many Christians from this oppressive and destructive idea. Sexual activity is essentially neither good nor evil; it is a normal biological activity which, like most other human activities, can be indulged in destructively or creatively.

Further, if we take impulses and experiences that are potentially wholesome and in a large measure unavoidable and characterize these as sinful, we create a great volume of unnecessary guilt and an explosive tension within the personality. When, as so often happens, the impulse breaks through the restriction, it does so with a ruthlessness and destructive energy that might not otherwise have been there. A distorted Christianity must bear some of the blame for the sexual disorders of society.

A WAY FORWARD

In trying to summarize the feelings and judgments that have come to us in the course of our several years' deliberations, we must keep this historical survey in mind. It supports us in rejecting almost completely the traditional approach of the organized Christian church to morality, with its supposition that it knows precisely what is right and what is wrong, that this distinction can be made in terms of an external pattern of behaviour, and that the greatest good will come only through universal adherence to that pattern. Nothing that has come to light in the course of our studies has altered the conviction that came to us when we began to examine the actual experiences of people—the conviction that love cannot be confined to a pattern. The waywardness of love is part of its nature and this is both its glory and its tragedy. If love did not tend to leap every barrier, if it could be tamed, it would not be the tremendous creative power we know it to be and want it to be.

So we are concerned with the homosexuals who say to each other "I love you" in the hopeless and bitter awareness of a hostile criminal code and hypocritical public opinion, and also with the anguish of men and women who know they love one another when marriage is impossible and only suffering can be envisaged. We recognize that, while most examples of the "eternal triangle" are produced by boredom and primitive misconduct, others may arise from the fact that the very experience of loving one person with depth and perception may sensitize a man or woman to the lovable qualities in others.

We think it our duty, not to stand on a peak of perfectionism, asking for an impossible conformity while the tide of human life sweeps by us, but to recognize, in compassion, the complications and bewilderment that love creates and to ask how we can discover a constructive way in each of an immense variety of particular experiences. It is not by checking our impulse to love that we keep love sweet. The man who swallows the words "I love you" when he meets another woman, may in that moment and for that reason begin to resent his wife's existence; but it is also true that love may be creative if honestly acknowledged though not openly confessed. We need to know much more about ourselves and what we do to our inner life when we follow codes or ideals that do not come from the heart.

Those who have read so far will recognize how difficult it has been for us to come to definite conclusions as to what people ought or ought not to do. But although we cannot produce a ready-made external morality to replace the conventional code, there are some things about which we can be definite. *The first is that there must be a morality of some sort to govern sexual relationships.* An experience so profound in its effect upon people and upon the community cannot be left wholly to private judgment. It will never be right for two people to say to each other "We'll do what we want, and what happens between us is nobody else's business." However private an act, it is never without its impact on society, and we must never behave as though society—which includes our other friends—did not exist. *Secondly, the need to preserve marriage and family life has been in the forefront of our minds throughout our work.* It is in marriage that sexual impulses have their greatest opportunity for joyful and creative expression, and where two people can enter into each other's lives and hearts most intimately. Here the greatest freedom can be experienced —the freedom conferred by an unreserved commitment to each other, by loving and fearless friendship, and by openness to the world. In marriage, two people thus committed can bring children into the world, provide them with the security of love and home and in this way fulfil their sexual nature. *Finally, we accept the definition of sin given by an Anglican broadcaster, as covering those actions that involve exploitation of the other person.* This is a concept of wrong-doing that applies both to homosexual and heterosexual actions and to actions within marriage as well as outside it. It condemns as fundamentally immoral every sexual action that is not, as far as is humanly ascertainable, the result of a mutual decision. It condemns seduction and even persuasion, and every instance of coitus which, by reason of disparity of age or intelligence or emotional condition, cannot be a matter of mutual responsibility.

It is clear that we need a much deeper morality, one that will enable people to find a constructive way through even the most difficult and unpredictable situations—a way that is not simply one of withdrawal and abnegation. There are many who say that when people find themselves in a situation where it is difficult to be consistently moral, they must practise self-denial and "bear their cross." This is often the right way; but it is a serious misconception of the Cross to suggest that it is related only to self-denial.

Morality should be creative. God is primarily Creator, not rule-maker. Quakerism from the beginning rejected the idea of particular observances, rituals or sacrament, and instead regarded the whole of life's activities as potentially sacramental. The Quaker movement arose in a time of spiritual stirring. By rejecting all authority save that of the Holy Spirit and the headship of Christ, its vital witness was to an authority which begins in personal experience, in the encounter of man and God in the human spirit and mind. Quakerism begins with a search and its method is experimental.

Every true Christian, of whatever branch of the Church, accepts that the whole of his life must be brought before God. The Society of Friends places particular emphasis on our individual and personal responsibility. We cannot accept as true a statement that is given us merely because it is given with the authority of tradition or of a Church. We have to make that truth our own—if it is a truth—through diligent and prayerful search and a rigorous discipline of thought and feeling. Man is intended to be a moral being. That is not to say that he should accept a formal morality, an observance of *mores,* but that his actions should come under searching scrutiny in the light that comes from the Gospels and the working of God within us.

There have been periods in our Quaker history when the effort to achieve consistency and integrity toppled over into a humourless scrupulosity, leading to a restricted life in which a pattern of conduct was secured at the expense of warmth and joy and creativeness. Friends, if they keep in mind the need to avoid this error, could help to discover that kind of conduct and inner discipline through which the sexual energy of men and women can bring health of mind and spirit to a world where man's energy always threatens to become destructive. We need a release of love, warmth and generosity into the world, in the everyday contacts of life, a positive force that will weaken our fear of one another and our tendencies towards aggression and power-seeking. We need to recognize fearlessly and thankfully the sexual origin of this force.

This search is a move forward into the unknown; it implies a high standard of responsibility, thinking and awareness—something much harder than simple obedience to a moral code. Further, the responsibility that it implies cannot be accepted alone; it must be responsibility within a group whose members are equally committed to the search for God's will.

Perhaps our last words should be to those, equally aware of

the tragedy, who may be distressed and put off by our rejection of a morality that has seemed to them a product of Christianity. We do know, from the intimate experience of several of us, that it is possible to give substance to the traditional code, to live within its requirements, enriched by an experience of love at its most generous and tender, and conscious of our debt to Christ in showing us what love implies. We would ask those who cannot easily follow our thoughts to recognize what has driven us—Christians and Friends, trying to live up to the high standard of integrity that our religious society asks of us —to our insistent questioning.

It is the awareness that the traditional code, in itself, does not come from the heart; for the great majority of men and women it has no roots in feeling or true conviction. We have been seeking a morality that will indeed have its roots in the depths of our being and in our awareness of the true needs of our fellows.

We believe that there is indeed a place for discipline, but that it can only be fully healthy as well as fully Christian when it is found in application to the *whole* of life. The challenge to each of us is clear: accustom yourself to seeking God's will and to the experience of his love and power, become used in your daily life to the simple but tremendous spiritual fact that what God asks he enables, provided only and always that we want to do his will.

Men and women thus accustomed will not be less exposed to sexual difficulties—heterosexual or homosexual—than others whose lives are not "under discipline" in this way. As we see it, the difference lies in their response to the claims of sexual urges. Whereas the emotional or "moral" response focusses attention on the control of the sexual urge in isolation, the way of life we have described makes it likely that the particular sexual problem will be seen in the full context of ordinary daily living, and thus be kept in perspective as something for which God has not only a solution but a positive purpose.

Such positive purpose may—and often does—involve the acceptance of suffering by the person concerned. We have no unity with those who regard all tension and all frustration as being by definition bad or unhealthy: such a view is utterly without psychological foundation. The mental and spiritual well-being of a person depends rather on his or her developed capacity to deal with tensions and frustrations as and when they arise. The Christian cannot escape the implications of the Cross. In the power of the Holy Spirit, there are no dangers from which strength cannot be gained, no apparent disaster which cannot be transformed into spiritual opportunities.

CONCLUSION

WHAT we have put forward already, and what appears in the appendices, give some idea of the great range of problems which may be brought by troubled people to those whom they trust and respect. Helping to alleviate disorders of the sort we have described is profoundly difficult, let no one doubt that: other problems such as poverty or physical ill-health are nothing compared with the more deeply ingrained sexual disorders which root themselves within the personality and seemingly defy the best attempts at relief. Individual counsellors may feel uncertain and unprepared, and it is to them that this section is directed. An understanding humility is no bad equipment. Such understanding of these disorders as we are able to share in these pages is directed towards a single aim, to give help.

Experience from discussions in our own group, the help we have had over the past five years from those within and without the Society of Friends, and the correspondence in *The Friend* and elsewhere, convince us that the desire to understand, to think deeply and to help, is widespread both amongst Friends and in other churches, but mere personal concern is not enough in a counselling situation. The over-confident or clumsy "do-gooder" can do much damage by treading with heavy feet among the tender problems of those in trouble. It is, however, also true that it is unnecessary for all enquirers to be sent automatically to the nearest marriage guidance bureau or psychiatric clinic. Such facilities already have more work than they can cope with in handling the more serious disorders, and such a step may magnify a problem that could be dealt with through ordinary understanding friendliness.

Men and women in sexual trouble usually feel that they are alone, cast out and rejected. Sympathetic friends may be of inestimable help, and indeed with many passing problems a listening ear and the reassurance which that can give are often all that is required. Most of those, for example, who are anxious about masturbation do not need psychiatric treatment but they may need help in overcoming a dominating habit. In only a few will this anxiety be a symptom of deeper disturbance. Sexual worries are often short-lived. They may be stirred up by life's passing crises (overwork, an examination, courtship, the death of a relative) and soon pass into oblivion.

Counselling at any level makes certain demands: first and foremost that of accessibility. It is hard to discuss one's sexual difficulties with others and it can be assumed that anyone wishing to do so is in some desperation, only coming after much heart-searching and plucking up of courage. Tuesday week, or even tomorrow evening, may be too late: the magic moment passes, courage may fail, a temporary but ultimately unsatisfactory solution may offer itself or, as in a few known cases, actual suicide may occur. Accessibility is thus both crucial and a dual problem: the "right" person must also somehow be readily reached.

Next is the need to listen with compassion but without judgment. Sexually troubled people are often overloaded with guilt about their condition: automatic censure is nothing new to them and serves only to increase their distress and isolation. Emotional reactions from the counsellor, arising mostly from origins of which he or she is not aware, are unhelpful. The realities of sexual conduct are far more complex than many yet realize, as we have tried to show; the counsellor must therefore be interested but unshockable, neither gleefully inquisitive nor blatantly horrified. The interest shown by some counsellors has a vicariously erotic flavour, and this can help neither party. Finally there is the need for absolute discretion, a secrecy equal to that of the confessional. Intimate details must only be given away with the person's consent, and in effect this means only to those who may be called on to help more expertly in treatment. With homosexual disorders in particular, the illegal nature of certain types of conduct may place some counsellors in a difficult position, but their duty is as clear as it is to the priest.

Because of the complexity of many of the matters herein discussed, we believe it right that for Christians, especially in larger congregations, one or two experienced counsellors should be known to be available, but we recognize that in sparsely populated rural areas this may not be possible.

Those who are called upon to give intimate and personal counsel will soon be aware of changing attitudes to morality among their fellow-members and they may feel it necessary to initiate group discussion on sexual matters. There is a danger that any compassionate view that is published—like this present essay—may be misread. A reader here and there may accept *some* of our ideas, and then proceed to put his interpretation of them into action—imposing on his victims the consequences of a permissiveness that we appear to support. It must therefore be said that at no point does our approach approve of mere permissiveness. To the question "May we do what we like?" we do *not* answer "Yes, you may." We have been led to ask what may be the actual and ultimate result in the persons concerned of love affairs involving coitus, and have implied that the result is not necessarily or invariably destructive. We do not, however, encourage anyone to think that it would be "perfectly all right" to make love with a casual friend who equally desires the experience.

The true answer to our open question might prove to be as critical of "free love" as of mere obedience to an external morality. Sexual actions can never be primitively "innocent." We are not in the Garden of Eden. We are a complex race of people with the imprint of a long history on our spirits. Sexual actions stir us far below the level of consciousness, and may do more than we know to shape our future. There is an almost overwhelming urge throughout society towards the trivializing of sexual actions and the separating of them from the rest of life. A young man, whose whole working life is given to preparation for a responsible career, may nevertheless think it all right to propose "going to bed" to a girl he has only just met and whose surname is unknown to him. We think it probable that to use one's capacity for love-making in so tenuous a relationship is to reduce ultimately one's capacity for any depth of feeling or commitment. For in many such liaisons there is a deliberate intention to steer clear of being involved, to have fun without commitment.

In trying to work out the implications of the high standard of responsibility demanded in this essay, we have been unable to avoid the continual challenge of the questions—*when is it right to have sexual intercourse?* and, *is it ever right outside marriage?* The problem of sexual behaviour outside marriage is everywhere under discussion at the present time, and the needs of many who want guidance are not met by the simple statement that chastity is right and un-chastity wrong. Such a statement leaves many untouched and some desperate.

We condemn exploitation in any form. Exploitation is using the partner to satisfy a physical or an emotional need without considering the other as a person. There are many forms of exploitation from the extreme of prostitution for material gain to exploitation in marriage. It is exploitation if the insecure boy enhances his sense of masculine adulthood by sexual adventures, without considering the girl's feelings. It is equally exploitation if the girl leads the young man into marriage by using her attraction as a bait without thinking about his welfare. Exploitation can also happen in non-sexual relationships when the stronger character accepts adoration from the weaker and the less mature, or when one person uses the other to enrich his or her status or self-confidence. This can occur not only between unequal, but also between equal partners. In marriage it is also exploitation if the man uses the woman to show his masculine prowess or the woman uses the man to establish her social status as a married woman, or as one who is attractive and valued. Neither partner has stopped to consider the other's value.

In seeking to find a truly Christian judgment of this problem, we have again and again been brought to the quality of human relationships as the only final criterion. To base our judgment on whether or not the sex-act has taken place is often to falsify that judgment fantastically. Is the girl who remains chaste, but leaves would-be lovers stimulated to the point where desire would almost certainly seek relief elsewhere, more or less blameworthy than the girl who surrenders, whether in mistaken generosity or in the pathetic desire to "keep her boy"? *The Christian standard of chastity should not be measured by a physical act, but should be a standard of human relationship, applicable within marriage as well as outside it.*

Moreover, the problem of what to say to the early developing, over-stimulated youth of the present time is not the same as the problem of what to say to the responsible young men and women equipped by experience and education to analyse and evaluate a situation in which they find themselves. A simple "thou shalt not" meets the needs of neither.

When human relationships are judged by this criterion, it is found to result in an assessment of behaviour not very different from that of conventional Christian morality, but it brings us to a new realization of the true nature of chastity. True chastity is a quality of the spirit: it entails the deepest respect and a profound value for human relationships. It involves the most generous giving, which may mean the restraint of withholding, but it is not solely measured in physical terms. Further, there are lives which are being lived unconventionally with more true chastity than some lived in obedience to conventional codes.

If chastity means respect for oneself and others, then promiscuity is the final denial of it. It denies the importance of personality, and those who seek relief in this way of life imprison their true selves—they are sexual deviants damaging both themselves and their transitory partner by divorcing the physical from the spiritual and keeping impersonal what should involve the whole personality. Yet wherever the most transient relationship has, as it may have, an element of true tenderness and mutual giving and receiving, it has in it something of good.

Promiscuity cannot be countered by the mere statement that it is sinful: its causes need to be sought and understood. It is often the expression of loneliness and insecurity, born of a lack of experience of real relationships with others. Promiscuity is exploitation—one-sided or mutual—but the wrongfulness of exploitation cannot be realized unless the significance of personality is perceived, until it is recognized, as Von Hügel put it, that "caring is the greatest thing, caring matters most."

Easier to judge with compassion, but in some ways more difficult to contend with, are the boy and girl relationships where both believe themselves totally committed and so have intercourse together. Today the dangers of pregnancy must and should be clearly set forth, and the wrongfulness of irresponsibly creating a life is something which boy and girl should know before they are deeply involved. Even were society's attitude to the child born out of wedlock to become more charitable, still the fatherless child is deprived of the family background that is its natural, right environment.

We must be prepared, however, to look ahead to the time when contraception is completely reliable and pregnancy is not a danger, and consider what sanctions and what motives can then be put forward. It is right and proper that many boys and girls and young men and women should fall in and out of love a number of times before they marry—and this process will involve emotional heights and depths. If these experiences are to be educative, they must involve all the personality, but such a series of experiences will be, generally, less disruptive if the final sexual commitment is avoided. Society can and should offer educational relationships by giving opportunities for the young to do things together. While they have no resources but to sit entwined in the cinema, watching huge photographs of impassioned love scenes, they will learn no outlet for their feelings for each other save those of passionate love-making.

But an activity shared with other couples may help a pair to look outward at life together rather than inward at each other, and so save them from being deeply committed physically before they are otherwise ready.

Impersonal exploitation, the dangers of pregnancy, the disruptive effect of a series of love affairs involving intercourse— these are heavy arguments in favour of continence in the young unmarried. Should we go further and say unequivocally that it is utterly wrong to have intercourse outside marriage, and if so on what grounds? Only those who remain virgin until marriage can tell the value of this in their married lives, and the number of couples who express their joy at having done this, constitutes an impressive argument to offer to the young unmarried. As one couple has said, "the trouble is that until you are married, you don't realize why it is so important not to beforehand." We feel, however, constrained to say, what we believe to be true, that many deeply rich and happy marriages exist when one or both partners has had previous sexual experience, and that it would be both cruel and untrue to suggest otherwise. This same truth is borne out in the experience of the many happy second marriages which abound. It is, of course, easy to say that the individual who has moved carelessly from one liasion to another is unlikely to be successful or faithful in marriage. Even this does not necessarily follow if the transitory affairs were the expression of an insecurity or immaturity which genuine love later enables him to supersede. Moreover, it must be recognized that there are those who before marriage allow themselves a sexual freedom which they would indignantly repudiate as permissible within the marriage bond.

It has indeed been claimed that marriages are more successful where there has been previous sexual experience. This claim can be neither proved nor disproved. Those who are happily married may attribute their happiness to whatever previous experiences they have had. Those who believe in sexual freedom before marriage may claim that their marriages are happy rather than admit the possibility that they were wrong; the same may be true of those who came virgin to marriage, and would be unwilling to acknowledge, or might even be unaware of, a lack of adjustment due to their inexperience. Where an experience previous to marriage has been one of depth and integrity, where the individual has learnt from it, even if the lesson were one of suffering, then the resulting growth of personality could be a strength and not a weakness in the marriage.

We have so far considered only pre-marital relationships with others than the future wife or husband. For a couple to have intercourse before marriage merely to see whether they really want to marry, is likely to be a disastrously misleading experiment. For some, harmony experienced before marriage disappears once they are committed in marriage; others may mistake for failure what is, in fact, a lack of mutual adjustment which experience could overcome. More important than either, perhaps, the atmosphere of tentativeness prevents the mutual abandonment essential to happy adjustment.

We have felt that a distinction should be drawn between this situation and that of the couple, who, with their wedding day fixed and imminent, deliberately anticipate it, in order that the moment when they take each other as man and wife shall be completely private to themselves alone. For them, their marriage begins then and there. Censure seems, in such a case, impertinent; yet it must also be said that for others their great joy is to wait until they have gladly and publicly exchanged their promises. It should be stressed that, where either partner feels doubt or guilt, it would be dangerous for them to anticipate their wedding night.

Finally, something must be said of those whose are adult and unmarried and find themselves deeply in love, in a situation where marriage is impossible. When two people are deeply committed to each other, but for some reason unable to marry, then the level of judgment is a totally different one. They may, in fact, live as husband and wife and their union may, in its inherent quality, be indistinguishable from that of a legally married couple. There are faithful, permanent and rich partnerships of this sort that deserve our deepest sympathy and often our respect. Yet such a relationship can affect others beside the couple concerned and the full cost of this has to be counted.

What then is chastity? It is the antithesis of what was recently described to one of us as "the hire purchase attitude of this age"—the attitude that implies: "I want it *now* and I must have it. I will pay later—perhaps—if I can." It is not rigid restraint nor refusal to be involved; it is not arid self-discipline nor living according to a moral pattern. It is a wholeness of personality, courtesy and charity, sincerity and purity of heart. It is not necessarily measured in physical terms; it is a total absence of exploitation; it is as necessary a part of marriage as of a single life.

There are no clear-cut answers to the questions we have posed, and this nearly every counsellor will be forced to admit if he seeks to understand fully a particular situation. This is precisely because we are dealing with human relationships at their deepest, the point where rules are irrelevant. But the point where rules cease to apply is also the point at which our first and greatest need is to seek the will of God. This at least we can say to our fellow members of the Society of Friends: that if the traditional code seems now to be of little value, either in restraining us or in pointing out the way to generous living, then more than ever we need the presence of God in our judgments and decisions. And Christianity, precisely because it is concerned with the quality of human relationships, is more relevant to the unforeseen and the intensely difficult than it is to the neatly patterned way of life.

What now can we say to those who do not accept God in their lives and may indeed reject any religious influence?—to the numerous boys and girls who tumble into sexual intimacy when they are little more than children, who are confused by what it does to them and escape from confusion into toughness; to the young adults whose bottle parties are followed by indiscriminate sexual indulgence; to those whose marriages are unsatisfying and who seek distraction elsewhere; to the homosexuals living in a hell in which they are torn between a genuine impulse to tenderness and an overwhelming sense of lust? For those who are already involved we can do little, except in so far as we meet particular cases; and then our approach has to be through compassion—the reverse of moral judgment. Through this we may be admitted to their lives and their problems, and our questions may become worthy of their consideration; it is by helping them in their self-questioning rather than by giving judgment that truth can be brought to light.

The response of Friends and counsellors generally to the problem as a whole must obviously be through a clearer concept of the purpose of education and of life in community. The fulfilment of our nature as distinctively human beings is through relationships that are *personal,* through the kind of friendship that is its own justification. To some this must seem so obvious as to make them forget that to an enormous extent the structure of society and the incentives it offers constitute a flat denial of this view. Almost the whole of the time spent in educational training is directed towards the study of groups and not of individuals; that is, towards a functional relationship, not a personal one, and significance is thought of as social significance, in terms of power and prestige. The recognition of personal relationship and the understanding of its nature are left to chance. This subject has been fully discussed by Rhymes (1964, pp. 53-56).

Some schools now admit counsellors trained by the Marriage Guidance Council to talk to their pupils about problems of sexual conduct and marriage, and a very important part of their work has proved to be a discussion of the nature of personal relationships, showing how young people can grow to maturity through them. It is clear that this is not self-evident to young people; the recognition of what is personal is not provided by instinct or common sense and it is confused by the meretricious attractions and influences of our urban and affluent society. A personal relationship is a loving relationship in its most meaningful sense—the sense implied by *"Thou shalt love the Lord thy God . . . and thy neighbour as thyself."* This is a love that has no ulterior purpose. It contains its own fulfilment in itself. Much has yet to be done to understand and clarify the nature of love. Too much attention has been given to love as an ideal, good or bad, noble or sentimental; too little to it as a form of action, a continuing and developing experience. Most novels are devoted to the analysis of the breakdown of love, the working out of its painful or tragic aspect in stock situations; few describe its fulfilment through the difficulties and crises of ordinary life. Everyone knows the passion, the excitement, the adoration that are the content of sexual experience in the first stage; but the nature of love as an established relationship is less easy to demonstrate in a convincing way to those who are caught in these first obsessions. This demonstration is an urgent necessity, for much more needs to be known as to what gives love stability and endurance and, conversely, what may leave it open to destruction.

The philosophic and religious approach to the nature of personal relationship has been explored by two outstanding thinkers in our time: Martin Buber and John Macmurray. It is to the latter that we owe the clearest exposition in English. His *Reason and Emotion,* first published in 1935, threw a new and startling light on sexual and general morality at a time when, because of the collapse of Western economy, many people were thinking furiously, and constructively, about the purpose of life and society. This book is equally relevant to our problems today. Those who wish to share our search for a new and effective morality will benefit from reading it, and, if obtainable, its predecessor *Freedom in the Modern World.*

Macmurray puts forward a new definition of chastity as "emotional sincerity," linking it with the sense in which a work of art can be said to be chaste and with the meaning of the words of Jesus, "Blessed are the pure in heart." Chastity, he says, is "sincerity in the expression of what we feel; and it is the fundamental virtue, from one point of view, of a Christian morality . . . It is the condition of personal integrity." The awareness with which our group has done its work may well be put in these lines from *Reason and Emotion:*

Though Europe has developed itself intellectually with a steady growth upwards, has progressed in its grasp of principle, in scholarship and understanding, in the organisation and control of life and the world, it has remained all but completely barbarous on the emotional side. Our civilization, for all its scientific and administrative capacity, has remained emotionally vulgar and primitive, un-chaste in the extreme. We do not recognize this, of course, because it is simply the reflection of our own inner insensibility. That insensibility is the inevitable result of a morality based upon will and reason, imposing itself upon the emotions and so destroying their integrity. Until we insist upon emotional sincerity, until we cease playing ducks and drakes with our feelings in the mistaken desire to dragoon them into conformity with what we conceive to be our "duties," until we begin to trust our emotional life, this state of affairs will necessarily go on. Our sex-morality, in particular, will remain blind, barbarous and unreal, a vulgarity and scandal.[2]

It might be added that our sex-morality, because it has not met the needs of people as persons, has been unable to prevent, and may indeed have caused, a great measure of personal tragedy between men and women and in the lives of their children.

Often it is the very idealism of a religious group that prevents its members from understanding the actions and needs of people. Idealism can be a sign of spontaneous and selfless devotion in an integrated personality. But too often it is the attachment of emotion to a pattern of ideas or morals, and this kind of idealism can be an escape from having to face the darker levels of our own nature. In this shadowed region of the personality, all that we consciously repudiate lives on, for the time being so overlaid by fine sentiments that we are unaware of its existence. It is in a crisis, when controls give way, that this shadow-life tends to become active and ravaged feelings make communication impossible just when it is most needed. A deeper morality must be concerned with the whole nature of man, not merely with his conscious intentions and sentiments.

In view of this, those who genuinely wish to give help to others in sexual confusion and distress will—if they really understand what their task is—be compelled to consider every aspect of family life and especially the relationships through which young people grow up. They must always reflect on the experiences that will decide whether their impulses and feelings remain confused and destructive under the surface of apparently good behaviour, or whether they will come to know themselves and discover the discipline through which their feelings and impulses can work towards a creative end.

by Paul Ramsey

ON TAKING SEXUAL RESPONSI-
BILITY SERIOUSLY ENOUGH

THE "Essay by a group of Friends" entitled "Towards a Quaker View of Sex"[1] reached profoundly into the question whether there are any rules of action embodying Christian responsibility in sexual behavior, or whether there are only acts that embody such responsibility. But then it flinched and drew back from the conclusions to which its argument was about to lead—indeed, to which it had led. This document provides, therefore, a significant "case study" in how we should understand the meaning of *Christian* responsibility, or the *Christian* meaning of responsibility.

THE MEANING OF RESPONSIBILITY

When is it right for intercourse to take place? asked the Quakers.

It should not happen until the partners come to know each other so well that the sexual contact becomes a consummation, a deeply meaningful total expression of a friendship in which each has accepted the other's reality and shared the other's interests.[2]

Reprinted from *Christianity and Crisis*, Vol. XXIII, No. 23, Jan. 6, 1964, pp. 247-51. By permission. PAUL RAMSEY is Payne Professor of Religion at Princeton University. He has been president of the American Society of Christian Ethics (1963). Among his publications are *Basic Christian Ethics, War and the Christian Conscience,* and *Nine Modern Moralists.*

If that is when *not,* when *should* it?

In these Friends' answer to this question, *responsibility embodied in the act* reached the border where it had to become *responsibility embodied in a general rule,* or where act-agapism, fully explored, was about to be replaced by rule-agapism:

> Could we say also that at least in spirit each should be committed to the other—should be open to the other in heart and mind? This would mean that each cared deeply about what might happen to the other and would do everything possible to meet the other's needs and lessen any suffering that had to be faced. It would mean a willingness to accept responsibility. . . .
> Should not there also be a commitment to a shared view of the nature and purpose of life?[3]

Why not affirm all this, reminiscent as these words are of the marriage vow? Precisely because they are. Precisely because that would be a rule or a pattern embodying responsibility. Therefore, these Friends say:

> At once we are aware that this is to ask for nothing less than the full commitment of marriage; indeed most marriages begin with a much less adequate basis.[4]

Thus the question of the meaning of responsibility in sexual ethics was simply begged in behalf of act-agapism or act-responsibility. Some such words might still be used as a "challenge" to sexual acts within marriage and to sexual acts outside of marriage, but we cannot "legislate" or "draw clear lines between good and evil," not even when an ethics of responsibility is probed to the point—and beyond the point—of drawing them.

THE MEANING OF MARRIAGE

Clearly, one cannot explore the meaning of Christian responsibility very profoundly without suddenly finding himself discussing, in this connection, the moral meaning of *marriage* itself. He will therefore find himself discussing *marital* relations, and not *pre*-marital relations.

In making a judgment upon all this, a Christian view of sex and of marriage never was a theology of the marriage *ceremony.*

Ours is not the task of defending bourgeois respectability or legal paper or church ceremonies and registers. None of these things has anything to do with defining a pre-marital or a conjugal relation. The man and the woman marry each other in fact when their consents are the response to and the responsibility for each other's reality which these Friends describe. Sexual consummation is then the consummation of an existing marriage, whether or not they have ever been—as we err in saying—"married."

This is acknowledged both in the sphere of the State and in the sphere of the Church. In most state jurisdictions in this country, one can get married according to all the regulations of the 20-odd volumes of the state's marriage law or he can get married without them. This is provided by the last paragraph on the last page of Vol. 20, which usually states: "None of the foregoing is intended to abolish the common law," i.e., the unwritten law that leaves people free to make their marriages simply out of their will to be responsible to and for one another. (The rules of evidence that can later establish that they did this need not be brought into the question.)

And in the sacrament of marriage in the Roman Church, the couple are the priests administering the sacrament to one another (if they are baptized and if their consents are as responsible as their words say). When the Council of Trent wanted to prohibit "clandestine marriages" (which were not "secret" but ordinary Christian sacramental marriages brought into being without a priest), it touched the sacrament "co-donated" by the two only by requiring a priest as a witness.

If anyone—after seeing clearly what makes a marriage and the only morally important distinction between pre- and post-marital intercourse—still wants to defend the need of a civil or religious ceremony, he will have to do this for practical reasons that are ethically insignificant, if indeed they are not entirely non-moral. He will have to link somehow an ethic of responsibility in love with the need for practical, public tests of this.

However important legalities and ceremonies may be, they are only external checks, which exhibit to others the fact that the lovers are married and which may help the lovers themselves to be steadfast in the responsible resolve that alone made them married. They may, of course, need some such external test simply to know whether what they are talking about as lovers is the question of *pre*-marital relations and not actually, in the ethical sense, a question only of their marital relations, or the consummation of their marriage.

AN OPENING TOWARD SEXUAL IRRESPONSIBILITY

But these Friends drew back when they saw that to ask what they were driven to ask from within an ethics of responsibility was "to ask nothing less than the full commitment of marriage." They chose act-responsibility when a rule of action embodying responsibility appeared on the horizon and was obviously required by their own analysis.

For the Friends to return to acts only required a weakening of their ethics of responsibility. It required less than the fullest response for them to reopen the question of genuinely pre-marital relations after that question had been closed by the emergence of full commitment to the other's reality in what amounted to marriage. Their sensitive reflection upon the moral life itself leads them to a rule of action embodying responsibility. This is an interesting demonstration of the fact that act-responsibility can be established only by arbitrarily rejecting rule-responsibility.

So the authors of the Quaker essay drew back from clarity about sexual responsibility. They chose rather a twilight zone where (according to their own description of human experience in this zone) not all is responsibility or full response. "A deliberate intention to avoid responsibility" is, of course, ruled out. (Even that is some sort of rule-morality!) But for irresponsibility to be absent, responsibility need not be present. Only in this twilight zone does act-responsibility again become possible for Christian conscience. The words now justifying the act are "openness" to and a "seed" or "measure" of responsibility:

Where there is genuine tenderness, an openness to responsibility, and the seed of commitment, God is surely not shut out. Can we not say that God can enter any relationship in which there is a measure of selfless love?[5]

I suppose that no Christian since Augustine has denied that God is present where there is any measure of beauty or order to seed or any being at all!

In order to exclude as "unrealistic" a proposal of a rule of behavior embodying *agape*-responsibility that was made by Sherwin Bailey in his *Common Sense about Sexual Ethics,* the authors reach down to something even less a measure of responsibility, and far more "wayward."

He (Bailey) holds that to say "I love you" means nothing less than this: "I want you, just as you are, to share the whole of my life, and I ask you to take me, just as I am, to share the whole of your life." He further says that it ought never to be said unless marriage is possible, right and at the time of speaking intended. That such a statement is unrealistic is at the root of our work.[6]

One would have thought that whether a rule of conduct is realistic is not the first or the main point to be proven. Even so, what the Quakers refer to in order to refute Bailey is not acts that are governed by a measure of responsibility but instead the conviction, drawn from "the actual experiences of people," that

Love cannot be confined to a pattern. The waywardness of love is part of its nature and this is both its glory and its tragedy. If love did not tend to leap every barrier, if it could be tamed, it would not be the tremendous creative power we know it to be and want it to be.[7]

There are, however, two steps by which these Friends withdrew from an analysis of the entire meaning of responsibility. First, they withdrew from full to only a measured responsibility (and this is correlated with flinching from rule-responsibility and an acceptance of act-responsibility in their underlying moral theory.) Secondly, they bring into prominence love's asserted tendency to go further down the slope or up into the heights; and they substitute for even a seed of responsibility in action love's own waywardness, its untameability, and the glory and tragedy of tending to leap every barrier and escape every pattern.

If sincere Christian people including theological ethicists can be found simply refusing to take responsibility seriously enough when rules of action, and not acts alone, threaten to emerge from this, is it to be expected that adolescent boys and girls will take any measure of sexual act-responsibility seriously? Was the editorial comment upon this Quaker document by the Jesuit weekly *America* altogether wrong:

> In plain English, they mean that it is right for two kids to commit fornication if they *really* love each other. . . . If the sex act is only an act of love and not, in the intention of God and nature, an act of generation, there is no reason why people should not make it a gesture comparable to a kiss.[8]

I do not mean that the only way to avoid this conclusion is to affirm, with Roman Catholics, that an act of sexual love is primarily a procreative act. But if we Protestants take the view that sexual love is primarily an act of union between the man and the woman, then this viewpoint may still take two forms: act-unition and rule-unition.

Nor do I assert that an ethics of act-unition is at once to be accused of being "a purely subjective evaluation of the rightness and wrongness of sexual relationship" (as *America* said of the Quaker statement). Nevertheless, it may be that rules of action are to be found in an ethics of sexual love *qua* unitative; and this ought not *prima facie* to be excluded, as so often happens today among those who pride themselves on knowing all about the sexual revolution and want to be compassionate or only contemplate the "situation."

An act-personalism or an act-responsibilism or an act-agapism or act-*koinonia* (community) ethics or an act-unitive sex ethic is not a subjective vagary. It is simply wrong.

Marriage as a rule of action embodying everything that Christian responsibility means in sexual life may be defined as the mutual and exclusive exchange of the right to acts that of themselves tend to establish and to nourish unity of life between the partners. The fact that Christian ethics knows this to be the truth about sexual responsibility ought not to be withheld from young people, no matter how much sexual behavior may be in revolution.

THE SOURCE AND MEANING OF CHRISTIAN RESPONSIBILITY

Somewhat contradicting the complete waywardness of human sexual love, these Friends report

from the intimate experience of several of us, that it is possible to give substance to the traditional code, to live within its requirements, enriched by an experience of love at its most generous and tender, and conscious of our debt to Christ in showing us what love implies.[9]

If Christ shows us what love implies, and if this comes not only from an experience of love at its most generous and tender, it may be asked why we are not obliged to affirm that the (so-called) traditional code contains rules of action that simply embody Christian responsibility when this is full and strong?

The reason given for *not* affirming this is "the awareness that the traditional code, in itself, does not come from the heart." Yet the experience of living within its requirements did come from the heart and from these Friends' debt to Christ in showing them what love implies. Actually, underneath their rejection of "the traditional code" is the human heart in the modern, post-Christian age. Undoubtedly, it is the case that "for the great majority of men and women it has not roots in feeling or true conviction" today.

Christian ethics must certainly be able to do more than to take note of this fact, else there is no hope of restoring any sort of Christian *ethos* to the churches, let alone the world at large. It can certainly be demonstrated that, historically, the traditional code came from the human heart as men were taught by Christ what love implied.

The theologian is blinded and in error if he imagines that from Ephesians 5 came only an act-agapism and not the rule-agapism that established in the minds of Christendom its laws of marriage—elevating, for example, Roman contractual marriage to the full measure of the requirements of steadfast covenant. And he is a poor constructive ethicist who, without much argumentation, rules out the possibility that rules of action may still be fashioned by hearts instructed by Christ to know what love itself implies.

In launching the discussion of this Quaker statement among American Protestants in *Christianity and Crisis* Prof. Tom F. Driver made a profoundly penetrating remark upon the quandary of the minister confronting the heart of modern man.

. . . When traditional religious authority is not felt by a man to be binding upon his conscience, then it is not possible to preach to him the Law and the Gospel at the same time. Well aware of the disasters created by preaching the Law only, ministers tend to say more about the Gospel. But in the long run this has the effect of undermining the Law itself, at least in so far as the Law must be spelled out as a specific rule of conduct.[10]

Why not, for once, try the preaching of "the Gospel contained in this Law," the law of marriage as a rule embodying Christian responsible action.

The fact that this is not done, and today can scarcely be done, requires explanation. It is due to the erosion of Christian substance from our churches, from the ministry, from theological ethics itself. This, in turn, explains the question-begging prejudice in favor of act-agapism or act-responsibility ethics, or else the prejudice in favor of a merely situational ethics explains the erosion of Christian ethical substance. Which, it is difficult to tell.

ON TAKING CHRISTIAN ETHICS SERIOUSLY ENOUGH

The Quaker pamphlet is a fine case study in how to do and how not to do Christian ethics. The main question it raises is whether, among the many options in ethics, there is a uniquely Christian understanding of moral responsibility.

Christian ethics, it is often said, has its distinctive character in Christian love (*agape*). If other ethics rest upon a conception of moral duty or upon a goal to be achieved, Christian ethics finds its basis in *agape*. The question whether there is such a thing as Christian ethics is the question whether *agape* instructs us concerning the moral life, and whether agapism is a third type of normative theory besides the ethics of duty and the ethics of goal-seeking.

But the Christian errs if he thinks he has solved the whole moral problem by speaking up for love. The question remains: How does Christian love express itself?

Thus Prof. William K. Frankena of the University of Michigan points out that if Christian ethics is a possible theory of ethics it must take two forms, which he calls act-agapism and rule-agapism. These are two possible views of how love best exhibits itself in practice.

Act-agapism, says Frankena, holds that we are never to appeal to rules. Instead, "we are to tell what we should do in a particular situation simply by getting clear about the facts of that situation and then asking what is the loving or the most loving thing to do in it."

Rule-agapism, by contrast, seeks "to determine what we ought to do . . . by determining which *rules of action* are most love-embodying. . . ."[11]

Theologians are playing tricks when they pit *agape* (or convenant-obedience, or *koinonia,* or any other primary ethical concept) against rules, without asking whether *agape* can and may or must work through rules. The same two options remain in Christian ethics, no matter what term is used to replace *agape* in indicating the reality upon which the Christian life rests. The Christian life may take two forms: it may be productive of acts only or of rules also.

For example, if Christian ethics is *koinonia* (community)— ethics and if this can be demonstrated to be in any way different from *agape* ethics, then some Christian moralists in elaborating the ethics of the Christian community (the ethics of *koinonia*) will affirm that we are to tell what we should do in a particular situation simply by getting clear about the facts of that situation and then asking what is the fellowship-creating or the most fellowship-creating thing to do. Others will affirm that we are to determine what we ought to do by determining which *rules of action* are the most fellowship-creating or most aligned with the *koinonia* God is creating through his work with men. Thus, there may be an act-*koinonia* ethics and a rule-*koinonia* ethics. The same decision must be made if any other term is believed to be the illuminating one to use in an analysis of the ethical reality of the Christian life.

Now, no philosopher who is an act-utilitarian would think of making his case by simply accusing the rule-utilitarian of having abandoned the principle of utility. He would not charge, at the beginning of the argument and to avoid any contest, that the rule-utilitarian is not applying the test of utility in his ethics, or that utility is any the less sovereign or the sole sovereign over right conduct, or that lordship of utility has been weakened and divided where there are any utility-embodying rules. It remained for theologians to invent these un-logics, in the debate (which as a consequence never ensues) between act-agapism or act-*koinonia* ethics and rule-agapism or rule-*koinonia* ethics. The real issue is whether there are any *agape*- or *koinonia*-embodying rules; and, if there are, what these rules may be.

Of course, theologians these days have a professional allergy to rules. But it is sheer emotionalism to object to the word "rule" simply because it is habitual to philosophers and is strange, even offensive, to theologians. If "rule" is unusable, another word has to be found, perhaps "principle," "middle axiom," "ideal," "directive," "guidance," "ordinance," the "structures" of *agape* or of *koinonia* life, or the "anatomy" or "pattern" of responsibility.

Finally, taking Christian ethics with utmost seriousness requires that we consider the importance of the *ethos,* the social habits, the customs and laws of any society—whether this be church or civil society. Before, we asked whether individual responsibility is embodied in acts only or also in general rules of conduct. Now, we must ask whether there are any *societal* rules that embody the highest general responsibility and which are the most fellowship-producing rules for society as a whole, or whether this is a matter of "situational" acts only.

The Quaker essay notes that

There must be a morality of some sort to govern sexual relationships. An experience so profound in its effect upon people and upon the community cannot be left wholly to private judgment. It will never be right for two people to say to each other, "We'll do what we want, and what happens between us is nobody else's business." However private an act, it is never without its impact on society, and we must never behave as though society—which includes our other friends—did not exist.[12]

How can Christians nourish the seeds of a wider social responsibility while seeming to praise only acts and never rules that embody personal responsibility between the two parties to sexual relations? Plainly the waywardness of the human heart works against any *ethos,* customs or laws that are generally good for all and not only against "the traditional code."

The glaring inconsistencies in the Quaker document are only an instance of the fact that Protestant Christian ethics is often too profoundly personal to be ethically relevant. Ordinarily, we do not take Chrisitan ethics with enough seriousness to illumine the path men, women and society should follow today.

by Kyle Haselden

SEGREGATION AND THE RIGHT TO BELONG

from *The Racial Problem in Christian Perspective*

WHAT determines the morality and the immorality of segregation? Specifically, what primary order, what sacred principle, what will of God is violated by the segregation of the Negro in church and in society? If we are to answer these questions correctly, if we are to see clearly that it is sometimes wrong to separate people from people, then we must see first that it is not always wrong to separate people from people; we have a case against certain forms of segregation only when we see the case for certain forms of segregation.

Therefore, in our search for a criterion by which to judge racial segregation let us remember first that some of the dearest and most beautiful experiences of life required the deliberate, absolute, and permanent exclusion of all other people. Marriage and family life, for examples, are such experiences; and against these exclusive social unities the charge of segregation in its ugly tones is never leveled. It is taken for granted that there are special kinds of unions of life and that the nature of such unions requires the absolute exclusion of those who are not integral parts of them. Segregation, then, the separation of

Reprinted from *The Racial Problem in Christian Perspective,* excerpt comprising Chap. 6 (pp. 118-30). Copyright © 1959 by Kyle Haselden, used by permission of Harper & Row. KYLE HASELDEN is editor of the *Christian Century.* In addition to the above volume he has written *The Urgency of Preaching* and *Death of a Myth.*

people from people, cannot be condemned as such. There is a love which has the right, the duty, to say "no" to many applicants so that it may say a proper "yes" to some.

Secondly, let us see that the test of the rightness and wrongness of segregation cannot be made by consulting the desires of people. Racial segregation is not evil because the wishes of human beings have been denied or because the range of their lives has been restricted by force. This occurs all the while in a social order, and sometimes such a denial and restriction is legitimate and right and at other times it is illegitimate and wrong. For example, if a society is to be stable there are areas of the life of that society into which people must not be admitted indiscriminately. Society, therefore, prevents the impersonating of officers of the law, the practicing of medicine by those who are not quaified to do so, the marriage of minors. Thus one of the exigencies of social welfare requires that certain people be prohibited from areas of life occupied by other people; to do otherwise is to invite anarchy and jeopardize the common welfare. What the people want, including the desire of the people for unfettered lives, is, consequently, not the test of the morality or immorality of racial segregation.

Finally, we might assume that if this is not the answer it at least suggests where the answer is to be found. It is concluded, in other words, that the evil of racial segregation lies in the fact that it excludes people on the basis of circumstances which are beyond their control. After all, a man does have the possibility of becoming an officer of the law; a student can aspire to the medical profession with reasonable hope; minors do grow up; but racial characteristics are indelible. Dr. Benjamin E. Mays, toward whom many of us have often turned with confidence and respect, has made this point a major argument against racial segregation: ". . . to segregate a man because his skin is brown or black, red or yellow, is to segregate a man for circumstances over which he has no control. And of all the immoral acts, this is the most immoral."[1]

We admit that it is immoral to segregate a man because of his color; but the immorality is not rooted in the fact that his color is beyond his control. Frequently within society people are rightfully separated from other people on the basis of circumstances over which they have no personal control. For example, the insane must for their own good and the good of society be segregated from the sane for the duration of their insanity, and the diseased who have contagious diseases are quarantined. The fact that such people are excluded from the company of other people on the basis of circumstances which they cannot control does not brand that exclusion as immoral. The test by which racial segregation is condemned must evidently be found elsewhere.

These cases which show segregation justified have, however, a most instructive common factor: in each one the segregated are rightfully excluded from that to which they do not belong. The impostor who impersonates an officer of the law, the layman who practices medicine, the minor who pretends that he is of marriageable age are all excluded from a relationship to which they aspire and they are excluded because they do not qualify; they do not belong. The insane and the infectious are quarantined and thus kept from the sane and healthy because they cannot qualify; they do not belong with the sane and the healthy. To cast them entirely beyond the bounds of society, beyond its care and concern, as was done in medieval and ancient times, would be immoral; to segregate them within society is not immoral. The intruder and the stranger are shut from the intimate circle of marriage and family because they are not integral parts of marriage and family; they do not belong.

This indicates that segregation has to do with the right to belong. Union is the relationship of those who belong to each other or who have oneness because they are mutually related to that to which they both belong; segregation is the denial of the right to belong on the basis of irrelevant considerations. It is the breaking of a union which ought to be, on grounds which have nothing to do with the union or with those who should participate in it. The abandoned child, the outcast brother, the neglected parent, the betrayed Lord, the forsaken country—these are spectacles of broken union which carry in them the essence of the evil of segregation. Segregation breaks the union of those who ought to be united by the arbitrary exclusion of the one party by the other. And we are here using the word *ought,* not in the sense of expediency or need, but to connote a primary order of life, an elemental rightness, an eternal will. Segregation is that act, or those acts, which separate a person or persons from those to whom they belong on the ground of circumstances irrelevant to the union which ought to be. Discrimination, in our definition, has to do with the unjust separation of people from things and circumstances; segregation, in our definition, has to do with the immoral separation of people from people.

Racial segregation falls under this judgment and under no other. It is evil for the simple reason that it severs a person or a people from those to whom they belong on the basis of capricious, arbitrary, and irrelevant considerations of race. In the mind of the segregationist, minor and superficial human distinctions are accounted sufficient to warrant the rupture of major and basic human identities. The Negro is a man but he is prohibited from a free association with other men because of his race and he is thereby excluded from man's estate. The Negro is a citizen and in the civil order all other considerations are secondary to that fact; but he is denied a full participation in the rights of citizenship because of his race and he is thereby cut off from that civil body to which he belongs. The Negro is a Christian, which means that he belongs to the Christian community, to the whole fellowship of those who are one in Christ; but by his color he is kept from communing with some parts of the household of faith and he is thereby barred from a primary union by an incidental distinction. This is the immoral aspect of racial segregation: it denies and violates on the ground of race that human oneness which is proclaimed by the highest order of government, and which is a central doctrine of the Christian religion.

The obvious relationship between discrmination and segregation must now be noted. Discrimination is the impertinent denial of the right to have; segregation is the irrelative denial of the right to belong. Since there are vast areas of life in which you cannot have without belonging, it is plain that segregation usually involves all the evils of discrimination and that it is a most convenient tool for those who, for whatever reason, seek to deprive their fellow man. Whether segregation is an expression of racial pride or merely an absent-minded, habitual observance of custom, it ends in the Negro's losing what is rightfully his by his being excluded from that humanity, that citizenship, or that spiritual community to which he rightly belongs. Segregated schools, buses, playgrounds, hotels, restaurants, churches, etc., are denials not merely of the right to belong but also of the right to have.

But we have given our attention to the problems and to the cures of discrimination and must examine now those evils which would be inherent in segregation even though in keeping certain people apart it still allowed them to have in full what is properly theirs. What can we say to that majority of Americans who believe that the answer to the racial problem is to be found in the establishing of parallel societies which are separate but equal? A surprising number of conscientious American minds, both white and Negro, hold to this view. They do not suggest, of course, as they once did, that these parallel societies occupy separate geographic areas, but they hope that one nation can somehow be made to embrace two distinct societies. To them discrimination is wrong but a segregated social system purged of all discrimination would be right.

So we must ask why it is that a Negro wants his child to attend a white school even though the Negro school is just as good or better. In my home county in South Carolina and in neighboring Clarendon County, where one of the cases which carried to the Supreme Court arose, the schools for Negro children are now in some instances equal or superior to the schools for white children. A fear of desegregation and a desire to delay or outrun court decisions, as well as a conscientious interest in the Negro on the part of some white people, have prompted the equalizing of school facilities. But there are still Negroes who do not want their children to attend these superior but segregated schools. Why? Are they just being "uppity" or is it because they sense in segregated schools a profaning of a deep and sacred right to belong which has nothing to do with inferior, equal, or superior schools? We must ask why Negroes resent their exclusion from membership in white churches. Don't they have good churches and aren't they happier with their own? And if some Negroes are content *to have* whether they *belong* or not, as some of them are, should they be content? What can we say to such questions and to the rather general notion that separate but equal societies, paralleling cultures, would be an eminently just solution to the problems of race in America?

We know, of course, that the supposition is false from the beginning; paralleling societies cannot be just. This is the correct philosophical assumption underlying the Brown v. Board of Education decision of the Supreme Court in 1954; segregation on the basis of race deprives a person of constitutional rights even though the " 'tangible' factors may be equal" and even though the Negro himself may have no objection. Moreover, if there were paralleling societies, the floor from which the Negro would have to begin his cultural and economic development and the ceiling to which he could rise would be considerably lower in his restricted racial grouping than they would be in the adjacent white society. But by supposing that such paralleling and equal societies would be just we can determine whether segregation is per se an evil or whether it is evil only when it results in discrimination, taking from people what they have a right to have.

The fundamental fact which denies the hope for Negro and white social orders which are equal to but isolated from each other is that the lives of Negroes and whites are already so thoroughly merged that the separation of the one from the other would be literally impossible. The roots of the histories of Negroes and whites in this country run so deep into a common past and are so intricately intertwined as to be virtually indistinguishable and certainly inseparable. In point of time the Negro is second only to the Indian and the Englishman in claiming America as a homeland, and the Negro arrived only a few years after the Englishman. In patriotism the Negro has a unique honor, being the first to shed his blood for American independence. (It would be interesting to know how many descendants of Crispus Attucks, the ex-slave who was the first to fall in the Boston Massacre in 1770, if he had descendants, have been invited to join the Sons and Daughters of the American Revolution.) Moreover, Negroes and whites are sharers and producers of a common culture. The impact of the white man upon the life of the Negro has been tremendous and dramatic. But there has also been a reciprocal influence, less extensive and deep and less dramatic, perhaps, but nonetheless real; the Negro by his presence on the American scene has had a large part in molding that culture which the white man believes to be entirely his own. The influence of the Negro upon the white man's conventions, his customs, his songs, his language, his accent, his temperament, his religion, has been such that there is no white man in the South today, however "pure" his blood, who is not to some extent culturally a Negro. The whites must count the Negroes among their spiritual ancestors whether they like it or not and the Negroes must acknowledge that in the whites they have the larger part of their cultural paternity. If by some miracle a complete physical separation of the races were effected, we could not in a thousand years undo what we have done to each other.

Indeed, however indelicate the subject may seem to some and however much the racial purists try to ignore the fact, this is true not only spiritually and culturally but also to a degree biologically. The Negro, biologically, is today not genetically the same Negro that landed in Jamestown in 1619, and, with the "passing" of thousands of Negroes into the white community each year, neither is the white man *as a race* genetically the same white man who came to this land a few years earlier. The visible and invisible mixture of the races has been and still is in process. Moreover, the economic lives of Negroes and whites are of one piece. What the prejudiced white man desires psychologically—the annihilation of the Negro—would be disastrous for the white man agriculturally, industrially, and economically. Cut the economic jugular vein of the Negro and the white man bleeds. And, to speak of nothing more, the two races are in the main embraced by a common faith, worship the same God, read the same Bible, endorse the same code of morality, hope for the same heaven, drink the same Cup, and serve the same Lord. This is a broken kinship but it is nevertheless a kinship which is rich in fact and tremendous in possibility. To speak of separating two races which are thus caught up in one bundle of life into separate and paralleling societies is to ignore that long intermixture which has made them one; and to hope that such a separation of the two races could be brought about without doing a deep injury to the body and soul of one race or the other or of both is obviously a delusion. Indeed, Negroes and whites are involved in a biological, cultural, social, economic, and spiritual oneness which cannot be broken.

Therefore, if we think for a moment in paradoxical terms, segregation in its deeper definition is the separating of that which cannot be separated; in other words, it splits on the circumference of life that which cannot be split at the center. It denies on the edges of human existence that which cannot be denied at the core. Perhaps we can illustrate this thought in the following way. We know that the relationship of mother and baby is one of biological and psychic "belongingness." If mother forsakes child or child be kidnapped from mother, their oneness is disrupted at one level but it is not disrupted at another. If the oneness of mother and baby could be completely destroyed, then mother would not mourn for child and child would not cry for mother. The agony, the anxiety, the tension, the sorrow of separation are a result of the fact that oneness which can never be destroyed has been somewhat destroyed.

Tillich has said that "illness, in the largest sense of body, soul and spirit, is estrangement."[2] This is a beautiful and searching statement from an authoritative theologian; but I must nevertheless add the suggestion that "illness, in the largest sense of body, soul and spirit, is estrangement" from that from which one cannot be estranged. It breaks on the surface a relationship which cannot be broken at the center. Physical illness is alienation from that physical nature from which one cannot escape except in death. Spiritual sickness is flight from a God whose presence is everywhere. Social sickness is alienation from a human union from which one cannot be separated. And, in the train of this thought, racial segregation is a temporal behavior which assumes that it has cancelled the eternal fact of the oneness of man; it separates on the social, or economic, or civil level that which cannot be separated in the deeper reaches of the human soul. And the result for white man and Negro is an illness, the illness of those who are estranged from those to whom they belong. For however fine we may draw out the nerve which connects man to man, it does not break. If it did, all the agonies, the aches and sorrows of human separation would break with it; but it does not break; it holds forever, thin and taut; and along this nerve throb the anxieties, the fears, the pangs of human estrangement.

From the anxieties of this separation the white man has in the past tried to escape, not by restoring and completing the broken union, but by seeking to make the severance complete. Said the white man to himself, "If I can debase this creature to a subhuman level, make him one with the beasts of the fields, then these intolerable vexations in my heart and mind will disappear and I shall be at ease." He set his clergy to the task of showing that the relationship between white and Negro, is by divine order, not one of man and man but one of master and servant. He showed through the studies of his anthropologists that there are in the physiognomy of the Negro plain evidences of the mental and physical inferiority of the Negro and even subtle hints that the Negro may be a subspecies midway between man and animal, naturally endowed for hard labor but fitted for nothing else. He declared through his scholars that the mental incapacities of the Negro deny that he is man, saying in the words of John C. Calhoun, "If I could find a Negro who knew Greek syntax, I should believe that the Negro was a human being and ought to be treated as a man." He wrote it into his law, as Justice Taney put it in the Dred Scott case, that the Negroes "had for more than a century . . . been regarded as being of an inferior order; and altogether unfit to associate with the white race, either in social or political relations; and so far inferior that they had no rights which the white man was bound to respect."[3]

Thus the white man has sought to ease his own vexed spirit by wiping from the table of his memory all records of that one-ness in which God has forever bound all of his children. The seat of the white man's misery in regard to the Negro is the fact that he has tried and is still trying to break what cannot be broken, to shatter at its center a relationship which he has severed on the surface. It is an embittering and frustrating task, doomed to failure; for the brother whom God has put and keeps in the heart, at the center of all exclusive circles, you cannot with sweet conscience exclude from your life. Three hundred years of failure should have convinced the white man that his poignant uneasiness about his relationship to the Negro has its solution, not in further estrangements of the one from the other, but in a reconciliation which acknowledges on the surface of life that oneness, unbreakable and imperishable, which is the central fact of all human intercourse. The answer to the anxieties of separateness, says Erich Fromm in *The Art of Loving*, "lies in the achievement of interpersonal union, of fusion with another person, *in love*."[4]

Seen from the Negro's point of view, the anxieties of sepa-rateness are different from those apparent in the troubled conscience of the white man. What the white man as the segre-gator wills to deny, the Negro as the segregated is not permitted to affirm. The white man bears the major guilt of segregation; the Negro bears the major burden of segregation. The white man is in the role of the mother who has willfully forsaken her child; the Negro is in the role of the willfully forsaken child. The mother can but will not return to that one-ness which she has flouted; the child would but cannot be restored to that oneness from which it has been expelled. The agonies of the Negro under segregation are the agonies of suffoca-tion; he is cut off from the sources of full life by being separated from that to which he belongs. To be his whole and healthy self he must be able to identify himself in free and complete associa-tion with that of which he is a part. To the extent to which the Negro as a man is isolated from being and acting as a man, to the extent that he can think of himself as a citizen but is deprived of the duty and privilege of a citizen, to the extent that he as a spiritual being is denied fellowship in worship and service with those who worship and serve the same God, to that extent he lives in a tent in which the oxygen of his being is slowly exhausted and in which he becomes pallid semblance of his real self. What William Temple said of the unemployed applies even more to excluded Negroes: ". . . they are not wanted! That is the thing that has power to corrupt the soul of any man not already far advanced in saintliness."[5] We shall see in a later chapter what discrimination and segregation do to the human soul, and we are now merely establishing the fact that man has a psychic need to belong to that to which he belongs and that the Negro through racial segregation is cut off from those associations which are indispensable to his being.

The need to belong requires little demonstration; it is the theme of psychological textbooks; forms the plots of novels and dramas; explains the bizarre dress and eccentric speech of adolescents; supports multitudinous fraternities and sororities; promotes church membership, patriotism, mob violence, and class reunions. There are numerous patterns of human behavior which make sense only because of the universal human need to belong. This is well known; but we must be impressed once more by the fact that the urge to belong, even in hermit and recluse, is a dominant and basic urge of the human soul and that its satisfaction is indispensable in the development of wholesome personality. The need to belong is a psychic need—deep, primary, and original. Human beings can tolerate an extraordinary amount of physical deprivation and even a physical separation from people provided that they know themselves to be directly and intimately related to those people or to those associations of people to whom they know that they belong; but sanity and personality are in serious jeopardy wherever people are not allowed to be identified with those communities of humanity of which they know themselves to be part and parcel. Racial segregation seriously jeopardizes the personality of the Negro and is a vicious threat to his mental and moral stability because it is forever thwarting his psychic need to belong to that to which he belongs and apart from which he cannot be what by nature, citizenry, and the grace of God he is. . . .

by E. Clinton Gardner

JUSTICE AND LOVE

ALTHOUGH the major denominations have come out in support of the 1954 Supreme Court decision banning segregation in the public schools, the Southern pulpit in general has been silent on the issue of racial segregation. There have been many exceptions, of course. On the one hand, some of the more liberal clergy have attempted to deal constructively with the problems involved. They have presented forced separation of the races as un-Christian and have dealt with the problems of freedom of speech and the basic need to honor the law of the land in order to prevent mob rule as well as with the need to bring about greater justice for Negroes. They have sought to keep lines of communication between the races open and to arrive at constructive steps whereby the mandate of the Supreme Court might be carried out in good faith. On the other hand, some of the more conservative clergy have defended legally enforced separation upon Biblical grounds and have supported the organization of White Citizens' Councils.

Reprinted from *Theology Today*, July 1957, pp. 212-222. By permission. E. CLINTON GARDNER is Professor of Social Ethics at Candler School of Theology, Emory University, Atlanta, Ga. He has been president of the American Society of Christian Social Ethics (1961-62), and is the author of *Biblical Faith and Social Ethics*.

I

In the main the ministers of the large urban Churches in the South have been silent upon the issue until recent months. Many of them have been considered friendly to the Court's ban on segregation, and some observers have supposed that they were part of a large group of liberal moderates who were not being heard from either because of the many pressures upon them to keep silent since they were unwilling actively to oppose integration, or because they believed that it would only accentuate prejudice and discrimination to attack segregation directly under the present circumstances. However, in recent months some of those who had previously held their peace have taken their stand in support of enforced separation,[1] and they have sought to justify their position upon Christian grounds. Unlike the theologically more conservative ministers who appeal to the Biblical account of the curse of Ham's descendants, these theologically more sophisticated and enlightened clergy generally reject the Biblical curse as the basis of their position. The argument which they use is much more serious than the appeal to the Old Testament curse, for not only is it made in the name of the Gospel, but it also undercuts the Christian concern for social justice in general and not in the field of race relations alone. For these reasons the present tendency, not just to be silent in the face of the claims of social justice but positively to defend the *status quo* and to proclaim that in any event the Christian faith is concerned only with personal salvation and with the practice of neighbor love exclusively in "one-to-one" relationships, must be resisted, for it makes the Gospel irrelevant to the basic social problems of the day.

While there was a paradoxical sense in which those who were not actively opposed to the efforts to bring about a greater degree of social justice could be considered supporters of such efforts ("he that is not against you is for you"), those who are now taking their stand in support of the *status quo* are clearly no longer neutral allies. And what is more, the very fact that they did not oppose the Court's school decision immediately after it was first rendered in May, 1954 as many avowed racialists did, but were ostensibly brought to their position reluctantly after much thought and prayer, seems to imply that their "realism" has stood the tests of truth and love. Moreover, this change on the part of "moderate" leaders becomes even more consequential when it is remembered that they frequently represent the spiritual leadership of the moderate-liberal urban congregations which would be most likely to respond to genuine guidance in the direction of greater social justice between the races. Thus while it is obvious that in the metropolitan area of Atlanta, for example, resistance to certain specific changes in the pattern of race relations would be great in any church, it is also clear that resistance to *some* steps would be far less than it would be in many other parts of the state. Witness the interracial groups in the area, the opening of the municipal golf courses to members of both races, the employment of Negro policemen, the election on a city-wide basis of Dr. Rufus Clement, President of Atlanta University, to the Atlanta school board, and the widespread opposition to the county unit system which plays into the hands of the more conservative political forces.

The basic issue which is raised by the current controversy over segregation is, of course, not new, but it urgently needs to be re-examined, not so much in the specific terms of race relations as the terms of the more general Biblical, theological, and ethical considerations involved in the relationships of justice to love. For the entire relevance of the Gospel and the Church to the social order is involved in the present controversy. It would be possible for many to see the issues involved far more objectively if such an analysis of the basic question were undertaken in a context other than that of defending and attacking racial segregation. Hence we shall direct our attention to a more general examination of the relations of love to justice in the light of the Biblical understanding of these concepts and also in the light of the related Christian doctrines of sin, salvation, and justification.

II

In the first place, it needs to be made clear that *in the Christian view love is the fulfillment of justice, never a substitute for justice.* More specifically, love in the New Testament sense of *agape* (uncalculating, self-giving love) is the fulfillment of justice in the classical sense of giving to each according to his due. The Christian is bound by a higher obligation which transcends the requirements of justice both as the latter is understood in an ideal sense apart from the Gospel and as it is exemplified in historical systems of civil law and convention. In relation to the latter in particular there is an element of truth with which we shall have to reckon in the argument advanced by those who seek to limit Christian morality to the area of personal relations, for the Christian norm of love is never fully embodied in a historical system of law. But the difficulty with this argument taken by itself is that it is so easily used to justify the acceptance of even less than the achievable justice in the social order. Love, if divorced from the attempt to establish social justice, becomes sentimental. It attempts to atone for social injustice by the practice of love—which requires more than the actual system of legal justice—in individual relationships. As the Oxford Conference on Church, Community, and State declared in 1937: "undue emphasis upon the higher possibilities of love in personal relations, within the limits of a given system of justice or an established social structure, may tempt Christians to allow individual acts of charity to become a screen for injustice and a substitute for justice."[2]

The attempt to substitute personal love for justice stems out of a basic cynicism concerning the social order which represents a *de facto* denial of the Christian doctrines of salvation and justification. It leads, on the one hand, to Pharisaism on the part of those who thus make this attempt and, on the other hand, to disillusionment on the part of the victims of injustice. This effort to substitute love for justice rests upon the belief that all of the alternative systems of justice are so inferior to love that the latter cannot constitute a principle of discrimination between them; it can only be a principle of judgment upon all possible systems of law and social justice. But such a policy of aloofness inevitably gives the advantage to the existing system as over against any effort to improve it. At the same time it beguiles the self-styled noninterventionists in social affairs into a Pharisaism which assumes that its ostensible neutrality is actually innocent of the injustices which flourish unopposed. The victims of the injustice which thus goes unchallenged are not so easily misled, however, for they soon become dubious of the salvation which is proclaimed in the name of a faith which appears to be utterly indifferent to social injustice, and it becomes increasingly difficult effectively to proclaim the Gospel to them.

The fallacy of this attempt to substitute personal love for social justice in the name of the Christian faith becomes clear when the Biblical teaching concerning human justice (*mishpat*) is examined in relation to the divine justice or righteousness (*tsedeq*). Paul Ramsey has shown how the judgmental righteousness (*tsedeq*) of God is normative for human justice (*mishpat*).[3] Indeed, so deeply is the Biblical definition of human justice penetrated by the Biblical conception of the righteousness of God, he maintains, that the two concepts are used in perfect parallelism and interchanged for each other in certain passages (Amos 5:24; Psalm 72:1-4; Psalm 82:3-4, for example). Furthermore, God's righteousness is so closely linked with his mercy (*chesed*) that the former cannot be understood apart from the latter. God's righteousness includes partiality for the weak and the poor, and the Biblical conception of the justice which is required of man differs from all other conceptions of justice in that it demands the same partiality for those in special need. As Rabbi R. L. Kahn declares, justice (*mishpat*) and mercy (*chesed*) are equally characteristic of God, and they are equally demanded of men.[4] It is following Micah's pleas to do justly and love mercy that man fulfills the divine commandment, "Ye shall be holy; for I Jehovah your God am holy." Thus while the Biblical conceptions of justice (*mishpat*), righteousness (*tsedeq*), and mercy (*chesed*) "perhaps never entirely coalesce into bare identity," they are "not at all clearly distinguishable in their meaning and never separable in fact."[5]

In the teaching of Jesus the tendency of "justice" to topple over into benevolence is completed. Professor Richard Niebuhr maintains that the special character of the ethical teaching of Jesus stems out of his conviction that "the God who rules nature and history is holy love."[6] For Jesus God is, emphatically, just. He judges each man by his own standards (Matt. 7:2); but his justice is also evidenced by the manner in which he makes up for the unfair inequalities among men, granting to the poor, the meek, the hungry, and the mourners what they have lacked (Matt. 5:3-11). His justice is holy justice, demanding complete inward integrity (Matt. 5:17-6:6); but his justice is also holy love, for what he demands he gives before making any demands: love, mercy, forgiveness, kindness. His kindness is manifest in the indiscriminateness of nature, for "he makes his sun rise on the evil and on the good, and sends rain on the just and on the unjust" (Matt. 5:45). He bestows his good gifts upon those who turn to him more generously than does a parent upon his children (Matt. 5: 7-11). "This divine mercifulness is not for Jesus something added to God's justice; it is the very heart of the goodness with which God is good. This is what he is, mercy, and this is what he requires in the character of his children."[7]

In the Bible, therefore, the justice which is demanded of men in the social order gets its meaning from the righteousness of God, and the latter can be understood only in terms both of his justice and of his mercy. The divine love includes concern for social justice, and indeed the love of God is made known in his righteous judgments upon men. The justice which God both manifests and requires is redemptive justice, or what Paul Tillich suggestively calls "creative justice."[8] Creative justice "means more than proportionate justice." It "is expressed in the divine grace which forgives in order to reunite." Understood in terms of their ontology as well as in terms of their Biblical usage, not only is there no essential conflict between justice and love, but also love cannot be separated from justice. "Justice in its ultimate meaning is creative justice, and creative justice is the form of reuniting love"—the form in which and through which love performs its work."[9]

III

In the second place, *justice is a necessary instrument of love.* Neighbor love in the New Testament means ministering to the neighbor's need, and the neighbor is every man who is affected by what we do or leave undone. The neighbor may be encountered both as an individual and as a member of various institutions by us who are also related to him both directly as individuals and indirectly through institutions. In all of these relationships his welfare and his dignity are at stake. Hence, as Daniel Day Williams admonishes us, it is "a dangerous sentimentality to exalt a pure and unmediated meeting of subjects in the I-Thou relationship as the only true good." Social justice, like love, seeks the welfare of all persons in community. It aims directly at the good of the group and indirectly at the good of each person in the group; and, since most of our relationships with our neighbors are necessarily indirect, the most effective way of ministering to their total welfare is through the pursuit of social justice.

In his Gifford Lectures, Reinhold Niebuhr has analyzed the manner in which systems and principles of justice become the servants of love in so far as they extend the sense of obligation toward the neighbor in the following three ways. In the first place, they may transform the awareness of an obligation that is immediately felt in the presence of an obvious need into a continuing sense of obligation that is expressed in fixed principles of social justice. In the second place, they may extend the obligation which one feels in relation to a single neighbor to the complex relations of the self and a group of neighbors. And, finally, they may extend the obligation which the individual discerns to "the wider obligations which the community defines from its more impartial perspective."[10] Thus justice may be used as an instrument of love in relationships involving only two individuals by way of assisting us to discern with greater clarity and objectivity the neighbor's true needs, but as soon as a third person is introduced into the relation love *requires* some calculation of conflicting needs and interests. Even within the family some rational estimate of conflicting claims and interests is necessary in the interest of love. The Samaritan may not have to employ the concept of justice in dealing with the single neighbor by the side of the road, but the moment he becomes confronted with two neighbors both of whose needs he is unable to meet he must evaluate their respective claims in the interest of *agape*.

Instead of contradicting the ethic of love, the provision for justice through the state is the indispensable means to the welfare of society as a whole and thus indirectly of the neighbor as an individual. As George Thomas points out, systems of social justice as exemplified in the laws of a state have a dual value.[11] In the first place, they have the negative function of restraining egoism and aggressivenesss on the part of the constituent members of a society (cf. Rom. 13:4), and thus they make social order possible. In the second place, they have a positive function to which the negative one is subordinate, namely, the provision of the structural framework in which all of the members of society may more effectively seek the fulfillment of their nature and purposes. This is surely an indispensable concern of love, for without such a structure of justice and law there would be no order and no freedom which are necessary to undergird man's efforts to fulfill his physical and social and spiritual needs. And not only is some system of social justice essential as the framework for the development of man's physical and social and spiritual natures, but the structural framework itself also performs a work of love in so far as it is creative for good in the life of a community. Professor Gordon Allport concludes his illuminating study, *The Nature of Prejudice*,[12] with the arresting judgment that legislative action is "one of the major methods of reducing, not only public discrimination, but private prejudice as well." The state is, as Williams observes, "always creative for good or evil";[13] hence,

Christians ought to use it as a way of educating men, including themselves, in love.

Individualistic Protestantism ignores the creative role of the state when it argues that Christianity has no concern with efforts to legislate justice and righteousness. The hypocrisy of this claim is clearly shown, however, by the fact that the argument is generally advanced in only one area, race relations, while at the same time the very groups which make this charge in relation to one area of legislation are among the strongest supporters of similar efforts in other areas, for example, prohibition. The hollowness of this argument is also shown by the fact that none of these groups or individuals seriously advocates the abolishment of all laws designed to secure the blessings of liberty and justice (traffic laws, school laws, food and drug laws, laws protecting property, even most existing laws providing for a certain amount of justice for the Negro) for all men. Indeed, the very fact that these groups strongly urge their members to be lawabiding as a Christian duty in most regards strongly suggests that the dichotomy between love and justice is not actually as great as is alleged for the purpose of excluding a certain sphere of conduct from the area of Christian obligation.

There is another consideration involved in our claim that justice is a necessary instrument of love, and this relates to the Church's task of evangelism. For not only does love require the pursuit of social justice in order to meet the basic social, political, and economic needs of men, but it also requires the pursuit of social justice as a condition of effectively ministering to their spiritual needs. Without concern for justice the proclamation of love in the name of the Gospel becomes hollow. Hence, it is not surprising that large segments of society do not respond to the proclamation of the Gospel, and it is also not surprising that the spiritual power of the Church in our day is at a startlingly low ebb, for the love which is proclaimed in terms of God's requirements for man is not *agape* at all but, rather, a sentimental version of love which is in reality an escape from *agape* or what Professor George Kelsey calls "practical atheism."[14]

Social conditions frequently become so oppressive that they constitute almost insurmountable obstacles to the reception of the Gospel and the experience of salvation. Thus, as Professor John Bennett points out,[15] poor housing conditions, contrasts in a society between extreme wealth and extreme poverty, unemployment, and a corrupt moral climate in which undue emphasis is placed upon personal financial gain and success judged in terms of false standards constitute obstacles to the experience of salvation as the awareness of God's forgiveness and acceptance and growth in obedience and love. This is true even when this salvation is viewed entirely in terms of a personal relationship to God. Hence it would seem that a wise policy of evangelism, even if its sole aim were the salvation of men's souls, would necessarily be concerned with the removal of social impediments to the reception of the Gospel, and it would seem that this concern would be especially great in the case of a stumbling-block such as segregation which is commonly recognized as being un-Christian even when withdrawal from the effort to eliminate it through social action is defended.

IV

Finally, *love is for the Christian the ultimate norm of justice.* As Reinhold Niebuhr declares, love is "both the fulfillment and the negation of all achievements of justice in history."[16] Individualistic Protestantism is quite right in seeing a certain negative relationship between love and justice, for all actual laws and systems of justice contain contradictions to *agape.* But it errs in failing to see the positive relationship whereby love is at the same time the fulfillment of the justice which the historical system of laws seeks. Hence individualistic Protestantism is always threatened with the danger of withdrawal from culture.

Viewed then in relation to concrete systems of justice, love reaches beyond justice and provides a standard for judging all historical schemes of justice. While recognizing the necessity for the concrete systems of justice, love always seeks to raise these expressions of justice to new heights, for it recognizes that each system of justice represents something less than perfect justice or perfect love. Yet love does not attempt to take the place of justice in group relationships, for it recognizes that even in the family or the Church the attempt to live by spontaneous love alone is self-defeating. For this reason love makes use of the structures of justice, not as "eternal norms to which life must perennially conform" but rather as "*ad hoc* efforts to strike a balance between the final moral possibilities of life and the immediate and given realities."[17]

For the Christian the distance between what is actually possible in a particular situation and the divine will under which all of our action stands in judgment is covered by grace. The central meaning of the classical doctrine of justification by faith is that no man—either the pietist or the monk or the reformer—is justified by works, even works of withdrawal to avoid compromise, but only by faith.[18] The person who withdraws from social responsibility in the name of a perfectionist ethic is always in danger of falling into pride and self-righteousness because he so narrowly limits the scope of the application of this ethic. Moreover, the attempt to withdraw from the pursuit of greater justice (greater equality, for example) just because perfect justice (perfect equality of opportunity) is unattainable in the present represents a serious misunderstanding of the nature of love, for it starts at the wrong center. It seeks to save one's life in eternity by keeping oneself unspotted from the world. The New Testament *agape,* on the other hand, begins with an orientation of the self toward God's will and the neighbor's need, "For whoever would save his life will lose it, and whoever loses his life for my sake will find it" (Matt. 16:25). The service of the neighbor under God is what is required of man.

Not only does love seek the welfare of all through the pursuit of social justice, but it also seeks the welfare of each member of the group as an individual, and in dealing with the needs of the individual neighbor in an I-Thou relationship it finds the highest possibilities for sacrificial love. "Naturally, the justice and harmony which is achieved in this way (social justice) is not the harmony of the kingdom of God, nor yet identical with the highest possible harmony between individuals in their personal evaluations." "For this reason," writes Reinhold Niebuhr, "there must always be a final distinction between what the Gospel demands of us in our individual and spontaneous relations and what is demanded in the institutions and structures of society."[19] Thus, in addition to—not instead of—the love which is expressed in the provision for community justice, the Christian is called upon to seek a fuller expression of *agape* above and beyond the civil law. To limit love to the relative justice of any historical system is to put love in a strait jacket. Love that is thus restricted and systematized becomes cold and calculating. It becomes something less than *agape*. But, on the other hand, to divorce love from justice is to turn it into pious sentimentality so that instead of being more than justice it ends up being less than justice.

II

Economic Community

THE production and distribution of goods constitutes a community of need and desire. The essays in this section deal with various ways of ordering this community, proposing values which should inform the further development of man through economic activity. Clark Kucheman develops the notion of a common end—rational freedom. He generalizes this to all men by a principle of fairness or equality. He then evaluates a compulsory or market economy as best setting the conditions for the development of freedom. He concludes that the market economy best furnishes the conditions of freedom, appealing to Paul Tillich's three mediating norms of self-determination, equality, and community in making his evaluation. This is a clear, systematic argument which enables the reader to make his own judgments.

Self-determination, equality and community are common values in the three statements, although *Populorum Progressio* and Paul Tillich's essay treat the religious vision as central to ethical judgment. Paul Tillich evaluates the technological organization of society differently. He sees loss of personhood and human community under the objectifying forces of a competitive society. Since Kucheman draws heavily on Tillich for his moral values, this disagreement indicates a radically different appraisal of the effects of the market economy. *Populorum Progressio* lifts up community and global solidarity as the central value; human community, thus, becomes the end of economic life. This leads to planning and allocation for human need. Kucheman is in sympathy with this concern in his prescriptions for dealing with poverty. However, the encyclical also attacks the materialism inherent in the competitive market system, whereas Kucheman glosses over this element. Despite his own argument that being a person, being free, and being rational means mastering one's drives and impulses, Kucheman seems untroubled by the materialism of the market. Thus, Kucheman lifts up self-determination as the critical value and plays down both personhood and community as these are stressed in the other perspectives, revealing the centrality of his own religious vision in choosing among various values.

by Clark Kucheman

TOWARD A THEORY OF
NORMATIVE ECONOMICS

DURING the past several years, perhaps more than ever before, discussion has turned to the problem of evaluating social arrangements and policies and, among these, especially economic arrangements and policies. By what standards should we evaluate economic systems, such as "capitalism" and "socialism?" Within such an overall system, how should we decide what economic policies to adopt in pursuit of what specific goals? These are the main questions at stake, and it goes without saying that the answers we give to them will affect the quality of human life. The policies we adopt—and even the choice of an overall system is a policy decision in the long run—will have much to do with how human life is lived both now and in the distant future.

In what follows I hope to contribute to this vital discussion by suggesting a normative scheme in terms of which economic arrangements and policies can be evaluated. I hope to provide at least a tentative solution to the problem posed above and, with it, a brief indication of what it means in practice.

First, how can we arrive at normative standards of this sort?

Paper given at the Conference of the Ethics and Society Field, January 1967, on the occasion of the 100th Anniversary of the Divinity School, University of Chicago. It will appear in the volume on social ethics, "Essays in Divinity," series to be published by the University of Chicago Press. CLARK KUCHEMAN is Associate Professor of Christian Ethics at Claremont Men's College and Claremont Graduate School.

One negative point is clear. Even though religious traditions—especially the Christian tradition—are often rich sources of ideas, we cannot regard them as authoritative. We cannot accept a norm on the grounds that it is Christian, or Jewish, or Buddhist, or, for that matter, "American." The reason for this is simply that if *we* are entitled to appeal to such an authority, so is anyone else. Since it is obvious that judgments reached by such a method need not agree, and since two contradictory judgments cannot both be true, the method itself is not acceptable. Furthermore, it will not do to say that only our *own* tradition is authoritative, or that only our *own* tradition contains "revealed" truth. For anyone else could make the same claim about *his* tradition, and this leaves us with the same difficulty as before. To avoid this we would have to give reasons for regarding our tradition as true. If we do this, however, we are appealing not to the tradition itself but to the reasons for appealing to it; that is, we are "selecting" on rational grounds what we regard as revelatory or authoritative. In order to justify or verify our judgments about norms, we must do so—ultimately—on rational grounds.

I

By what standard should we evaluate economic institutions and policies? The point of view I intend to present and defend can be stated briefly as follows.

1. Each of us has a moral end, i.e., a goal he ought to seek, or a potentiality he ought to realize. This moral end is "rationality," or, to use an alternative term, "freedom."

2. This end is a common end; it is an end that we all as human beings have in common.

3. Since it is a common end, freedom, or rationality, is the foundation of our rights and duties with respect to one another.

4. Social arrangements and institutions, including economic systems and policies, are means to this common end. They are good, or valuable, to the degree to which they contribute to the realization of the common end; they are bad, or disvaluable, to

the degree to which they prevent the realization of the common end.

In other words, my argument is that there is a common moral end, and that institutions are valuable in so far as they are conducive to achieving it. Economic systems and policies, then, should be judged from the point of view of their contribution to this end.

It goes without saying that this argument is not immediately convincing; indeed, without further explanation, the propositions themselves are not sufficiently clear. For example, how can it be that an institution that is conducive to the common end is also necessarily conducive to, or at least compatible with, the performance of duties and the exercise of rights? Is it not conceivable that these are different sorts of things, such that what is conducive to one is not conducive to the other? The answer must be that since the common end is the basis of rights and duties, in the sense that it determines what specific—substantive —rights and duties we ought to acknowledge, to be conducive to the common end is *ipso facto* to be conducive as well to the performance of duties and the exercise of rights. But why is this so? How does the common end determine what rights and duties should be acknowledged and respected?

Since it is so crucial for the argument, I shall begin by considering this problem of our rights and duties relative to one another and how they are established.

Upon what principle can we determine how we ought to treat one another? There is one necessary, albeit formal, principle to which we can appeal: the generalization principle, or the principle of fairness. If something—an act or a "rule"—is right for one person, it is right also for all relevantly similar persons in relevantly similar circumstances. If we observe a practice, or follow a rule, in one case, we ought to follow it in every case where it applies. This principle, I submit, is necessarily true. For to say that what is right for one person is *wrong* for a similar person in a similar circumstance is to say that what is right is wrong, and this is plainly self-contradictory. Thus the principle *must* be true. It is wrong, therefore, to be partial; it is wrong to apply a rule in one case and not in another, unless it can be shown that there is a relevant difference between the two cases. We ought to be impartial, or fair.

Even if it is true, however, can such a formal principle be very helpful? After all, it does not tell us *what* is right (or wrong); it only tells us that we must be consistent. It does tell us that if we adopt the rule, say, "Negroes should not be permitted to vote," then it would be wrong for us to permit some particular Negro, who might happen to be a friend, to vote. But, at least on this level of mere consistency, the generalization principle does not tell us whether the rule itself is right or wrong, or fair or unfair. Fortunately, however, it is possible to apply the principle in a more significant way as well. For rules must be applied to ourselves as well as to others; we must be willing to have others apply the rule to us that we wish to apply to them. For example, if we say—or act on the rule—that it is permissible for us to steal from others, then, to be consistent, we must also say that it is permissible for others to steal from us. This, too, follows from the requirement to be consistent; it is an application of the principle that what is right for one person is right for similar persons in similar circumstances.

Even carried to this level, however, there are difficulties in this line of reasoning. For if such a prescriptive rule is to make a difference for our conduct toward one another, we must in fact be unwilling or disinclined to have it applied to us. Yet we may indeed *be* willing to have such a rule applied to ourselves. In the case of stealing, we may be quite willing to have others try to steal from us, especially if we think we are strong enough to prevent them from succeeding. If so, then we could, without inconsistency, try to steal from them. Clearly, while this application of the principle of fairness is helpful—it forbids actions we do not want done to us—it is not definitive. Prescriptive rules derived in this manner would be conditional, not unconditional; they would be hypothetical rather than categorical. That is, they would be dependent upon our empirical wants or inclinations and could always be suspended if only your wants were strong enough. In fact, there would be no limits to what we could do, provided we would be willing to have it done to us as well.

Nevertheless, when properly interpreted the generalization principle does yield unconditional "oughts." This can be seen, for example, in the rule against stealing. As the rule was just formulated, stealing is permissible if we are willing to have others steal from us. But this formulation is faulty. To steal from someone is to take his property from him *against his will*. If he is willing to give it to us, then we are not stealing it! But when we add this important fact about stealing, it becomes clear that stealing cannot be permissible, regardless of our empirical desires or wants. The reason is that to apply the rule to ourselves it is not enough to be willing to have our property taken from us; we must be willing to have our property *forcibly* taken from us. That is, we must be *willing* to be *unwillingly* deprived of our property. And this is not merely a logical contradiction; it is literally impossible. We simply cannot be willing to be unwillingly deprived of our property. Either we are willing or we are not willing. We cannot be both. Therefore, since we cannot apply to ourselves the rule we would apply to others, the rule permitting us to steal must be false. Stealing is *prima facie* wrong; it cannot be generalized. The generalization principle does after all supply rules that do not depend upon empirical inclinations. The rule against stealing is merely one instance; all coercive actions, or rules of action, are similarly *prima facie* wrong. For they cannot be generalized. They cannot be generalized because we cannot be willing to be unwilling.

The preceding deliberations show that the generalization principle takes us at least a step in the direction of determining how we ought or ought not to treat one another. Certainly it establishes that we ought to be fair to one another and that this involves at least a *prima facie* rule that we ought not to coerce one another. Nevertheless, my claim is that a different principle —the principle of the common moral end—and not the generalization principle, is the ultimate foundation of rights and duties as well as of value judgments about social institutions and policies. How can this be so?

To begin with, it is easy to see that the principle of fairness is not by itself sufficient to evaluate social institutions and policies. This principle requires that we treat others in ways that we would, and could, be willing to be treated ourselves under similar circumstances. It demands equality of treatment, in the sense that rules derived from the generalization principle apply equally to all. But the generalization principle does not provide a criterion of content; it does not supply a standard for judging what ends or goals ought to be pursued. Apart from regulating our formal relations with other people, i.e., determining that we ought to treat them fairly, the generalization principle makes no prescriptions. It leaves open the question of how we ought to treat ourselves, or of what we ought to do with our lives. Any purpose or end is permissible, so long as we can pursue it fairly. Clearly, therefore, in order to evaluate institutions and policies, which are instruments we create and use in the pursuit of ends, we need a criterion in addition to the criterion of fairness; we need a standard for assessing ends or goals.

But this is not all. It can also be seen now that the generalization principle does not serve finally to establish substantive, or actual, rights and duties. For if human beings have no end that they ought morally to seek, then the generalization principle does not determine how they ought to be treated. The fact that the generalization principle does not say how human beings ought to treat themselves, or what they ought to do with their lives, implies that it cannot determine how they ought to treat one another. It does require that they treat one another fairly. But this is merely a formal requirement; its content depends upon the empirical wants or desires of the *recipient* of treatment, even if not upon the empirical wants or desires of the *agent*. Under the principle of fairness, if a person wants to be treated in a certain way, or is willing to be so treated, then it is not wrong to treat him in that way. For example, if a person is willing to sell himself into slavery, to commit himself forever to do someone else's bidding, then it is permissible to treat him accordingly. As a matter of fact, under a rule derivable from the generalization principle, namely, that we ought to help others achieve their purposes, it might even be an obligation to treat such a person as a slave. Similarly, it is permissible, and perhaps an obligation, to give dope to a potential addict, provided only that he wants it. Further, it is possible to imagine an entire society whose members mutually agree to administer opiates to one another, and, according to the generalization principle, this is a justifiable state of affairs; it is a perfectly "fair" arrangement.

We can see, then, that the generalization principle does not establish substantive rights and duties; it prescribes a form—fairness—but no content. The generalization principle does not tell us what specific rights and duties ought to be acknowledged and acted upon.

For these reasons, therefore, the principle of fairness alone is insufficient. By itself it does not prescribe a moral end—it says nothing about how we ought to live our lives—and, since it does not, it cannot establish substantive rights and duties. Now, is there such a criterion of content to which we can appeal? Can we discover a moral end? That is, is there an end we all ought to seek not because we may happen to want to but purely and simply because we ought to?

The prescriptive rules derived from the generalization principle apply to acts. They tell us whether actions of various kinds toward other people are right (permissible), wrong, or, in some cases, obligatory. They say what is fair, unfair, or, in the case of obligations, what is unfair *not* to do. But we yet may ask: Why should we do as the rules prescribe? Why ought we to do what the rules *say* we ought to do? At this point still another question comes to mind: What do the rules of fairness really give us? The answer is that they give us *reasons* for acting or not acting in certain ways; they give us *rational grounds* for regarding acts as right, wrong, or obligatory. The generalization principle, upon which the rules are based, states that if an act is right (or wrong) for one person, it is also right (or wrong) for similar people in similar circumstances. If we should hold, then, that a certain act is right for ourselves and yet wrong for a relevantly similar person in a relevantly similar circumstance, we are involved in a contradiction. We cannot *rationally* make such a claim. It would be irrational to do so, since in making such a claim we would violate a fundamental "law of thought," namely, the law of contradiction. Not to conform to the rules of fairness, therefore, is to be irrational; it is to refuse to order our thoughts and actions by reason. Why should we obey the rules? It is irrational not to do so.

But what has been accomplished by this line of reasoning? It is irrational not to obey the rules; it is rational to be fair. So what? After all, what if we do not want to be rational? This question changes the terms of the discussion somewhat. Up until now we have been speaking of actions, and we evaluated them as right, wrong, or obligatory. Now, however, the object of discussion is not an act but a condition, or a state of being. The issue concerns *being* something rather than *doing* something. The question is not about what we ought or ought not to *do;* it is about what we ought to *be.* Ought we to *be* rational? Is rationality a value we ought to pursue, embody, and express? Obviously, we are actually rational in some measure. To be rational is to order thought and action by reason, and, hopefully at least, that is what we are doing right now. To this degree we are indeed "rational animals." But ought we to perfect our nature as rational beings?

On this point the following passage from the work of Paul Tillich is suggested.

Whenever thought thinks about itself, it does not merely observe, as it does all other being, but it at the same time determines itself, criticizes itself, and imposes norms upon itself. From the standpoint of thought, its own existence is not strange and distant, as is the existence of a stone or an optical law. When thought becomes aware of itself, it cannot merely be a disinterested observer; it is always at the same time a participant.[1]

In other words, in the process of thinking we are not and cannot be indifferent about our thought. We necessarily judge the adequacy of our thought; that is, we judge it and order it in accordance with its own form—the "laws of thought." That we are in fact rational in some degree is clear; we are, and must order our thought rationally. For even to raise a question of any kind whatever is to think about our thought; it is to ask for reasons why we ought or ought not to think in certain ways. Rationality is thus our nature; we cannot do otherwise. Yet we can fall short; we can order our thought with varying degrees of adequacy. We can—and do—fail to conform to the "laws of thought." Rationality confronts us as a norm and as a goal as well as an accomplished reality; it is a potentiality we have partially actualized and which ought to be actualized more completely.

This contention can be supported dialectically. Consider the following question. Could we respond to an application of the generalization principle by saying that it would be binding upon us only if we *wanted* to be rational? We could say such a thing, of course, in that we would be able to utter the words, but our statement would not and could not be *true*. To claim that a statement is true is to assert that an argument can be made in its support. But no argument *can* be given in this case. To make an argument for an assertion is to give reasons for believing it, and, in this case, to make an argument would be to give reasons —or to have reasons—for not accepting reason. It would be to offer an argument for rejecting all arguments, including this argument. It would be to claim to be rational in rejecting rationality. And this is plainly absurd. Since it is false—nay, absurd— that we ought not to govern our thinking (and acting) by reasons, it must be true that we ought to do so. If any argument that we ought not to be rational is absurd, then we ought to be rational. And in so far as we are not rational, we ought to strive to become so. Moreover, this "ought" is categorical, not hypothetical; its "oughtness" is independent of our empirical wants or inclinations. Even if we do not want to, we ought to perfect our rationality. Rationality is a moral end, not merely a prudential one.

It is apparent, of course, that our conduct, as well as our thought, is not in fact fully rational. It is apparent not only that we violate the rules of fairness in our actions but also that we seeks ends that are in conflict with rationality considered as an end. Indeed, typically we employ an aspect of our actual rationality—the ability to adapt means to end, or to "calculate"—in the pursuit of irrational or self-destructive ends. Rationality, then, in the sense of conforming fully to the demands of reason, or even of being *able* to do so, is not a given state of affairs; it must consciously be sought and perfected. Rationality is always a goal; it is never fully achieved. Like the Kingdom of God, it is always "at hand," never here. Just as we must seek the Kingdom of God, so we must strive to be rational.

It may be useful at this juncture to relate the concept of rationality to a pair of more frequently used concepts, namely, "freedom" and "personality." In its ordinary usage, the term "freedom" refers to relations between separate human beings. A human being is said to be free if he is not subject to coercion by another human being. But "freedom" has a wider use as well. For just as we can distinguish between ourselves as agents, or actors, and other human beings, so we can distinguish between ourselves considered as agents and our empirical drives, impulses, and inclinations. We are slaves if these impulses master us; we are free if we master them. To be sure, such impulses are a part of us; they belong to our "destiny." They cannot—nor should they—simply be eliminated, but they can be mastered. Such mastery, or self-control, is freedom. Once again Professor Tillich can be of some help.

. . . [A] large amount of material is present in the psychological center—drives, inclinations, desires, more or less compulsory trends, moral experiences, ethical traditions and authorities, relations to other persons, social conditions. But the moral act is not the diagonal in which all these factors limit each other and converge; it is the centered self which actualizes itself as a personal self by distinguishing, separating, rejecting, preferring, connecting, and in doing so, transcending its elements. The act, or more exactly the whole complex of acts, in which this happens has the character of freedom, not freedom in the bad sense of the indeterminacy of an act of the will, but *freedom in the sense of a total reaction of a centered self which deliberates and decides.*[2]

To be free is to be master of these "psychological" materials by "distinguishing," "separating," "rejecting," "preferring," and "connecting." It is to deliberate and decide or, to use my language, to govern thought and action rationally. In short, to be free is to be rational. For to be rational is to be liberated from "natural" compulsion, i.e., from enslavement to one's own psychological drives and impulses.

Similarly, to be personal is to be rational. A person, to quote Tillich again, is "an individual embodiment of creative freedom."[3] To be a person is to be master of one's own drives and impulses; it is to be able to stand apart from one's empirical self, as well as from the world generally, so as to "grasp" and "shape" it rationally. We are persons, then, in so far as we are or can be rational; we are personal beings to the degree that we can and do regulate our lives on the basis of reason. To be personal is a demand upon us as well as an actual condition. We *are* partly personal; we ought to become *fully* personal.

The point at stake throughout the preceding discussion has been whether there is a moral end, i.e., an end that ought to be pursued for its own sake regardless of any prudential purpose or empirical inclination we might have. It should be clear now that there is such an end. It is rationality itself, or, to use the alternative terms, "freedom" or "personality." And it should also be clear from the discussion that this end is a common end. It is the same for all human beings. That is to say, it ought to be realized in all potentially rational beings.

Returning to the question of what rights and duties we ought to have relative to one another, we now have a criterion of content. Since rationality—freedom—is an end that all men ought to seek, they must also have the right to seek and express it. That is, they ought to be respected and treated as potentially rational beings—by *themselves* as well as by others. Under the generalization principle alone, as we saw, slavery, e.g., is justified so long as the person enslaved agrees to be so treated. But under the principle just presented—the "principle of the common end"—it is not. For no one can justifiably sell himself into slavery, no matter how badly he wants to do so. Slavery violates the principle of the common end, even if it does not violate the generalization principle. No one can have the right *not* to respect the "fundamental" right of his own person, namely, to

become rational—that is, to govern his own thought and conduct rationally. Similarly, a society whose members agreeably
administered opiates to one another could not be justified.
Opiates destroy the capacity to think and act rationally; we
have no right to do such a thing either to ourselves or to others.
Human beings have no right—no *moral* right—to treat either
themselves or others inhumanly.

Thus the common end is the basis of substantive rights and
duties. It is the basis of rights and duties for the simple reason
that it establishes the fundamental rights of all human beings
to be treated as human, i.e., as potentially or actually rational
beings. It establishes the fundamental right of all human beings
to be treated as persons rather than as "things." And it determines that all human beings are in this respect relevantly similar
to one another. Accordingly, the fundamental duty is to treat
others—as well as oneself—as persons. All other rights and
duties depend upon this fundamental right and its corresponding duty.

An example may be helpful here. Should we acknowledge a
right to the private ownership of the material means of production? The answer to this depends upon the consequences of
private ownership for the realization of human potentiality. If,
as Marx contends, private ownership involves exploitation or
"thingification," then we should not acknowledge it as a right.
If, on the other hand, private ownership is compatible with and
contributes to the realization of freedom on the part of all men
—i.e., "fairly"—then it ought to be acknowledged as a right.
Similarly, since the common end justifies particular rights, it
can also restrict or even suspend them. If the accumulation of
property above some amount leads to exploitation or dehumanization, i.e., if it has the consequence of denying to some the
fundamental right to actualize their potentialities as persons,
then at this point the right to property must be restricted. Within
the formal limits set by the principle of fairness, the principle
of the common end both establishes and overrides particular
rights.[4]

So much for the general problem of rights and duties. Now,

how can we evaluate social institutions and policies? The words "institution" and "policy" themselves point to the answer. To institute something, or to adopt a policy, is to do something in pursuit of a purpose. Thus, institutions and policies are instruments or means to ends. We have seen what moral end human beings as such ought to pursue: they ought to become rational or free. Institutions and policies, therefore, ought to make possible the development and expression of freedom on the part of human beings. Institutions should contribute to the realization of this moral end in all human beings.

To be sure, institutions cannot *make* human beings rational; human beings cannot be forced to be free. This is a contradiction in terms, since to be rational or free is to govern *oneself* by rational considerations. Nevertheless, institutions can provide the social conditions of freedom, and, by doing so—even coercively—they can promote it. This, then, is the standard in terms of which social institutions and policies should be judged. Do they promote the realization of human potentiality, or do they inhibit it? We ought to favor those social arrangements and policies which best, and most fairly, give rise to freedom (rationality) in human beings. Stated somewhat differently, institutions and policies should provide the social context required by the equal right of all to actualize their freedom. Economic arrangements and policies, then, should contribute to the development and expression of rationality in individual human beings.

If we ought to have social and economic institutions and policies that promote freedom in individual human beings, what broad standards does this notion suggest? What conditions in general are conducive to the self-perfection of individuals as free or rational persons? We can concur, I believe, with the three "mediating" norms proposed by Professor Tillich, namely, historical self-determination, equality, and community.

First, if human beings are to be able to actualize their potentialities as rational persons, they must have the opportunity to think and act for themselves within the course of history. That is, they must have both the possibility and the power to affect their own destinies significantly, as well as the destiny of the society to which they belong. "Freedom which has ceased to be the power of determining itself in history has ceased to be freedom, and men who have lost this power have lost their full humanity. They are dehumanized. . . . Freedom must appear in history, must embody itself in history, or it is not freedom."[5] Men must have the power to determine themselves within the course of human events if they are to develop and express their true freedom.

Second, social conditions must allow for the "basic" equality of human beings as persons, i.e., as potentially and, in part, actually rational. "Man's nature, namely the structure of creative freedom, includes one basic equality: the equal claim to be acknowledged as person, namely as individual embodiment of creative freedom with all the consequences derived from it, above all the equal right of everybody to actualize his creativity, although in the limits of his finitude which are different for each individual."[6] This does not mean, to be sure, that inequality per se is bad, e.g., inequality in political power or economic wealth. Indeed, equity—"to each his due"—justifies and requires some degree of inequality. Certainly to appoint an idiot or an ignoramus as the John Nuveen Professor of Theology at the University of Chicago could *not* be justified! Rather, the normative condition of equality is violated only when factual inequality has "resulted in dehumanization, i.e., the destruction of man's creative freedom."[7]

Finally, freedom calls for community, or, more exactly, the possibility of community. In order to become persons, to actualize our freedom, we must have encounters with other persons. That is, "in the encounter of a person who is already and not yet a person with another in the same condition, both are constituted as real persons."[8] "The person as the fully developed individual self is impossible without other fully developed selves. If he did not meet the resistance of other selves, every self would try to make himself absolute. But the resistance of other selves is unconditional. . . . The individual discovers himself through this resistance. . . . Therefore, there is no person without an encounter with other persons. Persons can grow only in the communion of personal encounter."[9] Social conditions themselves cannot produce personal encounter, but they can and should provide the conditions needed for it; social arrangements can be conducive to personal encounter, just as they can stand in the way of it. Social conditions may in fact lead instead to "massification"; they ought to be constructed so as to lead to community.

II

If this is the normative standpoint from which to judge the value of economic arrangements and policies, how does it apply to the empirically existing economic world? The best way to answer this question is to offer examples, although here the examples must necessarily be brief and somewhat sketchy.

One general comment is in order, however. The norm of freedom in the sense of rationality does not call for "laissez faire" in the realm of economic organization and policy. Freedom as spoken of in this paper is a positive goal, not merely a negative condition; in particular, it calls for a positive role on the part of government in economic affairs. It requires that we provide conditions within which human beings can develop and express rationality, and these conditions are both positive and negative in character. Above all, freedom as employed here does not mean that human beings should be permitted to do whatever they want to do, although it does require, of course, that they have *some* significant opportunity for "historical self-determination." To cite an obvious example, compulsory education is not contrary to the norm of freedom; indeed, compulsory education is imperative from this point of view. The reason is that freedom in our sense depends at least upon some minimal amount of education since education is one of the essential tools of freedom. To compel someone to get an education is not to deprive him of his freedom; rather, it is to prepare the way for freedom. Freedom is not merely the absence of external restraint; instead, freedom is a positive condition—it is the power to think and act rationally. Compulsion can be justified if it promotes "true" freedom.

Returning now to the questions posed at the beginning of the essay, what sort of overall economic arrangement should we favor? Needless to say, to answer this question we must have empirical knowledge. We must know the relevant facts about economic life; we must make use of the findings of the social sciences and, in particular, of the science of economics.

To begin with, what is an "economy"? To state it as briefly as possible, the economic system of a society is the organization through which the society determines how its productive resources are to be used and who is to make the important decisions on this matter. In some way or other, within every society in which there is division of labor, the decisions must be made as to (1) what is to be produced and in what proportions, (2) how the productive resources—including human labor and initiative—are to be allocated, (3) to whom the resulting products are to be distributed, and (4) how much productive activity is to be devoted to expanding the productive apparatus itself as against producing goods and services for use in the present.[10]

Within any society these functions must be performed, and the activities of individuals must be organized accordingly. There are, for the present at least, only two ways of doing this. Either the decisions on these matters must be made by a central authority—who may or may not be democratically chosen —or by a multitude of individuals exchanging goods and services with one another, i.e., buying and selling, in a competitive market. We can have either a "military" economy or a "market" economy; in the long run we cannot have both.[11]

Now, from the normative standpoint presented earlier, and assuming that either system serves to perform the required functions, which system ought we to favor? Which type of arrangement most closely conforms to the normative standard?

Within a military economy all productive resources are in principle the "property" of the central authority, since he decides how they will be employed. This implies that with respect to the "economically" productive part of life, human beings have little, if any, opportunity for historical self-determination. In principle, if not always in fact—as any member of the military services will testify—the central authority decides what sort of work a person does, where he resides, and, in large part, even the sort of life he lives—i.e., how and what he "consumes." If it were to be carried through consistently in practice, a military system would seriously limit, if not abolish, effective historical self-determination. It is thus contrary to one of the essential conditions of human self-realization. Within a market economy, by contrast, individuals are—subject to certain limitations—their own "property." They decide for themselves from a variety of alternatives what sort of productive activity they will engage in, where they will reside, and what they will "consume." There is at least some—indeed, much—opportunity to affect their own historical destinies, although probably not as much as proponents of the system frequently claim there is. Given that it "works," the market system provides more adequately for historical self-determination than does the military system.

Similarly, of the possible alternatives, the market system more closely approximates the conditions of equality and community. While it is certainly true that much inequality of wealth and income can and does occur within a market economy—this can be ameliorated, however—the degree of inequality in political power, if not of wealth and income, is much greater in a military economy. In a military economy, in principle everyone is the "property" of the central authority; everyone is "at his disposal" no matter how enlightened his exercise of this power may be. He decides who produces what and who gets it. Finally, by allowing for a greater degree of freedom of association, the market system comes closest to the norm of community. In a market economy people may relate to one another as *persons;* in a military economy they are all *instruments* to be used by the central authority.

Given that both types of economic arrangement can succeed in performing the four economic functions, I think it is clear which we ought to prefer.[12]

To say that the market system is better than the military system is not to say either that everything about the market system is satisfactory or that intervention into its operation is always to be avoided. The opposite is the case. To begin with, intervention on the part of government is needed simply to make the system work. The market system requires an appropriate set of laws and customs, as well as policies designed to combat the growth of monopoly and avoid fluctuations in the level of business activity. And, what is more relevant here, the market system gives rise to certain social evils. It creates conditions that stand in the way of the self-perfection of human beings as free persons. Each of these facts points to a need for special remedial policies within the framework of market capitalism. The issue is not whether or not we ought to have economic "planning." Economic planning is necessary! Policies of one kind or another are needed in order to have conditions within which human beings can perfect themselves and, as well, to keep the system going. The only stipulation is that our policies be compatible with the market system. For we should not allow ourselves to be forced into a military arrangement.

One salient feature of the market system is that it awards money incomes to people roughly in proportion to the contribution they make to total output. People are paid in terms of what they have to sell, not in terms of what they need. But for various reasons there are many people who cannot contribute, at least not in ways that have any "price" in the market. In short, we have poverty. A large fraction of the total population —from one fifth to one third, depending on what figures are used—subsist on incomes less than what is required for a "decent" life.[13] Poverty is contrary to our norms. For historical self-determination is not merely the absence of external restraint; it requires power to affect one's destiny. In poverty there is almost no such power. Poverty also runs counter to the norm of equality; poverty-stricken people are unduly subject to the will of others, and this is so even if the will of others is charitable. Moreover, people in the condition of poverty cannot participate in significant ways in the life of the society as a whole; thus poverty conflicts also with the norm of community. From the standpoint of the common moral end, poverty is surely an undesirable social condition. To alleviate poverty should be a major goal of economic policy. We ought to recognize, and put into effect, a right to a decent standard of living.

How can this be done? As it happens there is much agreement today about the need to alleviate poverty; there is much less agreement about what policies will serve to achieve this goal. Indeed, I think it is safe to say that most disagreements about economic policy are in fact disagreements within economic analysis rather than within the realm of normative principles. This will no doubt become apparent in the remarks that follow.

First, a few critical remarks are in order. Many policies aimed at poverty do not have the desired effect. In fact, frequently they do just the opposite of what is intended. Moreover, sometimes they are even incompatible with the market mechanism itself, thus leading to much more serious problems in the long run. To mention just a few, social ownership of the principal means of production, stronger and more inclusive trade unions, and minimum wage laws are often proposed as anti-poverty measures. But none of these have the desired effects.

Perhaps the most extreme of these proposals is the one that suggests socialism—social ownership of the principal means of production—as an anti-poverty measure. The idea here is that property ownership is the major cause of economic inequality, and hence of poverty, and that therefore poverty would disappear if property were to be socially (governmentally) rather than privately owned. This argument conflicts with the facts. For labor services, not property ownership, account for most income differential. Only about 25 per cent of income payments are for the use of property, while about 75 per cent are for labor services of one sort or another.[14] Moreover, the incomes of high income families are, for the most part, wage and salary incomes, not incomes deriving from property.[15] This fact, plus the fact that socialization of property could include only a very small proportion of the total of productive property, means that social ownership is clearly inappropriate as a means of mitigating poverty. Social ownership is perhaps conceivable as a way of controlling monopoly power; but it is not helpful as an anti-poverty measure. In addition, too much social ownership of productive resources would be incompatible with the market system as an overall economic arrangement.

Another suggestion frequently made is that by strengthening trade unions—increasing their bargaining power—and extending union coverage to more industries we could push up the wage level and thereby raise the incomes of the poor. To begin with, we need only to note that a large proportion of the poverty population would not even be affected by this, since they do not and cannot have jobs. But even for those who can and do have jobs, this policy would have negative effects. By forcing up wages in an industry we reduce the number of jobs available in that industry. The recent demise of the *World-Journal-Tribune* is probably a case in point. This has the effect of increasing the supply of labor in other industries, which in turn drives wages in those industries lower. What if we then form a union in that industry as well? In all industries? Then we simply cause unemployment. In fact, this is the effect of another of the proposals, namely, minimum wage legislation. Workers whose marginal productivity is less than the minimum we set—whether by law or by union contracts—cannot get any job at all! Thus, neither trade unions nor minimum wage laws can alleviate poverty. If anything, they make matters worse by increasing the incomes of the not-so-poor at the expense of the really-poor.

Yet these negative remarks are not intended to suggest that there are no effective ways to combat poverty. There are! Here are some possibilities.

While much more study is needed, the so-called negative income tax plan, proposed by Professor Milton Friedman, appears to be the best short-run policy so far suggested.[16] The idea is that instead of *paying* an income tax, the poor would receive a payment from the Internal Revenue Service. The lower the income, the larger the payment, on a progressive scale, such that at least a minimum income—but above the poverty level—is assured for everyone. Moreover, in contrast to current welfare policies, this scheme would permit and encourage the poor to add to their incomes by accepting remunerative employment. For they could do so without jeopardizing their right to receive at least some support from the negative tax program. Finally, and what is perhaps even more important, this plan is quite compatible with the market system as an overall economic arrangement. It would not interfere with the competitive adjusting of prices and wages; it would operate over and above the market rather than against the market.

By way of long-run policies, several come to mind. For in the long run it is possible to deal with the causes of poverty as well as with its outward appearance. Here are just a few:

1. Encourage and promote family planning. One important cause of poverty is to be found in the fact that large families are unable to give adequate attention to their children. The neglected children of today often become the poverty-stricken adults of tomorrow.

2. Improve and expand education. This is obvious. Since labor productivity accounts for the largest part of income differentials, we can raise incomes by improving labor productivity. Education is probably the most effective way of doing this.

3. Remove job discrimination and restrictions on entry into the various trades and professions. We cannot expect people to have the incentive to get an education, or to acquire a skill, if they cannot have access to employment later on. We cannot abolish poverty if we do not *permit* people to escape from it.

It goes without saying that much more could be said about anti-poverty measures. I offer these only as suggestions, i.e., as examples of how we can promote human self-realization by removing the conditions that stand in the way. Poverty is only one case; there are many others—perhaps an infinite number. The criterion, however, is both single and simple: Economic policy, and social policy in general, should seek to create conditions within which human beings can actualize their potentialities as rational or free persons.

by Pope Paul VI

ON THE DEVELOPMENT
OF PEOPLES
(Populorum Progressio)

Development of Peoples. The development of peoples has the church's close attention, particularly the development of those peoples who are striving to escape from hunger, misery, endemic diseases and ignorance; of those who are looking for a wider share in the benefits of civilisation and a more active improvement of their human qualities; of those who are aiming purposefully at their complete fulfilment. Following on the Second Vatican Ecumenical Council a renewed consciousness of the demands of the Gospel makes it her duty to put herself at the service of all, to help them grasp their serious problem in all its dimensions, and to convince them that solidarity in action at this turning point in human history is a matter of urgency.

Social teaching of the Popes. Our predecessors in their great encyclicals, Leo XIII in *Rerum Novarum,*[1] Pius XI in *Quadragesimo Anno*[2] and John XXIII in *Mater et Magistra*[3] and *Pacem in Terris*[4]—not to mention the messages of Pius XII[5] to the world—did not fail in the duty of their office of shedding the light of the Gospel on the social questions of their times.

Reprinted from the Encyclical Letter, *Populorum Progressio,* of His Holiness POPE PAUL VI, 1967, translated by the Vatican Polyglot Press and published by the United States Catholic Conference, Washington, D.C. Paragraphs 1-21 (pp. 3-17), 43-55 (pp. 33-40), and 76-80 (pp. 51-53).

The principal fact. Today the principal fact that we must all recognise is that the social question has become world-wide. John XXIII stated this in unambiguous terms[6] and the Council echoed him in its Pastoral Constitution on *The Church in the Modern World.*[7] This teaching is important and its application urgent. Today the peoples in hunger are making a dramatic appeal to the peoples blessed with abundance. The Church shudders at this cry of anguish and calls each one to give a loving response of charity to this brother's cry for help.

Our journeys. Before We became Pope, two journeys, to Latin America in 1960 and to Africa in 1962, brought Us into direct contact with the acute problems pressing on continents full of life and hope. Then on becoming Father of all We made further journeys, to the Holy Land and India, and were able to see and virtually touch the very serious difficulties besetting peoples of long-standing civilisations who are at grips with the problem of development. While the Second Vatican Ecumenical Council was being held in Rome, providential circumstances permitted Us to address in person the General Assembly of the United Nations, and We pleaded the cause of poor peoples before this distinguished body.

Justice and Peace. Then quite recently, in Our desire to carry out the wishes of the Council and give specific expression to the Holy See's contribution to this great cause of peoples in development, We considered it Our duty to set up a Pontifical Commission in the Church's central administration, charged with "bringing to the whole of God's People the full knowledge of the part expected of them at the present time, so as to further the progress of poorer peoples, to encourage social justice among nations, to offer to less developed nations the means whereby they can further their own progress":[8] its name, which is also its programme, is *Justice and Peace.* We think that this can and should bring together men of good will with our Catholic sons and our Christian brothers. So it is to all that We address this solemn appeal for concrete action towards man's complete development and the development of all mankind.

THE DATA OF THE PROBLEM

Men's aspirations. Freedom from misery, the greater assurance of finding subsistence, health and fixed employment; an increased share of responsibility without oppression of any kind and in security from situations that do violence to their dignity as men; better education—in brief, to seek to do more, know more and have more in order to be more: that is what men aspire to now when a greater number of them are condemned to live in conditions that make this lawful desire illusory. Besides, peoples who have recently gained national independence experience the need to add to this political freedom a fitting autonomous growth, social as well as economic, in order to assure their citizens of a full human enhancement and to take their rightful place with other nations.

Colonisation and colonialism. Though insufficient for the immensity and urgency of the task, the means inherited from the past are not lacking. It must certainly be recognised that colonising powers have often furthered their own interests, power or glory, and that their departure has sometimes left a precarious economy, bound up for instance with the production of one kind of crop whose market prices are subject to sudden and considerable variation. Yet while recognising the damage done by a certain type of colonialism and its consequences, one must at the same time acknowledge the qualities and achievement of colonisers who brought their science and technical knowledge and left beneficial results of their presence in so many underprivileged regions. The structures established by them persist, however incomplete they may be; they diminished ignorance and sickness, brought the benefits of communications and improved living conditions.

Yet once this is admitted, it remains only too true that the resultant situation is manifestly inadequate for facing the hard reality of modern economics. Left to itself it works rather to widen the differences in the world's levels of life, not to diminish them: rich peoples enjoy rapid growth whereas the poor develop slowly. The imbalance is on the increase: some produce a surplus of foodstuffs, others cruelly lack them and see their exports made uncertain.

Increasing awareness. At the same time social conflicts have taken on world dimensions. The acute disquiet which has taken hold of the poor classes in countries that are becoming industrialised, is now embracing those whose economy is almost exclusively agrarian: farming people, too, are becoming aware of their "undeserved hardship."[9] There is also the scandal of glaring inequalities not merely in the enjoyment of possessions but even more in the exercise of power. While a small restricted group enjoys a refined civilisation in certain regions, the remainder of the population, poor and scattered, is "deprived of nearly all possibility of personal initiative and of responsibility, and oftentimes even its living and working conditions are unworthy of the human person."[10]

Conflict of civilisations. Furthermore, the conflict between traditional civilisations and the new elements of industrial civilisation breaks down structures which do not adapt themselves to new conditions. Their framework, sometimes rigid, was the indispensable prop to personal and family life; older people remain attached to it, the young escape from it, as from a useless barrier, to turn eagerly to new forms of life in society. The conflict of the generations is made more serious by a tragic dilemma: whether to retain ancestral institutions and convictions and renounce progress, or to admit techniques and civilisations from outside and reject along with the traditions of the past all their human richness. In effect, the moral, spiritual and religious supports of the past too often give way without securing in return any guarantee of a place in the new world.

Conclusion. In this confusion the temptation becomes stronger to risk being swept away towards types of messianism which give promises but create illusions. The resulting dangers are patent: violent popular reactions, agitation towards insurrection, and a drifting towards totalitarian ideologies. Such are the data of the problem. Its seriousness is evident to all.

THE CHURCH AND DEVELOPMENT

Work of the missionaries. True to the teaching and example of her divine Founder, Who cited the preaching of the Gospel to the poor as a sign of His mission,[11] the Church has never failed to foster the human progress of the nations to which she brings faith in Christ. Her missionaries have built, not only churches, but also hostels and hospitals, schools and universities. Teaching the local populations the means of deriving the best advantages from their natural resources, missionaries have often protected them from the greed of foreigners. Without doubt their work, inasmuch as it was human, was not perfect, and sometimes the announcement of the authentic Gospel message was infiltrated by many ways of thinking and acting which were characteristic of their home country. But the missionaries were also able to develop and foster local institutions. In many a region they were among the pioneers in material progress as well as in cultural advancement. Let it suffice to recall the example of Father Charles de Foucauld, whose charity earned him the title "Universal Brother," and who edited an invaluable dictionary of the Touareg language. We ought to pay tribute to these pioneers who have been too often forgotten, but who were urged on by the love of Christ, just as we honour their imitators and successors who today still continue to put themselves at the generous and unselfish service of those to whom they announce the Gospel.

Church and world. However, local and individual undertakings are no longer enough. The present situation of the world demands concerted action based on a clear vision of all economic, social, cultural, and spiritual aspects. Experienced in human affairs, the Church, without attempting to interfere in any way in the politics of States, "seeks but a solitary goal: to carry forward the work of Christ Himself under the lead of the befriending Spirit. And Christ entered this world to give witness to the truth, to rescue and not to sit in judgment, to serve and not to be served."[12] Founded to establish on earth the Kindom of Heaven and not to conquer any earthly power, the Church clearly states that the two realms are distinct, just as the two powers, ecclesiastical and civil, are supreme, each in its own domain.[13] But, since the Church lives in history, she ought to "scrutinize the signs of the times and interpret them in the light of the Gospel."[14] Sharing the noblest aspirations of men and suffering when she sees them not satisfied, she wishes to help them attain their full flowering, and that is why she offers men what she possesses as her characteristic attribute: a global vision of man and of the human race.

CHRISTIAN VISION OF DEVELOPMENT

Development cannot be limited to mere economic growth. In order to be authentic, it must be complete: integral, that is, it has to promote the good of every man and of the whole man. As an eminent specialist has very rightly and emphatically declared: "We do not believe in separating the economic from the civilisations in which it exists. What we hold important is man, each man and each group of men, and we even include the whole of humanity."[15]

The vocation to self-fulfilment. In the design of God, every man is called upon to develop and fulfill himself, for every life is a vocation. At birth, everyone is granted, in germ, a set of aptitudes and qualities for him to bring to fruition. Their coming to maturity, which will be the result of education received from the environment and personal efforts, will allow each man to direct himself toward the destiny intended for him by his Creator. Endowed with intelligence and freedom, he is responsible for his fulfilment as he is for his salvation. He is aided, or sometimes impeded, by those who educate him and those with whom he lives, but each one remains, whatever be these influences affecting him, the principal agent of his own success or failure. By the unaided effort of his own intelligence and his will, each man can grow in humanity, can enhance his personal worth, can become more a person.

Personal responsibility. However, this self-fulfilment is not something optional. Just as the whole of creation is ordained to its Creator, so spiritual beings should of their own accord orientate their lives to God, the first truth and the supreme good. Thus it is that human fulfilment constitutes, as it were, a summary of our duties. But there is much more: this harmonious enrichment of nature by personal and responsible effort is ordered to a further perfection. By reason of his union with Christ, the source of life, man attains to new fulfilment of himself, to a transcendent humanism which gives him his greatest possible perfection: this is the highest goal of personal development.

And communal responsibility. But each man is a member of society. He is part of the whole of mankind. It is not just certain individuals, but all men who are called to this fullness of development. Civilisations are born, develop and die. But humanity is advancing along the path of history like the waves of a rising tide encroaching gradually on the shore. We have inherited from past generations, and we have benefitted from the work of our contemporaries: for this reason we have obligations towards all, and we cannot refuse to interest ourselves in those who will come after us to enlarge the human family. The reality of human solidarity, which is the benefit for us, also imposes a duty.

Scale of values. This personal and communal development would be threatened if the true scale of values were undermined. The desire for necessities is legitimate, and work undertaken to obtain them is a duty: "If any man will not work, neither let him eat."[16] But the acquiring of temporal goods can lead to greed, to the insatiable desire for more, and can make increased power a tempting objective. Individuals, families and nations can be overcome by avarice, be they poor or rich, and all can fall victim to a stifling materialism.

The ambivalence of growth. Increased possession is not the ultimate goal of nations nor of individuals. All growth is ambivalent. It is essential if man is to develop as a man, but in a way it imprisons man if he considers it the supreme good, and it restricts his vision. Then we see hearts harden and minds close, and men no longer gather together in friendship but out of self-interest, which soon leads to oppositions and disunity. The exclusive pursuit of possessions thus becomes an obstacle to individual fulfilment and to man's true greatness. Both for nations and for individual men, avarice is the most evident form of moral underdevelopment.

Towards a more human condition. If further development calls for the work of more and more technicians, even more necessary is the deep thought and reflection of wise men in search of a new humanism which will enable modern man to find himself anew by embracing the higher values of love and friendship, of prayer and contemplation.[17] This is what will permit the fullness of authentic development, a development which is for each and all the transition from less human conditions to those which are more human.

The ideal to be pursued. Less human conditions: the lack of material necessities for those who are without the minimum essential for life, the moral deficiences of those who are mutilated by selfishness. Less human conditions: oppressive social structures, whether due to the abuses of ownership or to the abuses of power, to the exploitation of workers or to unjust transactions. Conditions that are more human: the passage from misery towards the possession of necessities, victory over social scourges, the growth of knowledge, the acquisition of culture. Additional conditions that are more human: increased esteem for the dignity of others, the turning toward the spirit of poverty,[18] cooperation for the common good, the will and desire for peace. Conditions that are still more human: the acknowledgement by man of supreme values, and of God their source and their finality. Conditions that finally and above all, are more human: faith, a gift of God accepted by the good will of man, and unity in the charity of Christ, Who calls us all to share as sons in the life of the living God, the Father of all men.

THE DEVELOPMENT OF THE HUMAN RACE IN THE SPIRIT OF SOLIDARITY

Introduction. There can be no progress towards the complete development of man without the simultaneous development of all humanity in the spirit of solidarity. As we said at Bombay: "Man must meet man, nation meet nation, as brothers and sisters, as children of God. In this mutual understanding and friendship, in this sacred communion, we must also begin to work together to build the common future of the human race."[19] We also suggested a search for concrete and practical ways of organisation and cooperation, so that all available resources be pooled and thus a true communion among all nations be achieved.

Brotherhood of peoples. This duty is the concern especially of better-off nations. Their obligations stem from a brotherhood that is at once human and supernatural, and take on a threefold aspect: the duty of human solidarity—the aid that the rich nations must give to developing countries; the duty of social justice—the rectification of inequitable trade relations between powerful nations and weak nations; the duty of universal charity—the effort to bring about a world that is more human towards all men, where all will be able to give and receive, without one group making progress at the expense of the other. The question is urgent, for on it depends the future of the civilisation of the world.

War against hunger. "If a brother or a sister be naked," says Saint James; "if they lack their daily nourishment, and one of you says to them: 'Go in peace, be warmed and be filled', without giving them what is necessary for the body, what good does it do?"[20] Today no one can be ignorant any longer of the fact that in whole continents countless men and women are ravished by hunger, countless numbers of children are undernourished, so that many of them die in infancy, while the physical growth and mental development of many others are retarded and as a result whole regions are condemned to the most depressing despondency.

Today. Anguished appeals have already been sounded in the past: that of John XXIII was warmly received.[21] We Ourselves repeated it in Our Christmas Message of 1963,[22] and again in 1966 on behalf of India.[23] The campaign against hunger being carried on by the Food and Agriculture Organisation (FAO) and encouraged by the Holy See, has been generously supported. Our *Caritas Internationalis* is at work everywhere, and many Catholics, at the urging of Our Brothers in the episcopacy, contribute generously of their means and spend themselves without counting the cost in assisting those who are in want, continually widening the circle of those they look upon as neighbours.

Tomorrow. But neither all this nor the private and public funds that have been invested, nor the gifts and loans that have been made, can suffice. It is not just a matter of eliminating hunger, nor even of reducing poverty. The struggle against destitution, though urgent and necessary, is not enough. It is a question, rather, of building a world where every man, no matter what his race, religion or nationality, can live a fully human life, freed from servitude imposed on him by other men or by natural forces over which he has not sufficient control; a world where freedom is not an empty word and where the poor man Lazarus can sit down at the same table with the rich man.[24] This demands great generosity, much sacrifice and unceasing effort on the part of the rich man. Let each one examine his conscience, a conscience that conveys a new message for our times. Is he prepared to support out of his own pocket works and undertakings organised in favour of the most destitute? Is he ready to pay higher taxes so that the public authorities can intensify their efforts in favour of development? Is he ready to pay a higher price for imported goods so that the producer may be more justly rewarded? Or to leave his country, if necessary and if he is young, in order to assist in this development of the young nations?

Duty of human solidarity. The same duty of solidarity that rests on individuals exists also for nations: "Advanced nations have a very heavy obligation to help the developing peoples."[25] It is necessary to put this teaching of the Council into effect. Although it is normal that a nation should be the first to benefit from the gifts that Providence has bestowed on it as the fruit of the labours of its people, still no country can claim on that account to keep its wealth for itself alone. Every nation must produce more and better quality goods to give to all its inhabitants a truly human standard of living, and also to contribute to the common development of the human race. Given the increasing needs of the under-developed countries, it should be considered quite normal for an advanced country to devote a part of its production to meet their needs, and to train teachers, engineers, technicians and scholars prepared to put their knowledge and their skill at the disposal of less fortunate peoples.

Superfluous wealth. We must repeat once more that the superfluous wealth of rich countries should be placed at the service of poor nations. The rule which up to now held good for the benefit of those nearest to us, must today be applied to all the needy of this world. Besides, the rich will be the first to benefit as a result. Otherwise their continued greed will certainly call down upon them the judgment of God and the wrath of the poor, with consequences no one can foretell. If today's flourishing civilisations remain selfishly wrapped up in themselves, they could easily place their highest values in jeopardy, sacrificing their will to be great to the desire to possess more. To them we could apply also the parable of the rich man whose fields yielded an abundant harvest and who did not know where to store his harvest: "God said to him: 'Fool, this night do they demand your soul of you.' "[26]

Planning. In order to be fully effective, these efforts ought not to remain scattered or isolated, much less be in competition for reasons of power or prestige: the present situation calls for concerted planning. A planned programme is of course better and more effective than occasional aid left to individual goodwill. It presupposes, as We said above, careful study, the selection of ends and the choice of means, as well as a reorganisation of efforts to meet the needs of the present and the demands of the foreseeable future. More important, a concerted plan has advantages that go beyond the field of economic growth and social progress; for in addition it gives significance and value to the work undertaken. While shaping the world it sets a higher value on man.

World fund. But it is necessary to go still further. At Bombay We called for the establishment of a great *World Fund,* to be made up of part of the money spent on arms, to relieve the most destitute of this world.[27] What is true of the immediate struggle against want, holds good also when there is a question of development. Only world-wide collaboration, of which a common fund would be both means and symbol, will succeed in overcoming vain rivalries and in establishing a fruitful and peaceful exchange between peoples.

Its advantages. There is certainly no need to do away with bilateral and multilateral agreements: they allow ties of dependence and feelings of bitterness, left over from the era of colonialism, to yield place to the happier relationship of friendship, based on a footing of constitutional and political equality. However, if they were to be fitted into the frame-work of world-wide collaboration, they would be beyond all suspicion, and as a result there would be less distrust on the part of the receiving nations.

These would have less cause for fearing that, under the cloak of financial aid or technical assistance, there lurk certain manifestations of what has come to be called neo-colonialism, in the form of political pressures and economic suzerainty aimed at maintaining or acquiring complete dominance.

Its urgency. Besides, who does not see that such a fund would make it easier to take measures to prevent certain wasteful expenditures, the result of fear or pride? When so many people are hungry, when so many families suffer from destitution, when so many remain steeped in ignorance, when so many schools, hospitals and homes worthy of the name remain to be built, all public or private squandering of wealth, all expenditure prompted by motives of national or personal ostentation, every exhausting armaments race, becomes an intolerable scandal. We are conscious of Our duty to denounce it. Would that those in authority listened to Our words before it is too late!

Dialogue to be started. This means that it is absolutely necessary to create among all peoples that dialogue for whose establishment We expressed Our hope in Our first Encyclical *Ecclesiam Suam*.[28] This dialogue between those who contribute wealth and those who benefit from it, will provide the possibility of making an assessment of the contribution necessary, not only drawn up in terms of the generosity and the available wealth of the donor nations, but also conditioned by the real needs of the receiving countries and the use to which the financial assistance can be put. Developing countries will thus no longer risk being overwhelmed by debts whose repayment swallows up the greater part of their gains. Rates of interest and time for repayment of the loan could be so arranged as not to be too great a burden on either party, taking into account free gifts, interest-free or low-interest loans, and the time needed for liquidating the debts. Guarantees could be given to those who provide the capital that it will be put to use according to an agreed plan and with a reasonable measure of efficiency, since there is no question of encouraging parasites or the indolent. And the receiving countries could demand that there be no interference in their political life or subversion of their social structures. As sovereign states they have the right to conduct their own affairs, to decide on their policies and to move freely towards the kind of society they choose. What must be brought about, therefore, is a system of cooperation freely undertaken, an effective and mutual sharing, carried out with equal dignity on either side, for the construction of a more human world.

Its necessity. The task might seem impossible in those regions where the cares of day-to-day survival fill the entire existence of families incapable of planning the kind of work which would open the way to a future that is less desperate. These, however, are the men and women who must be helped, who must be persuaded to work for their own betterment and endeavour to acquire gradually the means to that end. This common task will not succeed without concerted, constant and courageous efforts. But let everyone be convinced of this: the very life of poor nations, civil peace in developing countries, and world peace itself are at stake.

DEVELOPMENT IS THE NEW NAME FOR PEACE

Conclusion. Excessive economic, social and cultural inequalities among peoples arouse tensions and conflicts, and are a danger to peace. As We said to the Fathers of the Council when We returned from Our journey of peace to the United Nations: "The condition of the peoples in process of development ought to be the object of our consideration; or better: our charity for the poor in the world—and there are multitudes of them—must become more considerate, more active, more generous."[29] To wage war on misery and to struggle against injustice is to promote, along with improved conditions, the human and spiritual progress of all men, and therefore the common good of humanity. Peace cannot be limited to a mere absence of war, the result of an ever precarious balance of forces. No, peace is something that is built up day after day, in the pursuit of an order intended by God, which implies a more perfect form of justice among men.[30]

End to isolation. The peoples themselves have the prime responsibility to work for their own development. But they will not bring this about in isolation. Regional agreements among weak nations for mutual support, understandings of wider scope entered into for their help, more far-reaching agreements to establish programmes for closer cooperation among groups of nations—these are the milestones on the road to development that leads to peace.

Towards an effective world authority. This international collaboration on a world-wide scale requires institutions that will prepare, coordinate and direct it, until finally there is established an order of justice which is universally recognised. With all Our heart, We encourage these organisations which have undertaken this collaboration for the development of the peoples of the world, and Our wish is that they grow in prestige and authority. "Your vocation", as We said to the representatives of the United Nations in New York, "is to bring not some people but all peoples to treat each other as brothers. . . . Who does not see the necessity of thus establishing progressively a world authority, capable of acting effectively in the juridical and political sectors?"[31]

A well-founded hope for a better world. Some would consider such hopes utopian. It may be that these persons are not realistic enough, and that they have not perceived the dynamism of a world which desires to live more fraternally—a world which, in spite of its ignorance, its mistakes and even its sins, its relapses into barbarism and its wandering far from the road of salvation, is, even unawares, taking slow but sure steps towards its Creator. This road towards a greater humanity requires effort and sacrifice; but suffering itself, accepted for the love of our brethren, favours the progress of the entire human family. Christians know that union with the sacrifice of our Saviour contributes to the building up of the Body of Christ in its plentitude: the assembled people of God.[32]

Universal solidarity. We are all united in this progress towards God. We have desired to remind all men how crucial is the present moment, how urgent the work to be done. The hour for action has now sounded. At stake are the survival of so many innocent children and, for so many families overcome by misery, the access to conditions fit for human beings; at stake are the peace of the world and the future of civilisation. It is time for all men and all peoples to face up to their responsibilities.

by Paul Tillich

THE PERSON IN A
TECHNICAL SOCIETY

IT is my understanding of the movement which is called Existentialism and which is at least one hundred years old that it rebels in the name of personality against the depersonalizing forces of technical society. For the sake of my special subject as well as in the spirit of this volume, I want to begin with some references to the earlier history of Existentialism. This history, going on since the middle of the nineteenth century, has determined the fate of the twentieth century in all spheres of human existence. The immense tragedy of our political as well as the creative chaos of our spiritual situation are foreshadowed and deeply influenced by the Existentialist rebels of the nineteenth century. Moreover, the tradition, out of which this book is written and out of which he to whom it is dedicated has worked, is rooted in the protest of the lonely prophets of the nineteenth century against the threatening destruction of humanity and personality by technical society. Finally, it is my con-

Reprinted from *Christian Faith and Social Action,* John A. Hutchinson, ed., pp. 137-53. Copyright 1953 by Charles Scribner's Sons and used by permission. PAUL TILLICH was John Nuveen Professor of Theology at the University of Chicago until his death in 1965. Prior to Chicago he had a long and distinguished career at Union Theological Seminary and Harvard, as well as earlier in Germany. Among his numerous publications are *Systematic Theology,* 3 vols., *The Protestant Era,* and *The Courage To Be.*

viction that the new beginning, of which this volume is supposed to be a symbol, should be and, I hope, will be a continuation of this tradition under new conditions and with new means. But the aim should be what it was in the preceding movements of protest: a fight for humanity, which includes both community and personality, against the dehumanizing power of modern society.

I. Kierkegaard and Existentialism

It is usual to refer to Kierkegaard as the instigator of Existentialism. For the theologians especially this is the natural start. Historically, however, this is incorrect, since people like Pascal, Schelling and others had raised the Existentialist protest before Kierkegaard. They had done it for the same reason and with the same purpose as Kierkegaard: to resist a world in which everything was transformed into a thing, a means, an object of scientific calculation, psychological and political management. Kierkegaard saw that, in spite of many romantic elements in Hegel and in spite of his doctrine of freedom as the purpose of history, *this* was the meaning of his attempt to subject all reality to a system of logical forms: The existing individual was swallowed, the deciding personality was eliminated. The world-process, playing with the individual, gave him the feeling that he was deciding for himself, while the process, governed by dialectical necessity, had already decided about him. Kierkegaard's metaphor of the "leap" embodying his protest against Hegel's logically determined world process is the idealistic mirror of the realities of the modern world. This was its greatness and this was the reason why the revolt against our world found its most successful expression in the protest against this mirror. Kierkegaard made his protest on the basis of classical Protestantism. But classical Protestantism had ceased to be an immediate reality. It had been lost and had to be regained. How? By being put in its place in the whole of the dialectical process, answered Hegel. By being reached through the leap of faith, answered Kierkegaard. Hegel's answer makes classical Protestantism a useful element within the frame of technical society; Kierkegaard's answer asks the individual to break away from this society in order to save his existence as a person. Therefore Kierkegaard's loneliness, therefore the pathological traits in his dealing with marriage, vocation and Church, therefore the lack of any effect in his own time. All this is understandable if the existing person can only be saved by a leap. Our own period, in which Kierkegaard has shaped philosophy as well as theology in the Existentialist direction, has shown this clearly. Philosophical Existentialism demands the leap of the individual out of all traditions and social obligations into the freedom of normless decisions. Theological Existentialism demands the leap of the individual out of his given cultural and intellectual situation into the acceptance of a sacred tradition formulated hundreds of years ago. The leap liberates, but does it not enslave again? The personalities of Sartre's novels have absolute freedom, but it is actually the freedom of falling under the compulsion of the internal or external situation of the moment. And the Neo-Orthodox Christian subjects himself through the leap of faith to traditional ecclesiastical dogmas. He is free in the moment of his leap. But his leap into freedom involves the sacrifice of his freedom. The power of technical society is manifest in this conflict between rational necessity and the leap of freedom. The person is lost if rational necessity prevails. He tried to save himself by the leap which, however, leads to new forms of servitude, natural or supranatural ones. Only if we face realistically this situation, can we realize the seriousness of the problem: "The person in a technical society."

II. MARX AS EXISTENTIALIST

While Hegel provided the idealistic mirror of technical society, Marx gave its realistic description. This accounts for his ambiguous relation to Hegel, his opposition to him, insofar as the idealistic side is concerned, his dependence on him, with respect to the dialectical analysis of present day society. Marx saw much more clearly than Kierkegaard that it is not a system of thought, but the reality of modern society which is responsible for the reduction of the person to a commodity. His famous descriptions of the dehumanizing effects of economy in the industrial age center around the proletariat, but they are meant for all groups of society. Everyone, insofar as he is drawn into the all-embracing mechanism of production and consumption, is enslaved to it, loses his character as person and becomes a thing. Marx did not think that it is the technical method of production as such which destroys personal freedom, but that the social structure of the class society is responsible for it. He believed in possibilities of humanizing the technical process, but he did not believe that this could happen within the frame of the class society. Therefore he became a political rebel against the social and economic structure of bourgeois society and a tremendous historical force, not only in the countries which became "Marxist"—at least in pretense—but also in those which avoided a radical transformation by fulfilling demands of the Marxist movements within the framework of bourgeois society. This latter fact should not be forgotten by those who are still interested in an unprejudiced, scientific criticism of Marx. The way in which Marx envisages the salvation of the person in technical society unites in an highly ambiguous way dialectical necessity with political decision. Marx, the sociologist, follows Hegel's method of structural analysis and derives from it not what Hegel did, a systematic glorification of the present, but a necessary, calculable development into a glorious future. At the same time he appeals to the action of the proletariat, especially the vanguard which consists of proletarians and people from other groups who have joined them. Appeal is senseless without the presupposition that it can be accepted or rejected. He did not believe that the "person" in the proletariat was extinguished to such a degree that political appeals would be meaningless. This view is supported by the two concepts which characterize Marx's view of man, the concept of "dehumanization" and the concept of "real humanism." Both presuppose that man can be distorted by social conditions in such a way that his humanity is lost, and both presuppose that there will be a state of things in which his community is reestablished. Both show that Marx is concerned with the loss and the salvation of the "person" in the technical society as he experienced it.

But again, as in the case of Kierkegaard, the power of this society became manifest as soon as the question was: how can one break away from it? The answer seems to be easy: through the dialectical process and the revolution it will bring about. But social dialectics and revolution occur through human beings, and this introduces alternatives which are as difficult as those we found in Kierkegaard's doctrine of the leap. If those in a state of complete depersonalization are carried by the dialectical process into the "realm of freedom," how can they use it without radical transformation from thing to person? But if they are still persons they introduce an incalculable element into the situation. The proletarians may not see their real interest or their enemies may be unexpectedly strong or groups may become active who do not fit the simple class scheme, or the proletarians may carry through their demands to such a degree that they cease to be proletarians in the genuine sense of the word. All this has actually happened and has produced two contradictory reactions. The one is the reaction by what is called today "the free world," namely, the attempt to save the person within the frame of the bourgeois-capitalistic society by methods of reforms (whatever they may be called). The other is the reaction by what is called today Communism, namely, the attempt to save the person in a future state of history by removing in the present those personal elements which might endanger the future. This has led to the establishment of the communist system in which all technical refinements are used to eliminate the risks involved in personal resistance against the system. A type of technical society has been created in which the person of the present is completely sacrificed for the sake of the expected person of the future. A movement which started with a passionate fight against depersonalization has turned into one of the greatest powers of depersonalization in all history.

III. NIETZSCHE'S PROTEST

The fight of Existentialism against the dangers of the technical society was done, at the same time, on a third front, on that front which determines more than the two others the present fight against depersonalization. It was in the name of life that Nietzsche fought against the "nihilism" of the technical culture. Many followed him in all spheres of spiritual creativity. He and the movement of which he is the most conspicuous symbol saw more sharply than Kierkegaard and Marx the deepest roots of the dehumanizing and depersonalizing implications of modern society. Technical society—this is the message of all adherents of the "philosophy of life" (whether philosophers or poets or writers or artists)—destroys the creative power of life. Man becomes, according to Nietzsche, a cog in the all-embracing machine of production and consumption. This self whose center is the will to realize itself has nothing to will any more, and, therefore, it wills the "nothing." Only a new beginning of the will which wills itself can save life from a complete disintegration. This will (misleadingly called by Nietzsche the "will to power") is the self-affirmation of life as life against everything which transforms it into an object, a thing, a tool. Only a small group of people are the bearers of this new beginning, persons acting in the sense of heroic self-affirmation. They are the saviors of personal existence, through whom the power of life will reappear. On this basis the philosophers of life denounce the technical mass civilization, the egalitarian ideals, the subjection to the system of values which are accepted in this civilization, including the Christian values insofar as they are amalgamated with the ideals of the modern society. Only a few romanticists amongst the philosophers of life attacked the technical development as such (just as a few ecstatics amongst the socialists, and a few pietists amongst the followers of Kierkegaard). Generally speaking the technical world was accepted as a meaningful creation of life. But the way in which this creation turns against its creator produces the wrath of all philosophers of life. They want to restitute the integrity of creative life by looking for something below the split into the subject and object. On their way they meet the depth-psychology, the emphasis on the unconscious, or the instincts, or the demonic, or the unreflected and unbroken self-realization. From the beginning in the early nineteenth century to their full development at the end of the nineteenth and the first half of the twentieth century depth-psychology, philosophy of life and Existentialism were intimate allies. Their common enemy was and is the objectifying, depersonalizing power of technical society. They do not look for the religious liberation through the leap of faith as did Kierkegaard, nor to the political liberation through the social dialectics as did Marx, but they look at the liberation which comes out of the depth of the personal life itself, his unconscious ground, his drives and instincts, his unity with nature, his self-affirming will. Sometimes they look back into the past, not in order to return to it, but in order to discover in it examples of undistorted life, e.g., in the Middle Ages, or in the archaic periods of the ancient cultures, or in the so-called primitives. Some go even beyond this and use the un-reflected animal life to symbolize the ideal they put against the realities of technical society (note the use of animal symbols in Nietzsche's *Zarathustra*).

IV. CONTEMPORARY PROTESTS

Again the protest is profound and forceful. But is it able to pierce the walls of the society and its depersonalizing magic? Obviously not. It is driven to fateful self-contradiction. It has to fight the state of reflection with the tools of reflection. Politically the fight against the intelligentsia, and for the primitive and the genuine—in its extreme form for "blood and soil"—has produced the most sophisticated and technically elaborated tools for suppressing every genuine expression of life which did not fit the demands of the political system. Man in this society was pressed into a scheme of thought, action and daily behavior which reminds more of machine parts than of human beings. Even the faces of the storm troopers, for example, were as stereotyped as normal industrial tools. Any indication of personality and individuality was removed. The attempt, made in the name of life, to overcome the rule of depersonalized things, has produced the complete removal of humanity in the supporters of this attempt. And its victims (including many followers) were transformed by terror into slaves, not less obedient than the slave which is called machine. The only way in which the origial emphasis on life was maintained was the unrestricted realization of formerly repressed drives toward power, pleasure and destruction. This was done in the name of vitality, against rationality. But the result was a mutilated, self-destroying vitality united with bestiality and absurdity. The power of the technical world proved again to be overwhelming.

Recent Existentialism (Sartre) tried to break its power by isolating the individual from the embracing structure of technical civilization. It tries to save the person by asking him to create himself without norms, laws and principles, without anybody else or anything else. True humanism is declared to be the message of the individual making himself. Since "man's essence is his existence" no criteria are given to him for his self-creating activity. The will willing itself, the decision deciding for the sake of deciding and not for the sake of a content, the freedom maintaining itself by the rejection of any obligation and devotion— all the descriptions of the existential situation express the protest of Existentialism against our technical world. They are an analogy to Kierkegaard's "leap"; and their freedom is as much a leap into the dark as Kierkegaard's leap would have been without his participation in the Christian Lutheran tradition. By surrendering all norms they deliver the person to the contingencies of the situation, they depersonalize him.

Much more successful in saving the person from the dehumanizing power of technical society seems to be the third ally in the fight for genuine life, the depth-psychology, especially in its latest development in which all emphasis is put on the analysis and synthesis of the personal life. "Personality" has become the central concept of the post-Freudian psycho-therapeutic development. The analytic attempt to liberate the unconscious from the repressions, forced upon it by the society, to liberate the Ego from the authoritarian representatives of the "Superego," to liberate the person from the compulsive drives which subdue the personal center and eliminate its power of making personal decisions—all this seems to be the way to the salvation of the person in the technical society. Many people believe that it is, and feel that their own experiences support this belief. So we must ask: Is psychotherapy the way to break through the otherwise unconquerable fortress of technical society? Is it the way to save the person from becoming a thing amongst things? Or is there a similar problem as that in the other attempts to save personal existence, namely the problem of transition, "the leap," the breaking away from the tyranny of the technical civilization. For two reasons it seems to me that the situation is not essentially different: first, because the individual person is not isolated; second, because the method of liberating him may strengthen that from which it tries to liberate. The first reason points back to Marx, the second to Nietzsche. A philosophical analyst once said to me: "What is the use of my work with my patients even if most successful, when I have to send them back into *this* society?" More and more psychotherapists have discovered that the conflicts of their patients are partly and often largely conditioned by the social situation in which they live, the competitive, technical, post-puritan society with the repressions, the anxiety, and the compulsions it produces. This, however, means a limit to the healing power of analysis and the demand for a social transformation for the sake of the person and his salvation from the depersonalizing forces.

But psychoanalysis has not only its "Marxism" problem, it has also its "Nietzschean" problem. It is the question: can a method, a technically elaborate procedure, save the person from technical society? Two answers can be given to this question. The one would say that psychotherapy is indeed a technique and works like every technique through adequate means toward a definite end. The end is healing of pathological states of mind; the means are determined by their methodological adequacy to their end. If this answer is accepted, the psychoanalyst no more saves the person than does the internist in bodily medicine. The opposite answer would say that within the psychotherapeutic method elements are present which transcend the mere technical sphere, above all a person-to-person relationship which may be saving for the patient as person. If this answer is accepted it means that the analyst implicitly and indirectly exercises priestly functions. This is quite possible and certainly very often real. But then it is not a psychotherapy as psychotherapy which saves the person, but the spiritual substances in which both the analyst and the patient participate. And the question remains: What is this saving power?

V. Two Shortcuts

The result of all this seems to be quite negative. It seems that the Existential revolts against technical society have been futile. From Kierkegaard to present-day psychotherapy, the problem of transition is decisive for the failure to save the person within the technical society. The "leap" in all its variations is more an expression of despair than an answer. Nevertheless, the Existentialist revolt is the decisive event, theoretical and practical, of the last one hundred years. It has shown the problem and it has given different solutions, each of which proved the superiority of the technical society over all those who attacked it. But the attack itself was and is most significant. Whether victorious or not, it kept alive the consciousness that technical society is the great threat against the person. This is the reason why almost all important creations of the last decades were creations by those who belong to the movement of rebellion against the technical society.

These attacks have led to attitudes and systems of life and thought which challenge the contemporary bourgeois society. What, then, about this society and the attitude toward it by groups who largely agree with the criticism made by the one hundred years of Existentialist protest and who, at the same time, are aware of the tragic self-contradictions into which the protesting ideas were driven when they succeeded politically or spiritually? It seems to me that such groups, e.g., the contributors of this volume and the movement they represent, must avoid two shortcuts, the one to return, in a state of disappointment, to a full affirmation of present-day technical society, the other, to use the Christian message as a *deus ex machina,* which solves all problems, unsolved by the other movements!

The first shortcut is an understandable reaction to the chaos of disintegration and the horrors of attempted reintegration which we have experienced in our period. A conservative mood today pervades, not only the disappointed members of the older generation, but also the younger people who without a revolutionary impetus and without visions concerning the future adapt themselves, in a matter-of-fact way, to the concrete demands of the given reality. It is a practical positivism, but without the forward-looking enthusiasm of the earlier positivism. It is a realism of resignation. One hardly can resist this mood in a world in which small groups under the protection of political and military secrecy rule mankind; and in which the dependence on production of a highly technical character subjects everybody more and more to a new kind of fate—as incalculable and threatening as that towards the end of the ancient world. Nevertheless, one can resist this mood, not by closing one's eyes to this actual situation, not by glorifying our own reality because it is not as bad as the reality elsewhere—certainly it is better, yet the threat is the same—not by pointing to the improvements of the social situation in the western world—certainly there are improvements, yet the conflict between person and industrial society is not removed—but by transcending the whole situation and seeing it from a point beyond it.

This point, however, is not the Christian Church and her traditional message. To say this would be another shortcut. One must ask, especially on Christian ground, why the Church and her message are so powerless in their fight against the depersonalizing forces of the present world. The reason cannot be that they are in themselves without power. The opposite is true, not only for the vision of faith, but also for sociological and psychological observation. The reason that the Church and her message are unable to resist the progressive annihilation of the person within industrial society is something else. It is the unintended participation of the Church in the essential structure of industrial society. Step by step, the Church, including the way she has shaped and communicated her message, has been determined by the categories of life and thought which characterizes the industrial society. The Church became a section of that against which she was supposed to defend the person. The process of depersonalization has caught up even with the churches and their members. One should not close his eyes in face of this situation, and one should not glorify the churches as more protected against depersonalization. Certainly, they are more protected in principle, namely, by their foundation, their message, their community—but this is not a necessary protection in the actual churches. They have means of resisting depersonalization in their traditions, their symbols, their rites— but these means can be transformed into powerful tools of dehumanization. They emphasize the infinite value of the individual person—but they are in danger of depersonalizing the person in order to preserve his infinite value. One must transcend not only society but also that section in the society which is taken by the churches, in order to see the situation in its threatening power. Only from "beyond," can industrial society and its dehumanizing forces be resisted and finally overcome.

VI. MAN AND THE NEW REALITY

Two shortcuts have been rejected: the conservative acceptance of the state of things within the so-called "free world," and the ecclesiastical acceptance of the churches as the means of saving the person in the industrial society. It is obvious that the widespread combination of the two shortcuts does not provide for the right way. What, then, is the direction in which we must look for the right way? It is the Christian message of the New Reality, seen in the light of the Existentialist criticism of the old reality, and of its special expression in the industrial society. This, it seems to me, must be the program of a group such as that which is represented by this volume. It is now possible to point to some basic implications of this idea.

The first critical statement to be derived from it is directed against the reality of such a thing as "Industrial Society." Its meaning is a society whose character is determined by man's industrial activity. Man certainly is *homo faber,* industrial man. The being which invented the first tool *as* a tool for permanent use transcends by this act everything given and was potentially the creator of a world beyond the given world. The importance of this fact can hardly be exaggerated in a theological or philosophical doctrine of man. But this power of transcending the given is not an isolated element in man's nature. It is interdependent with many other elements within a total structure. The industrial man is at the same time the man who is able to speak because he has universals, and he is social man because he is able to have I-Thou relations, and he is theoretical man because he is able to ask and to receive answers, and he is moral man because he is able to make responsible decisions, and he is religious man because he is able to be aware of his finitude and of the infinite to which he belongs at the same time. Man is all this because of the basic structure of being which is complete in him; he has a centered self in correlation with a structured world. He looks at both of them, he is free from and for both of them, and he can transcend them both.

If one element in this structure is developed in isolation and put into control over the others, not only the whole structure is distorted, but the special element itself loses its power and its meaning. If, for instance, industrial society transforms the universities into places of research for industrial purposes, not only the universities lose their function of asking radically for the truth, but the technical development itself will be stopped in the long run—the danger of present-day America. On the other hand, if the universities isolate their function of asking for man's existential concern, e.g., the social, they lose their significance and fall victims to unanalyzed ideologies—the danger of past Germany. Many similar examples about the self-destructive consequences of the isolation and imperialism of a special function of the human mind can easily be given. In all of them the result is depersonalization, for the person is a centered whole to which all his functions are subjected. As soon as one function is separated from the others and put into control over the whole, the person is subjected to this function and through it to something which is not itself. It *becomes* this function. This is even true of religion. The abominable word "religionist" implies that a man has dissolved his personality into the religious function, that he is, for example, not free to ask radically even for the truth of religion, that he cannot transcend his functional limits —an implication which is not in vocational names as artist, economist, statesman, bishop. If religion make "religionists," it destroys the person as much as industry by producing an industrial age. Not industry but the isolation and imperialism of industry is the threat for the person in our age.

Homo faber, the industrial man, makes tools; this is the only thing he can "make." The "world above" the "world" he produces is the world of means, leaving open the question of the ends. One previous consideration has shown that the person is either the end for which everything else is means, or the person becomes a means and then not only the person but also the end is lost. There is no end in the chain of means and ends except the person. And if the person himself becomes a means, an endless chain of means-and-ends-and-means is established which crushes purpose, meaning and person. But one may ask the question: Is it not the person for whose comfort and well-being the whole technical world is produced; and even more, is not the creation and the use of tools, from the hammer to the artificial brain in itself an expression of man's power over nature and a confirmation of his personal superiority? To this one must answer that, certainly, only man as a person is able to produce this "second world," but that in doing so he can become himself a tool for the production of tools, spiritually as well as economically, centered in "gadgets" and considered as a part of the production and consumption power. And although the tool serves the comfort of the person, it cannot serve the person as person, that which makes him a person. It can make communication easier. But that which makes the person is the content of what is communicated, and it may well be that the ease and the content of the communication are inversely proportional. Another question could be raised, namely, whether the person is the end which cannot become means without being destroyed. Is not the glory of God or the Kingdom of God or, in more secular terms the realization of values, the ultimate end for which everything must become means, even the person? But such a question is self-contradictory. The meaning of, for instance, Kingdom of God is not the unity of things or functions, but it is the unity of persons including their relationship to the whole non-personal realm. Through persons, i.e., through beings who can decide for or against them, values and the glory of God are actualized. To say that God is the ultimate end is saying that the person is the ultimate end.

VII. CONFORMITY VERSUS MAN

Western technical society has produced methods of adjusting persons to its demands in production and consumption which are less brutal, but in the long run, more effective than totalitarian suppression. They depersonalize not by commanding but by providing; providing, namely, what makes individual creativity superfluous. If one looks around at the methods which produce conformity one is astonished that still enough individual creativity is left even to produce these refined methods. One discovers that man's spiritual life has a tremendous power of resistance against a reduction to prescribed patterns of behavior. But one also sees that this resistance is in a great danger of being worn down by the ways in which adjustment is forced upon him in the industrial society. It starts with the education of "adjustment" which produces conformity just by allowing for more spontaneity of the child than any pre-industrial civilization. But the definite frame within which this spontaneity is quietly kept, leads to a spontaneous adjustment which is more dangerous for creative freedom than any openly deterministic influence. At the same time, and throughout his whole life, other powerful means of adjustment are working upon the person in the technical society; the newspapers which choose the facts worth reporting and suggest their interpretation, the radio programs which eliminate non-conformist contents and interpreters, television which replaces the visual imagination by selected pictorial presentations, the movie which for commercial and censorship reasons has to maintain in most of its productions a conscious mediocrity, adjusting itself to the adjusted taste of the masses, the patterns of advertisement which permeate all other means of public communication, and have an inescapable omnipresence. All this means that more people have more occasions to encounter the cultural contents of past and present than in any pre-industrial civilization. But it also means that these contents become cultural "goods," sold and bought after they have been deprived of the ultimate concern they represented when originally created. They cease to be a matter of *to be or not to be* for the person. They become matters of entertainment, sensation, sentimentality, learning, weapons of competition or social prestige, and lose in this way the power of mediating a spiritual center to the person. They lose their potential dangers for the conformity which is needed for the functioning of the technical society. And by losing their dangers they also lose their creative power, and the person without a spiritual center disintegrates.

VIII. THE STRUGGLE FOR PERSONS

To struggle for the right of the person under the conditions of technical society should not become a fight against the technical side of mass communications; it should not even become a fight against their adjusting power. The technical development is irreversible and adjustment is necessary in every society, especially in a mass society. The person as a person can preserve himself only by a *partial nonparticipation in* the objectifying structures of technical society. But he can withdraw even partially only if he has a place to which to withdraw. And this place is the New Reality to which the Christian message points, which transcends Christianity as well as non-Christianity, which is anticipated everywhere in history, and which has found its criterion in the picture of Jesus as the Christ. But the place of the withdrawal is at the same time, the starting point for the attack on the technical society and its power of depersonalization.

It is the task of the Church, especially of its theology, to describe the place of withdrawal, mainly the "religious reservation." It is the task of active groups within and on the boundary line of the Church to show the possibilities of attack, to participate in it wherever it is made and to be ready to lead it if necessary.

Looking back at the three great movements of protest against the dehumanization in the technical society, we can say that he who fights today for the person has to become an heir of all three of them. He must join in the rebellion of creative life against the degradation of person into an object. This is the first frontier of a Christian action today. Together with the philosophers of life, the Existentialists, the depth-psychologists, and whatever new allies appear, it must show how the "structure of objectivation" (transforming life and person partly into a thing, partly into a calculating machine), penetrates all realms of life and all spiritual functions. It must show especially how even the religious symbols have been misinterpreted as statements about facts and events within the whole of objectivity, thus losing their inborn power to transcend this realm of the subjective-objective, and to mediate visions of that level of reality in which life and personality are rooted. Christian action must be as daring as that of the Existentialists in their analysis of the human situation generally and the present cultural and religious situation especially. It must be as conscious of the infinite complexity of the human soul as that of the depth-psychologists, fully aware of the fact that religion is responsible as much for the complexities and conflicts of the mind as it can contribute to the solution of the conflicts. Christian action today must, like the philosophers of life, have the courage to join the rebellion of life against internal repression and external suppression—in spite of the risk of chaos. But in joining these allies, Christian action must show that it comes from a place of withdrawal where it has received a criterion and a power able to overcome the danger of losing the person while attempting to save him.

And Christian action today must be aware of the second front: together with all movements for social justice whether they are called socialist or not, it must show how the competitive society produces patterns of existence which destroy personality because they destroy community, and which increase that all-pervading anxiety which characterizes our century. Christian action today must preserve, in spite of political and social odds against it, the tradition of social criticism which runs from the enthusiasts of the Reformation period through the bourgeois revolutionaries of the eighteenth century to the social critics of the nineteenth century of whom Marx was the most passionate, the most profound and the most dangerous. In alliance with all these movements Christian action must attack wherever social patterns become visible by which persons are treated as means or transferred into things or deprived of their freedom to decide and to create, or thrown into anxiety or bitterness or hate or tragic guilt. But in joining these allies, Christian action must show that it comes from a place of withdrawal where it has received a criterion and a power able to overcome the danger of sacrificing the person in order to save him.

And Christian action today must be aware of the third front: Together with all the movements within and outside Christianity which have rediscovered, partly in dependence on Kierkegaard, man's existential situation and the ultimate conflict which underlies all other conflicts, his estrangement from the ground of his being and meaning, Christian action must point to the ultimate roots of personal being. It must show that man can maintain his nature and dignity as a person only by a personal encounter with the ground of everything personal. In this encounter, which is the living center of religion and which, against rational as well as mystical criticism, has been defended by Christianity, the person is established. In showing this, Christian action shows also the place to which it withdraws from the technical society in order to attack this society. This place is that which transcends every place, even the Christian Churches. It is the New Reality which is manifest in Christ and against which even technical society and its power of destroying the person as person cannot prevail. Only out of the ground of the personal can the personal be saved. Only those who withdraw from action can receive the power to act. Christian action today rests on two poles, the one which transcends the structure of technical society—the new reality of which Christianity is the witness; the other which is present within the structure of technical society—the movements which struggle, from different sides, against its depersonalizing power. In the correlation of these two poles Christian action must find a way to save the person in the industrial society.

III

Political Community

THE political community is the articulation of particular interests in the realization of common interests; thus, it organizes particular centers of power in representative centers of authority, whether these be monarchic, aristocratic, or democratic. The political community is, in this respect, the community par excellence, since it seeks to bring to fulfillment through a common life the diverse interests and potentialities of individuals and communities. Lawrence Haworth's conception of moral power and growth locates the quality of the good city in an order that can furnish opportunity for the development of individual potentialities in an ordered way.

Reinhold Niebuhr's classic critique of democratic liberalism is also a defense of the possibility and necessity of democracy. In this brief essay he delineates man's struggle for survival in pursuing his particular interests and his search for fulfillment through community; from this dialectic Niebuhr carries through his attack on the liberal notion that self-interest eventuates in social harmony, and by the same dialectic criticizes collectivist hopes of fulfilling particular interests through a utopian community. In his view, the balance between self-interest and community may be preserved through a transcendent vision which relativizes both and sustains both in man's moral struggle.

Lawrence Haworth eschews a religious perspective, considering the problems of planning and the good city from the perspective of the philosopher; however, he affirms the equivalent of a religious vision or cause (maintaining our broad use of the term religious) in his chapter on Community: "The common cause that unifies the inhabitants of a city should be, simply, the city—as it is, so far as it is good; as it might be, so far as it falls short of the ideal."

These essays are rich in moral insight into the fabric of a democratic community. The continuing problem with Reinhold Niebuhr's dialectic is whether there is sufficient substance to his vision in order to gain more than a balance of interests; by contrast, Haworth's thoughtful and somewhat Aristotelian approach runs directly counter to the ethos of a pluralistic society which can agree on democratic process rather than a common cause or ideal. Nevertheless, the two perspectives pose thoughtfully and clearly the dilemma of a secular, pluralistic society as it seeks to develop an ordered city for man.

by Reinhold Niebuhr

THE CHILDREN OF LIGHT AND THE CHILDREN OF DARKNESS

I

DEMOCRACY, as every other historic ideal and institution, contains both ephemeral and more permanently valid elements. Democracy is on the one hand the characteristic fruit of a bourgeois civilization; on the other hand it is a perennially valuable form of social organization in which freedom and order are made to support, and not to contradict, each other.

Democracy is a "bourgeois ideology" in so far as it expresses the typical viewpoints of the middle classes who have risen to power in European civilization in the past three or four centuries. Most of the democratic ideals, as we know them, were weapons of the commercial classes who engaged in stubborn, and ultimately victorious, conflict with the ecclesiastical and aristocratic rulers of the feudal-medieval world. The ideal of equality, unknown in the democratic life of the Greek city states and derived partly from Christian and partly from Stoic

Reprinted from *The Children of Light and the Children of Darkness*, excerpt comprising Chap. One under the same title (pp. 1-41). Copyright 1944 by Charles Scribner's Sons and used by permission. REINHOLD NIEBUHR is Professor Emeritus of Applied Christianity at Union Theological Seminary in New York. Important among his innumerable articles and books are *The Nature and Destiny of Man, Moral Man and Immoral Society, An Interpretation of Christian Ethics, Faith and History,* and *The Irony of American History.*

sources, gave the bourgeois classes a sense of self-respect in overcoming the aristocratic pretension and condescension of the feudal over-lords of medieval society. The middle classes defeated the combination of economic and political power of mercantilism by stressing economic liberty; and, through the principles of political liberty, they added the political power of suffrage to their growing economic power. The implicit assumptions, as well as the explicit ideals, of democratic civilization were also largely the fruit of middle-class existence. The social and historical optimism of democratic life, for instance, represents the typical illusion of an advancing class which mistook its own progress for the progress of the world.

Since bourgeois civilization, which came to birth in the sixteenth to eighteenth centuries and reached its zenith in the nineteenth century, is now obviously in grave peril, if not actually in *rigor mortis* in the twentieth century, it must be obvious that democracy, in so far as it is a middle-class ideology, also faces its doom.

This fate of democracy might be viewed with equanimity, but for the fact that it has a deeper dimension and broader validity than its middle-class character. Ideally democracy is a permanently valid form of social and political organization which does justice to two dimensions of human existence: to man's spiritual stature and his social character; to the uniqueness and variety of life, as well as to the common necessities of all men. Bourgeois democracy frequently exalted the individual at the expense of the community; but its emphasis upon liberty contained a valid element, which transcended its excessive individualism. The community requires liberty as much as does the individual; and the individual requires community more than bourgeois thought comprehended. Democracy can therefore not be equated with freedom. An ideal democratic order seeks unity within the conditions of freedom; and maintains freedom within the framework of order.

Man requires freedom in his social organization because he is "essentially" free, which is to say, that he has the capacity for indeterminate transcendence over the processes and limitations of nature. This freedom enables him to make history and to elaborate communal organizations in boundless variety and in endless breadth and extent. But he also requires community because he is by nature social. He cannot fulfill his life within himself but only in responsible and mutual relations with his fellows.

Bourgeois democrats are inclined to believe that freedom is primarily a necessity for the individual, and that community and social order are necessary only because there are many individuals in a small world, so that minimal restrictions are required to prevent confusion. Actually the community requires freedom as much as the individual; and the individual requires order as much as does the community.

Both the individual and the community require freedom so that neither communal nor historical restraints may prematurely arrest the potencies which inhere in man's essential freedom and which express themselves collectively as well as individually. It is true that individuals are usually the initiators of new insights and the proponents of novel methods. Yet there are collective forces at work in society which are not the conscious contrivance of individuals. In any event society is as much the beneficiary of freedom as the individual. In a free society new forces may enter into competition with the old and gradually establish themselves. In a traditional or tyrannical form of social organization new forces are either suppressed, or they establish themselves at the price of social convulsion and upheaval.

The order of a community is, on the other hand, a boon to the individual as well as to the community. The individual cannot be a true self in isolation. Nor can he live within the confines of the community which "nature" establishes in the minimal cohesion of family and herd. His freedom transcends these limits of nature, and therefore makes larger and larger social units both possible and necessary. It is precisely because of the essential freedom of man that he requires a contrived order in his community.

The democratic ideal is thus more valid than the libertarian and individualistic version of it which bourgeois civilization elaborated. Since the bourgeois version has been discredited by the events of contemporary history and since, in any event, bourgeois civilization is in process of disintegration, it becomes important to distinguish and save what is permanently valid from what is ephemeral in the democratic order.

If democracy is to survive it must find a more adequate cultural basis than the philosophy which has informed the building of the bourgeois world. The inadequacy of the presuppositions upon which the democratic experiment rests does not consist merely in the excessive individualism and libertarianism of the bourgeois world view; though it must be noted that this excessive individualism prompted a civil war in the whole western world in which the rising proletarian classes pitted an excessive collectivism against the false individualism of middle-class life. This civil conflict contributed to the weakness of democratic civilization when faced with the threat of barbarism. Neither the individualism nor the collectivism did justice to all the requirements of man's social life, and the conflict between half-truth and half-truth divided the civilized world in such a way that the barbarians were able to claim first one side and then the other in this civil conflict as their provisional allies.[1]

But there is a more fundamental error in the social philosophy of democratic civilization than the individualism of bourgeois democracy and the collectivism of Marxism. It is the confidence of both bourgeois and proletarian idealists in the possibility of achieving an easy resolution of the tension and conflict between self-interest and the general interest. Modern bourgeois civilization is not, as Catholic philosophers and medievalists generally assert, a rebellion against universal law, or a defiance of universal standards of justice, or a war against the historic institutions which sought to achieve and preserve some general social and international harmony. Modern secularism is not, as religious idealists usually aver, merely a rationalization of self-interest, either individual or collective. Bourgeois individualism may be excessive and it may destroy the individual's organic relation to the community; but it was not intended to destroy either the national or the international order. On the contrary the social idealism which informs our democratic civilization had a touching faith in the possibility of achieving a simple harmony between self-interest and the general welfare on every level.

It is not true that Nazism is the final fruit of a moral cynicism which had its rise in the Renaissance and Reformation, as Catholic apologists aver. Nazi barbarism is the final fruit of a moral cynicism which was only a subordinate note in the cultural life of the modern period, and which remained subordinate until very recently. Modern civilization did indeed seek to give the individual a greater freedom in the national community than the traditional feudal order had given him; and it did seek to free the nations of restraints placed upon their freedom by the international church. But it never cynically defied the general interest in the name of self-interest, either individual or collective. It came closer to doing this nationally than individually. Machiavelli's amoral "Prince," who knows no law beyond his own will and power, is made to bear the whole burden of the Catholic polemic against the modern world. It must be admitted that Machiavelli is the first of a long line of moral cynics in the field of international relations. But this moral cynicism only qualifies, and does not efface, the general universalistic overtone of modern liberal idealism. In the field of domestic politics the war of uncontrolled interests may have been the consequence, but it was certainly not the intention, of middle-class individualists. Nor was the conflict between nations in our modern world their intention. They did demand a greater degree of freedom for the nations; but they believed that it was possible to achieve an uncontrolled harmony between them, once the allegedly irrelevant restrictions of the old religio-political order were removed. In this they proved to be mistaken. They did not make the mistake, however, of giving simple moral sanction to self-interest. They depended rather upon controls and restraints which proved to be inadequate.

II

In illumining this important distinction more fully, we may well designate the moral cynics, who know no law beyond their will and interest, with a scriptural designation of "children of this world" or "children of darkness." Those who believe that self-interest should be brought under the discipline of a higher law could then be termed "the children of light." This is no mere arbitrary device; for evil is always the assertion of some self-interest without regard to the whole, whether the whole be conceived as the immediate community, or the total community of mankind, or the total order of the world. The good is, on the other hand, always the harmony of the whole on various levels. Devotion to a subordinate and premature "whole" such as the nation, may of course become evil, viewed from the perspective of a larger whole, such as the community of mankind. The "children of light" may thus be defined as those who seek to bring self-interest under the discipline of a more universal law and in harmony with a more universal good.

According to the scripture "the children of this world are in their generation wiser than the children of light." This observation fits the modern situation. Our democratic civilization has been built, not by children of darkness but by foolish children of light. It has been under attack by the children of darkness, by the moral cynics, who declare that a strong nation need acknowledge no law beyond its strength. It has come close to complete disaster under this attack, not because it accepted the same creed as the cynics; but because it underestimated the power of self-interest, both individual and collective, in modern society. The children of light have not been as wise as the children of darkness.

The children of darkness are evil because they know no law beyond the self. They are wise, though evil, because they understand the power of self-interest. The children of light are virtuous because they have some conception of a higher law than their own will. They are usually foolish because they do not know the power of self-will. They underestimate the peril of anarchy in both the national and the international community. Modern democratic civilization is, in short, sentimental rather than cynical. It has an easy solution for the problem of anarchy and chaos on both the national and international level of community, because of its fatuous and superficial view of man. It does not know that the same man who is ostensibly devoted to the "common good" may have desires and ambitions, hopes and fears, which set him at variance with his neighbor.

It must be understood that the children of light are foolish not merely because they underestimate the power of self-interest among the children of darkness. They underestimate this power among themselves. The democratic world came so close to disaster not merely because it never believed that Nazism possessed the demonic fury which it avowed. Civilization refused to recognize the power of class interest in its own communities. It also spoke glibly of an international conscience; but the children of darkness meanwhile skilfully set nation against nation. They were thereby enabled to despoil one nation after another, without every civilized nation coming to the defence of each. Moral cynicism had a provisional advantage over moral sentimentality. Its advantage lay not merely in its own lack of moral scruple but also in its shrewd assessment of the power of self-interest, individual and national, among the children of light, despite their moral protestations.

While our modern children of light, the secularized idealists, were particularly foolish and blind, the more "Christian" children of light have been almost equally guilty of this error. Modern liberal Protestantism was probably even more sentimental in its appraisal of the moral realities in our political life than secular idealism, and Catholicism could see nothing but cynical rebellion in the modern secular revolt against Catholic universalism and a Catholic "Christian" civilization. In Catholic thought medieval political universalism is always accepted at face value. Rebellion against medieval culture is therefore invariably regarded as the fruit of moral cynicism. Actually the middle-class revolt against the feudal order was partially prompted by a generous idealism, not unmixed of course with peculiar middle-class interests. The feudal order was not so simply a Christian civilization as Catholic defenders of it aver. It compounded its devotion to a universal order with the special interests of the priestly and aristocratic bearers of effective social power. The rationalization of their unique position in the feudal order may not have been more marked than the subsequent rationalization of bourgeois interests in the liberal world. But it is idle to deny this "ideological taint" in the feudal order and to pretend that rebels against the order were merely rebels against order as such. They were rebels against a particular order which gave an undue advantage to the aristocratic opponents of the middle classes.[2] The blindness of Catholicism to its own ideological taint is typical of the blindness of the children of light.

Our modern civilization, as a middle-class revolt against an aristocratic and clerical order, was irreligious partly because a Catholic civilization had so compounded the eternal sanctities with the contingent and relative justice and injustice of an agrarian-feudal order, that the new and dynamic bourgeois social force was compelled to challenge not only the political-economic arrangements of the order but also the eternal sanctities which hallowed it.

If modern civilization represents a bourgeois revolt against feudalism, modern culture represents the revolt of new thought, informed by modern science, against a culture in which religious authority had fixed premature and too narrow limits for the expansion of science and had sought to restrain the curiosity of the human mind from inquiring into "secondary causes." The culture which venerated science in place of religion, worshipped natural causation in place of God, and which regarded the cool prudence of bourgeois man as morally more normative than Christian love, has proved itself to be less profound than it appeared to be in the seventeenth and eighteenth centuries. But these inadequacies, which must be further examined as typical of the foolishness of modern children of light, do not validate the judgment that these modern rebels were really children of darkness, intent upon defying the truth or destroying universal order.

The modern revolt against the feudal order and the medieval culture was occasioned by the assertion of new vitalities in the social order and the discovery of new dimensions in the cultural enterprise of mankind. It was truly democratic in so far as it challenged the premature and tentative unity of a society and the stabilization of a culture, and in so far as it developed new social and cultural possibilities. The conflict between the middle classes and the aristocrats, between the scientists and the priests, was not a conflict between children of darkness and children of light. It was a conflict between pious and less pious children of light, both of whom were unconscious of the corruption of self-interest in all ideal achievements and pretensions of human culture.

III

In this conflict the devotees of medieval religion were largely unconscious of the corruption of self-interest in their own position; but it must be admitted that they were not as foolish as their secular successors in their estimate of the force of self-interest in human society. Catholicism did strive for an inner and religious discipline upon inordinate desire; and it had a statesmanlike conception of the necessity of legal and political restraint upon the power of egotism, both individual and collective, in the national and the more universal human community.

Our modern civilization, on the other hand, was ushered in on a wave of boundless social optimism. Modern secularism is divided into many schools. But all the various schools agreed in rejecting the Christian doctrine of original sin. It is not possible to explain the subtleties or to measure the profundity of this doctrine in this connection. But it is necessary to point out that the doctrine makes an important contribution to any adequate social and political theory the lack of which has robbed bourgeois theory of real wisdom; for it emphasizes a fact which every page of human history attests. Through it one may understand that no matter how wide the perspectives which the human mind may reach, how broad the loyalties which the human imagination may conceive, how universal the community which human statecraft may organize, or how pure the aspirations of the saintliest idealists may be, there is no level of human moral or social achievement in which there is not some corruption of inordinate self-love.

This sober and true view of the human situation was neatly rejected by modern culture. That is why it conceived so many fatuous and futile plans for resolving the conflict between the self and the community; and between the national and the world community. Whenever modern idealists are confronted with the divisive and corrosive effects of man's self-love, they look for some immediate cause of this perennial tendency, usually in some specific form of social organization. One school holds that men would be good if only political institutions would not corrupt them; another believes that they would be good if the prior evil of a faulty economic organization could be eliminated. Or another school thinks of this evil as no more than ignorance, and therefore waits for a more perfect educational process to redeem man from his partial and particular loyalties. But no school asks how it is that an essentially good man could have produced corrupting and tyrannical political organizations or exploiting economic organizations, or fanatical and superstitious religious organizations.

The result of this persistent blindness to the obvious and tragic fact of man's social history is that democracy has had to maintain itself precariously against the guile and the malice of the children of darkness, while its statesmen and guides conjured up all sorts of abstract and abortive plans for the creation of perfect national and international communities.

The confidence of modern secular idealism in the possibility of an easy resolution of the tension between individual and community, or between classes, races and nations is derived from a too optimistic view of human nature. This too generous estimate of human virtue is intimately related to an erroneous estimate of the dimensions of the human stature. The conception of human nature which underlies the social and political attitudes of a liberal democratic culture is that of an essentially harmless individual. The survival impulse, which man shares with the animals, is regarded as the normative form of his egoistic drive. If this were a true picture of the human situation man might be, or might become, as harmless as seventeenth- and eighteenth-century thought assumed. Unfortunately for the validity of this picture of man, the most significant distinction between the human and the animal world is that the impulses of the former are "spiritualized" in the human world. Human capacities for evil as well as for good are derived from this spiritualization. There is of course always a natural survival impulse at the core of all human ambition. But this survival impulse cannot be neatly disentangled from two forms of its spiritualization. The one form is the desire to fulfill the potentialities of life and not merely to maintain its existence. Man is the kind of animal who cannot merely live. If he lives at all he is bound to seek the realization of his true nature; and to his true nature belongs his fulfillment in the lives of others. The will to live is thus transmuted into the will to self-realization; and self-realization involves self-giving in relations to others. When this desire for self-realization is fully explored it becomes apparent that it is subject to the paradox that the highest form of self-realization is the consequence of self-giving, but that it cannot be the intended consequence without being prematurely limited. Thus the will to live is finally transmuted into its opposite in the sense that only in self-giving can the self be fulfilled, for: "He that findeth his life shall lose it: and he that loseth his life for my sake shall find it."[3]

On the other hand the will-to-live is also spiritually transmuted into the will-to-power or into the desire for "power and glory." Man, being more than a natural creature, is not interested merely in physical survival but in prestige and social approval. Having the intelligence to anticipate the perils in which he stands in nature and history, he invariably seeks to gain security against these perils by enhancing his power, individually and collectively. Possessing a darkly unconscious sense of his insignificance in the total scheme of things, he seeks to compensate for his insignificance by pretensions of pride. The conflicts between man are thus never simple conflicts between competing survival impulses. They are conflicts in which each man or group seeks to guard its power and prestige against the peril of competing expressions of power and pride. Since the very possession of power and prestige always involves some encroachment upon the prestige and power of others, this conflict is by its very nature a more stubborn and difficult one than the mere competition between various survival impulses in nature. It remains to be added that this conflict expresses itself even more cruelly in collective than in individual terms. Human behaviour being less individualistic than secular liberalism assumed, the struggle between classes, races and other groups in human society is not as easily resolved by the expedient of dissolving the groups as liberal democratic idealists assumed.

Since the survival impulse in nature is transmuted into two different and contradictory spiritualized forms, which we may briefly designate as the will-to-live-truly and the will-to-power, man is at variance with himself. The power of the second impulse places him more fundamentally in conflict with his fellowman than democratic liberalism realizes. The fact that he cannot realize himself, except in organic relation with his fellows, makes the community more important than bourgeois individualism understands. The fact that the two impulses, though standing in contradiction to each other, are also mixed and compounded with each other on every level of human life, makes the simple distinctions between good and evil, between selfishness and altruism, with which liberal idealism has tried to estimate moral and political facts, invalid. The fact that the will-to-power inevitably justifies itself in terms of the morally more acceptable will to realize man's true nature means that the egotistic corruption of universal ideals is a much more persistent fact in human conduct than any moralistic creed is inclined to admit.

If we survey any period of history, and not merely the present tragic era of world catastrophe, it becomes quite apparent that human ambitions, lusts and desires, are more inevitably inordinate, that both human creativity and human evil reach greater heights, and that conflicts in the community between varying conceptions of the good and between competing expressions of vitality are of more tragic proportions than was anticipated in the basic philosophy which underlies democratic civilization.

There is a specially ironic element in the effort of the seventeenth century to confine man to the limits of a harmless "nature" or to bring all his actions under the discipline of a cool prudence. For while democratic social philosophy was elaborating the picture of a harmless individual, moved by no more than a survival impulse, living in a social peace guaranteed by a pre-established harmony of nature, the advancing natural sciences were enabling man to harness the powers of nature, and to give his desires and ambitions a more limitless scope than they previously had. The static inequalities of an agrarian society were transmuted into the dynamic inequalities of an industrial age. The temptation to inordinate expressions of the possessive impulse, created by the new wealth of a technical civilization, stood in curious and ironic contradiction to the picture of essentially moderate and ordinate desires which underlay the social philosophy of the physiocrats and of Adam Smith. Furthermore a technical society developed new and more intensive forms of social cohesion and a greater central-ization of economic process in defiance of the individualistic conception of social relations which informed the liberal philos-ophy.[4]

The demonic fury of fascist politics in which a collective will expresses boundless ambitions and imperial desires and in which the instruments of a technical civilization are used to arm this will with a destructive power, previously unknown in history, represents a melancholy historical refutation of the eighteenth- and nineteenth-century conceptions of a harmless and essentially individual human life. Human desires are ex-pressed more collectively, are less under the discipline of pru-dent calculation, and are more the masters of, and less limited by, natural forces than the democratic creed had understood.

While the fury of fascist politics represents a particularly vivid refutation of the democratic view of human nature, the develop-ments within the confines of democratic civilization itself offer almost as telling a refutation. The liberal creed is never an explicit instrument of the children of darkness. But it is sur-prising to what degree the forces of darkness are able to make a covert use of the creed. One must therefore, in analyzing the liberal hope of a simple social and political harmony, be equally aware of the universalistic presuppositions which underlie the hope and of the egoistic corruption (both individual and col-lective) which inevitably express themselves in our culture in terms of, and in despite of, the creed. One must understand that it is a creed of children of light; but also that it betrays their blindness to the forces of darkness.

In the social philosophy of Adam Smith there was both a religious guarantee of the preservation of community and a moral demand that the individual consider its claims. The religious guarantee was contained in Smith's secularized version of providence. Smith believed that when a man is guided by self-interest he is also "led by an invisible hand to promote an end which is not his intention."[5] This "invisible hand" is of course the power of a pre-established social harmony, conceived as a harmony of nature, which transmutes conflicts of self-interest into a vast scheme of mutual service.

Despite this determinism Smith does not hesitate to make moral demands upon men to sacrifice their interests to the wider interest. The universalistic presupposition which underlies Smith's thought is clearly indicated for instance in such an observation as this: "The wise and virtuous man is at all times willing that his own private interests should be sacrificed to the public interest of his own particular order of society—that the interests of this order of society be sacrificed to the greater interest of the state. He should therefore be equally willing that all those inferior interests should be sacrificed to the greater interests of the universe, to the interests of that great society of all sensible and intelligent beings, of which God himself is the immediate administrator and director."[6]

It must be noted that in Smith's conception the "wider interest" does not stop at the boundary of the national state. His was a real universalism in intent. *Laissez faire* was intended to establish a world community as well as a natural harmony of interests within each nation. Smith clearly belongs to the children of light. But the children of darkness were able to make good use of his creed. A dogma which was intended to guarantee the economic freedom of the individual became the "ideology" of vast corporate structures of a later period of capitalism, used by them, and still used, to prevent a proper political control of their power. His vision of international harmony was transmuted into the sorry realities of an international capitalism which recognized neither moral scruples nor political restraints in expanding its power over the world. His vision of a democratic harmony of society, founded upon the free play of economic forces, was refuted by the tragic realities of the class conflicts in western society. Individual and collective egotism usually employed the political philosophy of this creed, but always defied the moral idealism which informed it.

The political theory of liberalism, as distinct from the economic theory, based its confidence in the identity of particular and universal interests, not so much upon the natural limits of egotism as upon either the capacity of reason to transmute egotism into a concern for the general welfare, or upon the ability of government to overcome the potential conflict of wills in society. But even when this confidence lies in reason or in government, the actual character of the egotism which must be restrained is frequently measured in the dimension of the natural impulse of survival only. Thus John Locke, who thinks government necessary in order to overcome the "inconvenience of the state of nature," sees self-interest in conflict with the general interest only on the low level where "self-preservation" stands in contrast to the interests of others. He therefore can express the sense of obligation to others in terms which assume no final conflict between egotism and the wider interest: "Everyone," he writes, "as he is bound to preserve himself and not to quit his station willfully, so by the like reason, when his own preservation comes not into competition, ought as much as he can to preserve the rest of mankind."[7] This is obviously no creed of a moral cynic; but neither is it a profound expression of the sense of universal obligation. For most of the gigantic conflicts of will in human history, whether between individuals or groups, take place on a level, where "self-preservation" is not immediately but only indirectly involved. They are conflicts of rival lusts and ambitions.

The general confidence of an identity between self-interest and the commonweal, which underlies liberal democratic political theory, is succinctly expressed in Thomas Paine's simple creed:

"Public good is not a term opposed to the good of the individual; on the contrary it is the good of every individual collected. It is the good of all, because it is the good of every one; for as the public body is every individual collected, so the public good is the collected good of those individuals."[8]

While there is a sense in which this identity between a particular and the general interest is ultimately true, it is never absolutely true in an immediate situation; and such identity as could be validly claimed in an immediate situation is not usually recognized by the proponents of particular interest.[9] Human intelligence is never as pure an instrument of the universal perspective as the liberal democratic theory assumes, though neither is it as purely the instrument of the ego, as is assumed by the anti-democratic theory, derived from the pessimism of such men as Thomas Hobbes and Martin Luther.

The most naïve form of the democratic faith in an identity between the individual and the general interest is developed by the utilitarians of the eighteenth and nineteenth centuries. Their theory manages to extract a covertly expressed sense of obligation toward the "greatest good of the greatest number" from a hedonistic analysis of morals which really lacks all logical presuppositions for any idea of obligation, and which cannot logically rise above an egoistic view of life. This utilitarianism therefore expresses the stupidity of the children of light in its most vivid form. Traditional moralists may point to any hedonistic doctrine as the creed of the children of darkness, because it has no real escape from egotism. But since it thinks it has, it illustrates the stupidity of the children of light, rather than the malice of the children of darkness. It must be observed of course that the children of darkness are well able to make use of such a creed. Utilitarianism's conception of the wise egotist, who in his prudence manages to serve interests wider than his own, supported exactly the same kind of political philosophy as Adam Smith's conception of the harmless egotist, who did not even have to be wise, since the providential laws of nature held his egotism in check. So Jeremy Bentham's influence was added to that of Adam Smith in support of a *laissez-faire* political philosophy; and this philosophy encouraged an unrestrained expression of human greed at the precise moment in history when an advancing industrialism required more, rather than less, moral and political restraint upon economic forces.

It must be added that, whenever the democratic idealists were challenged to explain the contrast between the actual behaviour of men and their conception of it, they had recourse to the evolutionary hope; and declared with William Godwin, that human history is moving toward a form of rationality which will finally achieve a perfect identity of self-interest and the public good.[10]

Perhaps the most remarkable proof of the power of this optimistic creed, which underlies democratic thought, is that Marxism, which is ostensibly a revolt against it, manages to express the same optimism in another form. While liberal democrats dreamed of a simple social harmony, to be achieved by a cool prudence and a calculating egotism, the actual facts of social history revealed that the static class struggle of agrarian societies had been fanned into the flames of a dynamic struggle. Marxism was the social creed and the social cry of those classes who knew by their miseries that the creed of the liberal optimists was a snare and a delusion. Marxism insisted that the increasingly overt social conflict in democratic society would have to become even more overt, and would finally be fought to a bitter conclusion. But Marxism was also convinced that after the triumph of the lower classes of society, a new society would emerge in which exactly that kind of harmony between all social forces would be established, which Adam Smith had regarded as a possibility for any kind of society. The similarities between classical *laissez-faire* theory and the vision of an anarchistic millennium in Marxism are significant, whatever may be the superficial differences. Thus the provisionally cynical Lenin, who can trace all the complexities of social conflict in contemporary society with penetrating shrewdness, can also express the utopian hope that the revolution will usher in a period of history which will culminate in the Marxist millennium of anarchism. "All need for force will vanish," declared Lenin, "since people will grow accustomed to observing the elementary conditions of social existence without force and without subjection."[11]

The Roman Catholic polemic against Marxism is no more

valid than its strictures against democratic liberalism. The charge that this is a creed of moral cynicism cannot be justified. However strong the dose of provisional cynicism, which the creed may contain, it is a sentimental and not a cynical creed. The Marxists, too, are children of light. Their provisional cynicism does not even save them from the usual stupidity, nor from the fate, of other stupid children of light. That fate is to have their creed become the vehicle and instrument of the children of darkness. A new oligarchy is arising in Russia, the spiritual characteristics of which can hardly be distinguished from those of the American "go-getters" of the latter nineteenth and early twentieth centuries. And in the light of history Stalin will probably have the same relation to the early dreamers of the Marxist dreams which Napoleon has to the liberal dreamers of the eighteenth century.

IV

Democratic theory, whether in its liberal or in its more radical form, is just as stupid in analyzing the relation between the national and the international community as in seeking a too simple harmony between the individual and the national community. Here, too, modern liberal culture exhibits few traces of moral cynicism. The morally autonomous modern national state does indeed arise; and it acknowledges no law beyond its interests. The actual behaviour of the nations is cynical. But the creed of liberal civilization is sentimental. This is true not only of the theorists whose creed was used by the architects of economic imperialism and of the more covert forms of national egotism in the international community, but also of those whose theories were appropriated by the proponents of an explicit national egotism. A straight line runs from Mazzini to Mussolini in the history of Italian nationalism. Yet there was not a touch of moral cynicism in the thought of Mazzini. He was, on the contrary, a pure universalist.[12]

Even the philosophy of German romanticism, which has been accused with some justification of making specific contributions to the creed of German Nazism, reveals the stupidity of the children of light much more than the malice of the children of darkness. There is of course a strong note of moral nihilism in the final fruit of this romantic movement as we have it in Nietzsche; though even Nietzsche was no nationalist. But the earlier romantics usually express the same combination of individualism and universalism which characterizes the theory of the more naturalistic and rationalistic democrats of the western countries. Fichte resolved the conflict between the individual and the community through the instrumentality of the "just law" almost as easily as the utilitarians resolved it by the calculations of the prudent egotist and as easily as Rousseau resolved it by his conception of a "general will," which would fulfill the best purposes of each individual will. This was no creed of a community, making itself the idolatrous end of human existence. The theory was actually truer than the more individualistic and naturalistic forms of the democratic creed; for romanticism understood that the individual requires the community for his fulfillment. Thus even Hegel, who is sometimes regarded as the father of state absolutism in modern culture, thought of the national state as providing "for the reasonable will, insofar as it is in the individual only implicitly the universal will coming to a consciousness and an understanding of itself and being found."[13]

This was not the creed of a collective egotism which negated the right of the individual. Rather it was a theory which, unlike the more purely democratic creed, understood the necessity of social fulfillment for the individual, and which, in common with the more liberal theories, regarded this as a much too simple process.

If the theory was not directed toward the annihilation of the individual, as is the creed of modern religious nationalism, to what degree was it directed against the universal community? Was it an expression of the national community's defiance of any interest or law above and beyond itself? This also is not the case. Herder believed that "fatherlands" might "lie peaceably side by side and aid each other as families. It is the grossest barbarity of human speech to speak of fatherlands in bloody battle with each other." Unfortunately this is something more than a barbarity of speech. Herder was a universalist, who thought a nice harmony between various communities could be achieved if only the right would be granted to each to express itself according to its unique and peculiar genius. He thought the false universalism of imperialism, according to which one community makes itself the standard and the governor of others, was merely the consequence of a false philosophy, whereas it is in fact one of the perennial corruptions of man's collective life.

Fichte, too, was a universalist who was fully conscious of moral obligations which transcend the national community. His difficulty, like that of all the children of light, was that he had a too easy resolution of the conflict between the nation and the community of nations. He thought that philosophy, particularly German philosophy, could achieve a synthesis between national and universal interest. "The patriot," he declared, "wishes the purpose of mankind to be reached first of all in that nation of which he is a member. . . . This purpose is the only possible patriotic goal. . . . Cosmopolitanism is the will that the purpose of life and of man be attained in all mankind. Patriotism is the will that this purpose be attained first of all in that nation of which we are members."[14] It is absurd to regard such doctrine as the dogma of national egotism, though Fichte could not express it without insinuating a certain degree of national pride into it. The pride took the form of the complacent assumption that German philosophy enabled the German nation to achieve a more perfect relation to the community of mankind than any other nation. He was, in other words, one of the many stupid children of light, who failed to understand the difficulty of the problem which he was considering; and his blindness included failure to see the significance of the implicit denial of an ideal in the thought and action of the very idealist who propounds it.

Hegel, too, belongs to the children of light. To be sure he saw little possibility of constructing a legal structure of universal proportions which might guard the interests of the universal community and place a check upon the will of nations. He declared "states find themselves in a natural, more than a legal, relation to each other. Therefore there is a continuous struggle between them. . . . They maintain and procure their rights through their own power and must as a matter of necessity plunge into war."[15] It may be observed in passing that this is a more accurate description of the actual realities of international relations than that of any of the theorists thus far considered. But the question is whether Hegel regarded this actual situation as morally normative. Hegel's thought upon this matter was ambiguous. On the one hand he tended to regard the demands of the state as final because he saw no way of achieving a legal or political implementation of the inchoate community which lies beyond the state. But on the other hand he believed that a more ultimate law stood over the nation, that it "had its real content in *Weltgeschichte,* the realm of the world mind which holds the supreme absolute truth."[16] This mind, he believed, "constitutes itself the absolute judge over states." The nation is thus politically, but not morally, autonomous. This is no doctrine of moral cynicism. Rather it is a sentimental doctrine. Hegel imagined that the nation, free of political but not of moral inhibitions, could nevertheless, by thinking "in Weltgeschichte" (that is, by becoming fully conscious of its relation to mankind), thereby "lay hold of its concrete universality."[17] The error is very similar to that of Fichte and of all the universalists, whether naturalistic or idealistic, positivist or romantic. It is the error of a too great reliance upon the human capacity for transcendence over self-interest. There is indeed such a capacity. If there were not, any form of social harmony among men would be impossible; and certainly a democratic version of such harmony would be quite unthinkable. But the same man who displays this capacity also reveals varying degrees of the power of self-interest and of the subservience of the mind to these interests. Sometimes this egotism stands in frank contradiction to the professed ideal or sense of obligation to higher and wider values; and sometimes it uses the ideal as its instrument.

It is this fact which a few pessimists in our modern culture have realized, only to draw undemocratic and sometimes completely cynical conclusions from it. The democratic idealists of practically all schools of thought have managed to remain remarkably oblivious to the obvious facts. Democratic theory therefore has not squared with the facts of history. This grave defect in democratic theory was comparatively innocuous in the heyday of the bourgeois period, when the youth and the power of democratic civilization surmounted all errors of judgment and confusions of mind. But in this latter day, when it has become important to save what is valuable in democratic life from the destruction of what is false in bourgeois civilization, it has also become necessary to distinguish what is false in democratic theory from what is true in democratic life.

The preservation of a democratic civilization requires the wisdom of the serpent and the harmlessness of the dove. The children of light must be armed with the wisdom of the children of darkness but remain free from their malice. They must know the power of self-interest in human society without giving it moral justification. They must have this wisdom in order that they may beguile, deflect, harness and restrain self-interest, individual and collective, for the sake of the community.

by Lawrence Haworth

THE GOOD LIFE: GROWTH AND DUTY

from *The Good City*

I

INSTITUTIONAL control is not an end in itself, nor is the potentiality for guiding the development of urban institutions self-justifying. There are important questions of ends and means to be settled. We must determine whether the potentiality for institutional control can be pointed toward desirable ends, and we must discover whether acceptable means of pursuing those ends are available. We must decide what we wish to make of the city, and how we wish to organize the effort by which our goals are to be pursued. These problems form the subject matter of this and the following four chapters.

The underlying ideas to be developed have already been suggested. With the growth of the city human beings meet increasing opportunities for self-expression and achievement, and as a result new dimensions of human personality are called forth. The very magnitude of the scale of urban life creates a new order of problems. Life is far-flung, but spread thin. Disorientation becomes difficult to avoid, and the genuine opportunities

Reprinted from *The Good City* (First Midland Book edition; Indianapolis, Ind.: Indiania University Press, 1966), excerpts consisting of Chap. 4 (pp. 53-62), sec. VI of Chap 6 (pp. 84-85), and Chap. 7 (pp. 86-101). By permission. LAWRENCE HAWORTH is Professor of Philosophy at Purdue University.

for growth are unevenly distributed. In cities as in art, the difficulties of achieving order are in direct proportion to the magnitude and variety of the materials to be ordered. Yet by presenting a broader and richer canvas, the city presents a more meaningful challenge: the human settlement that would result from ordering the wealth of opportunities offered by urban institutions would form a far more valuable arena for the life of man than the family, the village community, the *polis,* or the manor.

The city's great variety of opportunities for significant action is a result of the differentiation and specialization of institutional rules. But another result has been the problems this diversity brings to the city. As opportunity grew, community withered. Differentiation brought dispersion and fragmentation of persons, and the human settlement became, instead of a community of persons, an organization of functionaries. The problem is to rediscover community while retaining and ordering opportunity. These remarks do not define the goal, but they identify the ground on which a definition must be sought.

II

There are two ordinary approaches to the problem of defining the good city. One is architectural in emphasis, the other sociological, though not all architects follow the first, nor all sociologists the second. The architectural approach is essentially pictorial. Worked out in terms of buildings and vistas, it encompasses what can be seen of the city. Certain elementary functional matters are taken into account. The location and the architectural design of buildings, shops, and factories are fixed upon. The over-all shape of the city, whether it should be circular or strung along a principal thoroughfare, is decided. Attention is given to problems of movement. One either, with Frank Lloyd Wright, accepts the automobile and spreads people out, an acre for every family; or, with Le Corbusier, packs them tightly together in circular "Garden Cities," two and three-fourths miles across and containing 1,600,000 inhabitants.[1]

It would be foolish to deny the relevance of these matters with which architecturally oriented city planners are concerned. But error creeps in when the limitations of architecture are imposed on the problem of conceiving a good city. Our ideal should include more than can be seen in an aerial photograph. Are the people rich or poor? Do the shiny buildings intimidate them, or do the people feel comfortable in their shelter? Are the people communicative? Do they form a community? Do the advantages of the city extend to everyone within it, or only to a privileged majority? Above all, what types of person are nurtured by the city's physical design and social arrangements? Are they sensitive, alert, and creative, or dull, unimaginative, passive, and lost? Architecture does not answer these questions, and it would not be reasonable to expect that it should. But neither would it be reasonable to expect that one can decide whether a city is good without such answers.

Although the sociological approach is not burdened with these limitations, its advantages over the architectural approach are few. The city is not viewed as merely buildings and streets, and the problems are not those of where to place things: the city is considered as an arena of activity, of human concerns and problems. But though the sociological approach correctly focuses on affairs rather than things, it has no awareness of the city as a whole and as a result is not able to conceive a *good* city. When one thinks of the city in architectural terms it is not difficult to keep the whole city in view, and the good one conceives can be expressed as a quality of the whole. When the city is defined in terms of activities, however, its wholeness cannot be pictured, but has rather to be thought. This is a much more difficult task, and if one fails to accomplish it, then instead of a unified view of a good city he is left with a list of goals or problems to be solved. The single objective of building a good city dissolves into a plurality of objectives associated with various trouble spots in the life of the city: traffic problems, housing problems, educational problems, delinquency, crime, dope addiction, poverty, slums, blight, and urban sprawl.

At some point in the process of improving conditions in the

city, each of these problems must be isolated and attacked separately. But this effort is greatly handicapped if there is no
synoptic view of the city to which the separate decisions may be
referred. There are dozens of possible solutions for each problem,
but while some reinforce the efforts made to solve other urban
problems, others hinder such efforts. A housing shortage can be
alleviated by constructing apartment buildings in a way that increases transportation problems, congestion, delinquency, and
blight. Or the need for more dwellings can be met in a way that
eases these conditions. A shortage of parking spaces is as effectively overcome by building parking garages as by rerouting
traffic so that the demand for space is reduced. But the first
solution will further choke the movement of traffic by encouraging increased use of already overloaded streets; the second will
free land for the construction of schools and playgrounds. A
synoptic view of the good city facilitates intelligent choice between alternative solutions.

Another weakness of the sociological approach is that it is
essentially a negative one: it offers not the realization of an ideal,
but simply the elimination of certain conditions—slums, blight,
congestion, and sprawl—that are deplorable. The negativity
and plurality of this approach could not be expected to elicit the
same enthusiasm as positive efforts toward achieving a unified
ideal. Even if this were not true, finding a solution to the various
urban problems would not mean so much that the city had become good as that it had overcome many of the respects in which
it was bad. There is a profound difference between seeing one's
efforts as an attempt to extricate oneself from a hole, and seeing
oneself as already standing on the ground and aiming at the
moon. In the first case, the accomplishment lies merely in having
climbed out; what matters is that one is not where one has been.
In the second case, the fulfillment of the objective makes all the
difference; the end has its value in itself, not in the fact that it
replaces an undesirable condition.

The conclusion suggested by these remarks is that the architectural and sociological approaches complement each other.
It is only necessary to translate the synoptic view, which char-

acterizes the former, into terms of the more adequate grasp of what a city is, which characterizes the latter. We must achieve a conception of a good city, an ideal whole, but in doing so we must keep in mind that the city is an arena of human activities and concerns.

When the facts of institution and structure in the city are taken seriously, this conclusion gains a special meaning. Seeing the city as an arena of human affairs and concerns requires seeing it as a settled system of institutions, or, what comes to the same thing, an institution of institutions. Since human affairs in the city are institutionalized, a good that is expressed in terms of human affairs should be expressed in terms of the traits urban institutions must acquire if they are to become good. The good city will be a city whose form or pattern of action possesses such traits to the fullest extent.

We seek, then, the *form* of a good city, in the sense not of a geometrical figure but of a style of life. What form does urban life take when it is ideal? What are the traits that distinguish it, the marks by which it may be known? Opportunity and community, we say. But what does this mean in structural terms? If opportunity and community are to become assured and stable features of urban life, then how must the city's institutions be altered?

These questions may be interpreted as a request for a concrete program of urban reconstruction, a statement of specific steps that need to be taken. But this is not my meaning. No sensible program so concrete that it could be immediately acted on in a specific place can be arrived at solely by thinking about the abstract ideals of opportunity and community. The program must be tailored to the place, designed with an eye to local problems and local resources. The conception of a good city that we seek is one which applies to contemporary cities in general rather than to only one city. It is our desire to establish a model which any city may follow, and which it must follow if it is to become a fit arena for human life. By being general, the model approaches universality; what it loses in the process is concreteness. The conception of a good city is an abstraction: it is

described in the language of abstractions—traits, universal prop-
erties, classes, types, essential characteristics—rather than the
language of particulars. But this is a virtue of the conception,
not a defect. If the model were concrete, as are those of the
architecturally oriented city planners, the result of its universal
acceptance would be that cities would become indistinguishable
from one another. I think almost everyone would agree that this
result would be intolerable.

The virtue of conceiving the form of a good city in abstract
terms is that it promotes diversity. Local traditions and resources,
distinguishing geographical details, the peculiarities of local institutions and even of the persons influential in city affairs fix
for each city the concrete meaning of the abstract model. The
fact that these conditions vary from one locality to another neces-
sitates a variety of solutions to the problem of rebuilding the city.
But each such solution is arrived at by looking not only to the
facts but to the form of the good, which alone discloses the im-
port of the facts.

If the practice of guiding the growth of urban institutions is
not regulated by reference to an ideal, abstract whole, then how
are the practitioners to know that a good city will result from
their efforts? Criticizing the city and attempts to reconstruct it
is rapidly becoming a profession; but how can such a critic hope
to function in a responsible manner except by relating the programs he evaluates to an abstract conception of a good city? The
answer is, I think, that city planners, official and unofficial, have
somewhere in their minds a conception of the form of a good
city, but it is not systematized; they hold it unconsciously, as a
set of mental reflexes. Until it is brought to consciousness, however, it cannot be evaluated and, if need be, modified. The need
is for deliberate, abstract thought. The difficulty is that, on the
one hand, city planners find their time too much taken up with
day-to-day urban problems to indulge whatever inclination they
may have to speculate on the larger issues of city planning; on
the other, those who enjoy both the time and the inclination for
speculative pursuits ordinarily occupy themselves with matters
less relevant to contemporary urban life.

III

Any conception of a good city must rest on a conception of individual good, of what it means for an individual to live a good life. The good city is, simply, one whose structure encourages such a life in every way possible. It provides an environment which grounds the good; it is so designed that a good life is on all sides the natural outcome of the way affairs are ordered.

We are led, then, to ethical theory and to the acceptance of Aristotle's view that ethics is an indispensable preface to politics. What is meant by individual good? The abstraction that answers the question in one word is self-realization: the good life for the individual is one wherein he develops his powers harmoniously and to the fullest extent. He realizes (makes real or actual) his potentialities, and he accomplishes this in a way that leaves him with an ordered self. Since there is no such condition as a completed self, a self whose potentialities are so fully realized that no further development is possible, the ideal of self-realization is one with the ideal of growth: the good life is one wherein the person is developing his potentialities, realizing an ordered self.

The objections generally raised against the ideal of self-realization are of two sorts. In the first place, objections are made to the conception of the self maintained by one or another upholder of the ideal. The issue is that of what it is one ought to be realizing when one is realizing one's "self." Since the answer to this appears as a matter of course in the succeeding chapters, it will be unnecessary to discuss it here. The second objection, however, cannot be deferred, and the answer to it bears on the first one. It is objected that there are two fundamental ethical categories, good and right, and that a different view of the moral life is associated with each of them. To say that a person leads "the good life" is to say that upon reflection he and others would find his life highly satisfactory. Then the problem of defining the good is nothing other than that of discovering in general terms the kind of life people may be expected to approve in this way. This was the approach of Plato, Aristotle, and more recently, John Dewey. When one says that self-realization is the good, it is to be taken as meaning that self-realization is what, above all else, satisfies reflective people. I mean that upon reflection it satisfies them. Thus we say it is what reason recommends.

But to say that one has done the right thing is to introduce connotations not evident in the idea of a good life. These new connotations are those of duty and obligation, and they form, for some people, the very core of morality. The difference here is between doing something that from every angle "satisfies," and doing something because one imagines it ought to be done. When we heed the call of duty we cannot be sure that what ensues will be satisfying to ourselves or to others. For those so moved by the calls of the inner voice that they ignore the claims of growth, the sense of duty may lead to a hermit's hut and an atrophy of one's powers, the very negation of self-realization. Ebullience, on the other hand, may signify moral failure. What some call personal growth, others call escape from one's duty.

This duality in the conception of morality, the evident opposition between an ethics of growth and an ethics of duty, poses a problem for anyone who would make a conscientious effort to give an ethical foundation to the notion of a good city. A city designed to nurture citizens who center their lives on a sense of duty would evidently be a different place from one designed to promote individual growth. Apparently a choice must be made between these two types of historically prominent ethical theory.

But to choose is also to reject, and I imagine that few are prepared to deny entirely the claims made by either type of ethical theory. There is room in a satisfying life for duty and obligation; and room for satisfaction and growth in a life that focuses primarily on duty. In both cases the addition represents a gain. To a life that centers on personal growth, a sense of duty adds firmness and an awareness that one's efforts have meaning beyond oneself. To the life devoted to duty, growth adds stature; it lends significance to the person and a dignity which he cannot claim if he has allowed concern for others to obscure his duties to himself.

Both duty and growth have a rightful place in the good city. We could not call a city good that is given over to the development of persons who take no cognizance of their duties in the world, who know no discipline other than that which their own growth requires, whose lives gain value not by their impact upon the city but only by their impact upon themselves. Neither could we call a city good where life is impoverished, where people, however "moral," do not fulfill the promise of man's nature, are not alive to the powers that reside within them and enabled by their circumstances to release those powers in a fashion which promotes their own growth.

So widely recognized is the need to accommodate both types of ethical theory that almost always provision is made in the formulation of one for a way of absorbing the other. Thus one says with Kant that among the duties one has is a duty to develop one's nature to the fullest extent, thereby assimilating the ethics of growth to the ethics of duty. Or one says with virtually every upholder of the ideal of self-realization from Plato to Dewey that the self to be realized is in some way a social self, so that recognition of the claims made upon us by others is a condition of our own personal development. It remains true, of course, that in the first case one should seek to grow because it is one's duty and that in the second case one should perform one's duty because it is a condition of growth. But this is a difference in the theoretical rationale for moral action, not in the action itself.

The conclusion is that our conception of a good city must be founded on an ethics of growth, but also on an ethics of duty; on the idea of the good life, but also on the ideas of discipline, responsibility, and obligation. In accepting these latter ideas, I have no particular ethical theory in mind and no specific notion of what our primary duties are. Our duties *vis-à-vis* the city are, simply, to act in ways which make the city better. They are derived from our conception of a good city and are designed to assure the realization of that ideal. This is not to say that the ideas of duty and obligation bring nothing new to the conception of a good city. Duty and obligation connote the individual's taking a distinctive stance in the world, one characterized by his centering his life on something outside himself, toward which he directs his efforts. His posture is that of one who undertsands that the meaning of events consists in their impact upon the world, not himself, and who conducts his affairs with an eye to their ramifications in the world. He acts for the sake of something which transcends him but which he regards as preeminently valuable, and his affairs gain significance from their tendency to sustain that value. In this way, he freely takes on duties and obligations and becomes, for the first time as some would imagine, a moral creature. The contrast is a fundamental one. When the individual recognizes nothing valuable outside himself which can serve as the organizing principle of his affairs, then either he is led by interest or habit, or else he flaccidly drifts with the currents in which he finds himself. But when the individual discovers something outside himself so valuable that he orders his affairs around it, then duty and obligation, discipline and responsibility, become real forces in his world. He is moved by a sense of what is needed, not of what he needs. This does not mean that he moves reluctantly: it is not uncommon to find persons whose devotion to a cause is wholehearted.

To see the implication of these remarks, we only have to reflect that the historical period during which duty and obligation have become de-emphasized in human settlements is also the period during which community in the settlement has dissolved. The era of individualism in the city coincides with the era when urban people have little sense of a common value or goal. It is no accident that the age of interest rather than duty, of narrow and personal goals, is also an age when community is so rare that many people cling until the end of their days to the memory of a war whose horrors led them to find a common cause with their neighbors. For community is the objective counterpart to what we recognize in personal life as duty, just as opportunity is the objective counterpart to individual growth and development. When the individual's world bears the marks of a genuine community, he confronts common values. In the course of events, he is led to perform functions which sustain these values, to participate in the affairs with which the community is overtly engaged. If the community is open, he is brought into it as naturally as he is brought into the world. His acquisition and acceptance of duties follow inevitably. By incorporating him, the community makes its value his value, and his devotion to that value is evidenced by the care with which he conducts his affairs. He apprehends a responsibility to sustain the common value and derives from this responsibility a series of duties that correspond with the ways in which the life of community is implicated by his life.

The family provides the best contemporary example, for here at least community is not unusual. If, as is often the case, the family's affairs are pervaded with a sense of a mutual value to which each family member makes a distinctive contribution, then in their joint effort they form a community. Their union is not merely an external one. It is a vital affair charged with a meaning for each member that is not limited to his personal advantage. If a person born into such a family does not enter into the familial community, we think it strange and seek an explanation for the anomaly. Normally the individual shoulders as a matter of course the duties corresponding to his place in the family. Within the circle of the family, if nowhere else, he finds the meaning of his involvement with others to lie not in what he personally gains from it, but in the goods that arise out of the joint effort and in which all share.

By restoring community to our settlements we incorporate into the order of affairs an inducement to the moral life, to a personal orientation that leads each inhabitant to find the point of his life in its impact on the settlement, not on himself. When this occurs within a community it is effortless, natural, and almost inevitable—not, as at present, a seldom-achieved feat of emotional gymnastics. Moreover, within a community such a posture does not entail self-sacrifice. The person is part of the community he serves and if it is rightly ordered, both grows by serving it and shares in the goods that the community sustains. In a genuine community the antithesis between living for oneself and living for others, selfishness and altruism, is transcended. The self and the others are incorporated in a venture that serves at once as the ground of their self-fulfillment and the focus of their duties. None lives for himself alone, nor yet merely for the others: all live for a community which is *theirs*.

The conception of a good city centers on two leading ideas: opportunity and community. On one hand, we look to the city for the social arrangements that individual growth requires; on the other, we ask that these arrangements be ordered in a way that answers to the ideal of community. So far as these two demands are met, the human settlement forms a community whose established patterns of action foster both the good and the right in individual life. We have now to develop the conception of such a community.

THE FREE CITY

.   .   .   .

IN analyzing the ideas of moral power and freedom, I have sought to discover an exhaustive list of institutional traits which, taken all together, form the objective ground of individual freedom and individual power in the city. So far as the city possesses these traits, it is itself free and morally powerful. Implicit in this approach, then, is a distinction between the freedom and power of the person and the freedom and power of the city. This distinction creates certain problems. Shall we say that the individual automatically becomes free when the objective ground of freedom is built into the structure of urban affairs? Does individual freedom inevitably result from the acquisition by the city's institutions of flexibility, voluntariness, and controllability? A similar question might be asked regarding moral power. The issue is whether the individual can fail to be free even though the formal ground of freedom is present in the city; or, more generally, whether he can fail to grow, to realize his nature, even though the city itself is both free and morally powerful. If this is possible, then one must inquire whether there are not certain subjective conditions of growth that must be met as well before the good life can become a reality.

When the city is free and morally powerful, the inhabitant finds there genuine opportunity for personal growth. Whether he does in fact lead the good life is another matter. The freedom and power of the city denote opportunities that are, from the standpoint of the individual, possibilities. The freedom and power of the individual is something actual. An individual enjoys freedom and power by acting in certain ways; a city possesses freedom and power by grounding the possibility for acting in those ways. To be sure, the existence of the possibility depends upon a number of actualities, including the personal characteristics of the city's inhabitants. Whether the inhabitant will in fact participate in the rich life of the city is in no way assured by the existence of an opportunity to do so.

But to supplement our conception of the good city with arrangements designed to induce the inhabitants to realize the opportunities it offers would be disastrous—a violation of the ideal it was intended to serve. If such inducements were successful, they would, in effect, impose the city on its inhabitants, and in so doing they would jeopardize the voluntary character of the city's institutions. The point is a fundamental one. A city becomes good by opening vistas, by widening and intensifying opportunity, not by narrowing and restricting life, by imposing arrangements, however desirable, upon the individual. What the individual makes of this open environment, assuming that he is mature and mentally competent, is entirely his own affair and quite beyond the legitimate domain of those who would build a better city.

COMMUNITY

I

IN a good city, opportunity appears within the context of community. Though the city as we find it betrays serious deficiencies in moral power and freedom, these are less noticeable than the disappearance of community. We must now seek to understand how community—or the possibility of community—may be restored. What we desire is an arrangement that, while making community possible, will enable the inhabitant to exclude himself from the community if he wishes. Unless this is accomplished, community will be bought at the price of opportunity; and the unique promise of the city, that it will form a community both powerful and free, will not be fulfilled.

In any genuine community there are shared values: the members are united through the fact that they fix on some object as preeminently valuable. And there is a joint effort, involving all members of the community, by which they give overt expression to their mutual regard for that object. In terms of prevailing philosophical categories, the first of these marks of community is subjective, the second objective. The duality in the idea of community is manifested in the terms one uses in discussing it —"care," "concern," "regard," "value." To care for something is to have a certain attitude toward it, and also to handle it in a certain fashion, "carefully." "Concern" designates a way of acting as well as a way of feeling. One *is* concerned and *shows* concern. Similarly, to regard something highly and to value it mean both to hold it in high esteem and to treat it with respect. A genuine community is formed whenever a group of people "care" for something in common, in both senses of the term: their overt caring unifies them in fact, they interact with one another; and their common attitude unifies them in mind, they form a unity of intent.

If the city is to become a community, then, the inhabitants must identify the settlement itself as the focal point of their individual lives. The overt component of community is already present in the settled structure of institutional affairs. The inhabitants lead a common life, participate in a joint effort that brings them together at every turn, but this extensive network of interaction does not unite them into a genuine community. The explanation lies in the fact that unity of effort is not matched by a corresponding unity of intent. They work together, but for diverse reasons, and so the life they jointly lead is external, not infused with mind.

It must be recalled that the city, as such, has no life of its own: its affairs are the affairs of the institutions that comprise it. Its life is formed by the religious, political, artistic, educational, industrial, commercial, familial, and recreational activities of its inhabitants. Each of these institutions has a reason for being, a purpose or end for whose sake those who participate in it are brought together. The institution exists to entertain and amuse, to instruct, to worship God, to investigate nature, to produce clothing, to distribute gasoline, or to govern the city. These are the purposes of the city, *its* reason for being.

Consequently, the idea that the city will become a community when the inhabitants identify their settlement as the focal point of their lives means that it will become a community when their purpose in participating in each of these varied institutional affairs becomes one with the public purpose served by the institution itself. Until those who participate in an institutional activity raise the public purpose of the activity to the level of a value, desired and aimed at, an object which gives point to their participation, that purpose is for them a mere result. It is the outcome of what they collectively do, and they may apprehend that the outcome serves their interests. They imagine themselves to be brought together as a matter of convenience. It is to their mutual advantage to work together—each is enabled to earn a living in this way, or to amuse himself. But these are private and personal aims. By entering into the activity for such reasons, the participants reduce the activity to the status of a means. There is then nothing in the activity which can unify them, no basis for community. On the other hand, when the public outcome of the activity is the aim of the participants, this outcome becomes a unifying and mutually held purpose. The fact that their efforts are centered on a common object draws the participants together into a community.

Community is ordinarily thought to involve a much closer union than these remarks suggest. One is led to picture an association whose members are bound by intimate emotional ties.

A community based solely on a common purpose is likely to seem hollow by contrast. This reaction results from a misunderstanding of the way his purposes penetrate the individual's activity. The person who is deeply committed to accomplishing something communicates this purpose in each step he takes toward its fulfillment. When a group possesses a common commitment to the public purpose of their activity, this appears overtly in what they collectively do. When an activity is thus penetrated by purpose, the institution gains atmosphere and spirit, a quality of mind. It can no longer be understood in purely mechanical terms as a pattern of interactivity made up of differentiated roles. The basis for the transformation lies in the manner in which the participants perform their allotted tasks: their concern for the public purpose of the institution finds expression in the care with which they do their work. The atmosphere or texture one apprehends in the institution is the whole formed by the totality of these individual expressions of care.

When a group of people who work together for a cause are moved by a strong sense of the value of their efforts, their entire undertaking is affected. The distinction between a subjective purpose and the overt activity by which the purpose is pursued becomes artificial. So integral is the purpose to the activity that the participants seldom need be conscious of the purpose as such. The primary significance of the fact that the participants have a common purpose is that they bring care and concern to their particular tasks, that they are personally involved in fulfilling the overt and public purpose of the activity. If the individual's concern for the purpose is not actualized in his performance of his work, however, the activity becomes as mechanical and external as if there were no value to be realized. It is not the conception of and attachment to the end, as such, which unites the participants. Rather, they are united by the way they participate, by the fact that the participation of each communicates a kind of care and concern that refers one to the public purpose of the activity.

We are able, from this point of view, to understand the absence from earlier forms of human settlement of any separately held, conscious idea of the purposes of the settlement. Probably, the inhabitants of a village community seldom, if ever, achieve a distinct awareness of why they act as they do; yet community is a pervasive fact of their lives. Lacking such an awareness, they are not able to isolate in their minds the public purposes of village life and hold them there as personal aims. Community with them is more integral. One would not think of denying that they have a common purpose, but it is not merely a mental fact. Instead, it is ubiquitous, a quality laid over the entire overt life of the village.

A second consequence of seeing the idea of community in this light is that the fallacy of identifying community with like-mindedness is exposed. If holding a common purpose required that a group of people simultaneously frame in their minds a conception of and attachment to the same purpose, then like-mindedness would be a necessary condition of community. When the basis for community is understood to lie in the common possession of a purpose that penetrates activity, however, like-mindedness becomes unessential. For, to the extent that each individual's mode of participation in an institutional activity differs from that of the other participants, the care he expresses in his participation differs too. It is of the sort required by his unique place in the institution. One individual may testify to his involvement by working with extreme deliberation and coolness, another by expressing strong emotion, and a third by adopting a withdrawn and casual air. They need have no emotion in common, no idea, and no feeling: no isolable mental state at all. It is necessary only that the concern they express in their activity be designed for accomplishing a common result, so that one looking on might say of the persons engaged in the activity that, whether they are aware of it or not, they are all pointing their efforts toward the same object.

The common purpose on which a genuine community is founded qualifies the whole interactive process in which the members are engaged. Thus achievement of community in the city means a transformation of the city itself, not merely a change in the private attitudes of its inhabitants. Life in the city gains integrity, and the established patterns of action are internalized.[2] The terms integrity and internalization refer to the same result— the first in the case of the person, and the second in the case of the institutions that form the person's life. The person gains integrity in the most immediate sense of that term: his life becomes integrated with the results of his overt activity. As we have seen, this implies a way of participating in the institutions. To the extent that the individual's purposes differ from those we attribute to his institutions, there is a rift in his life. He fails to be fully involved in the affairs that primarily occupy him. They are either a bleak routine, unavoidable but without color, or they engage his energies not for their own sakes but for some private and personal result. His life is compartmentalized into the times he is engaged in these activities and the times he is occupied with affairs to which he attributes intrinsic value but which, because they are compartmentalized in this way, he does not regard as having public significance.

When the city dweller's life gains integrity, his institutions become internalized. Again, this would not be understandable if having a common purpose were taken to refer to a merely subjective condition of the participants in an institution, instead of to their manner of participating. By becoming involved in the public life of the city for its own sake, the inhabitants internalize the city's institutions: the city acquires a mind. It becomes, instead of a mechanical system of contrivances for fulfilling the separately conceived purposes of the inhabitants, a vital whole, a settled order of institutions on which the inhabitants center their lives and for whose sake they conduct their daily affairs.

II

So long as it is assumed that the public purposes of urban institutions consist of such laudable and noncontroversial goals as instructing the youth, promoting the general welfare, investigating nature, and even providing the inhabitants of the city with shoes, there will be little opposition to the idea that the individual should internalize his settlement by taking those purposes as his own. But this is a naïve assumption from one point of view. The purpose of a shoe factory is not just to make shoes, but to make a profit, and it would seem that the latter is its real purpose and the former only a means to that end. Similarly, the actual purpose of a particular urban government may be to protect local commercial interests, or to perpetuate the reign of the dominant political party, rather than to order the affairs of the city in the public interest. Frequently it is only when institutions are viewed in the abstract and from a great distance that they appear to have desirable purposes. When one asks, on closer inspection, what the particular purpose of a specific institution is, one may discover that that purpose is, at the least, questionable. No fault will be found with the proposal that, in the interests of community, the workers in a shoe factory have the making of shoes as their purpose. But if the real purpose of the shoe factory is not making shoes but making profits, what then? Does the idea of restoring community imply that the workers should be encouraged to direct their efforts toward this end, to become "company men"? More generally, does the idea of internalizing the established patterns of urban life imply internalizing them as they are found in actual cities? If so, how can we answer those who rightly feel that in many instances the actual purposes of urban institutions are so distorted that it would be at the least sheer silliness and at the most gross immorality to breathe one's life into them?

There are only two ways around this difficulty. The first, though attractive at first glance, appears on analysis indefensible. It consists in arguing that the real purposes of our institutions are always desirable. When a particular organization seems to be working toward an undesirable end, this is explained by contending that somehow the real and desirable purpose of the institution has become submerged: though it is still present, immanent in the institution, it is not effective. An artificial and unatural purpose has momentarily come to the fore. The problem is to find a way of restoring the real purpose to its proper place, and community among the participants consists in their taking the real, abiding purpose as their own.

This solution cannot be reconciled with the facts of public life. Organized crime is as much an institution of the city as the family, and there are good reasons for regarding the urban slums as an institution, too. Though if one looks one can find positive values even in slums and crime, not even the beneficiaries of these practices would defend the proposition that, on the whole, our cities are better for having slums and crime syndicates. To insist that after all slums and crime syndicates are not really institutions is only to beg the question. The sole basis for refusing to call them institutions is that their purposes are not desirable, and this is the very point at issue: can an institution have an undesirable purpose?

Fortunately, there is a more realistic way around this difficulty, a way that allows one to accept the facts of urban life as he finds them. Undesirable patterns of action do exist in the city, and if the participants were to take the outcome of these institutions as their purpose in life, they would form a community just as authentic as that formed by the members of a family or church. But it would not be as good a community, and this is the whole point. When community is gained at the expense of the other facts of a good city, the gain is illusory. The ideal community requires more than the identification of personal with institutional purposes. It requires the construction of an order of urban institutions whose purposes it is reasonable to take as one's own, an order marked by moral power and freedom. The internalization of urban life must be matched by a reconstruction of the objective order, so that it becomes a fit receptacle for the mind with which one would infuse it. Unless this is done, it would be far better to leave the city, as we frequently find it, external and soulless.

III

Two reasons are commonly given for modern man's failure to internalize his institutions. Though not mutually exclusive, they represent differences of emphasis on the part of particular critics of contemporary urban life. It is said that modern life is both too materialistic and too mechanical. The point of the difference is that in the first case the critic focuses on people's tendency to enter into institutional activities for extraneous and private reasons. In the second, he focuses on the imputed aridity and aseptic quality of life in the city. It is a matter of either having the wrong purpose or having no purpose, of becoming involved for the sake of a personal result, or failing to become involved at all. For those critics whose *bête noire* is materialism, Emerson was a great prophet: "Things are in the saddle,/and ride mankind." The others find Eliot more to their liking: "This is the way the world ends/Not with a bang but a whimper."

Of the two sorts of criticism, that which stresses the materialism of urban life is the more sweeping. Three themes form its indictment: consumerism, conformity, and commercialization.[3] The "things" that are in the saddle, it is said, are things (and services) for sale—commodities—and the individual, by being saddled with commodities, finds his stance in the city to be essentially that of a *consumer*. He orders his experience by relating it with the acquisition and use of commodities. The meaning of work is that it provides him with funds to buy commodities; the meaning of friendship, that it provides market information regarding commodities; the meaning of leisure time, that it provides an opportunity to consume and, lamentably, repair, commodities. Because he is a consumer, he is also a conformist. The commodities on which he centers his life are, for the most part, standardized products designed for a mass market. When he consents to use such a product, he consents also to a certain way of ordering his life: putting a television set in one's living room or a car in one's garage makes a difference in how one lives. Standardization of the commodity leads to a corresponding standardization of life. Even the apparent exceptions can be made to support this thesis: the automobile allows one to travel farther than ever before, to see new places and have new experiences; and yet, increasingly, nothing in those new places is new, for the same commodities that are found back home are found there, too. The style of life the individual buys along with the commodity is one that his neighbors have also bought, or will buy. In buying it, he conforms with them not merely in the trivial sense that he makes a similar purchase, but in the more significant sense that he consents to style his life in a similar fashion. Not infrequently, of course, the sales appeal that precedes the transaction emphasizes that others use the same commodity, style their lives in the same fashion. Conformity as a psychological mechanism—the disposition to let one's attitudes and actions be guided by his sense of what others expect—provides the individual with a principle that perfectly complements his stance as a consumer. It makes him responsive to the sales appeals that activate him as a consumer, and by assuring that his attitudes and actions will not differ widely from those of his neighbors, keeps him firmly in place as a member of the mass market.

The image of the consumer-conformist has become a familiar one, but if the criticism implied in that image is considered to be applicable to the majority of city dwellers, it is wildly overstated. Its relevance depends on the fact that it identifies a trend. The consumer-conformist, though in a minority, is especially characteristic of contemporary urban life. Moreover, the conditions that nurture him are spreading, so that in the future he is likely to be even more prevalent. For this reason, the observation that not everyone is a consumer-conformist raises no serious objection to the literature of conformity. Its weaknesses are of a different sort. Conformity is generally regarded as a personal problem, requiring for its solution only a change of mind on the part of those who conform. In fact, the problem is basically social, and can be solved only through a change in the objective institutional order. The consumer-conformist is only the subjective counterpart of a commercialized city. We cannot reasonably expect to check the development of consumer-conformists without doing something to the public order which encourages this type of personality and to which it is appropriate. If the order of affairs in which people mature is shot through with inducements to live for the sake of consuming, the result is likely to be a wide-spread disposition to do so. It is no more complicated than that.

To be sure, there are people who escape their environment; but most do not. Moreover, the commercialization of the city is partial and incomplete. For these reasons the consumer-conformist is not everywhere in the city and probably never will be, even if commercialization becomes more intense. Though this may caution us against becoming unduly alarmed about present conditions, it does not touch the main point: if the transformation of the individual into a consumer-conformist is objectionable, then so also is the commercialization of his institutions. To minimize the former, it is necessary to minimize or in some way alter the latter.

The principal implications of this conclusion concern that sector of urban life called the economy. Commercialization in this realm means the dominance of a purpose to achieve a maximum flow of commodities. The commodity is originally designed with that end in view: it is designed to be sold, but it is also designed to be resold and to be superseded by another slightly modified commodity. This is not objectionable in itself. But it becomes objectionable when it leads, as frequently happens, to useless and shoddy products. In a commercialized city, the sales outlets for these products are ordered for accomplishing the same objective. The purpose is to make a sale. Standards of integrity and honesty are frequently maintained; possibly even higher ones than good business requires. But the stores are "in business," and to that extent not public purpose but some form of private return is their ordering principle. Similarly, the promoter stands between the factories and commercial outlets, on one hand, and the consumer on the other, advising the former how to design and distribute the product so that the consumer will want it, and attempting to manipulate the attitudes of the consumer so that he will want what the factories have produced for him. The immediate function of promotion is to bring the buyer and seller to terms with each other, to fit the product to the wishes of the consumer and the wishes of the consumer to the product. By fitting the two together, promotion further advances the interest in securing a maximum flow of commodities.

There is nothing new in this: people have been in business for a long time. What is new is its extent. Through mass communication and mass entertainment, it invades the home and affects the flow of family life. Moreover, ours is an economy of abundance. Our productive capacity is so great that the economic problem is no longer one of producing a sufficient supply of goods, but of distributing them. In the first instance, this is a problem of providing people with enough money to purchase the product of industry; in the second instance, of making them want the products that are available. The prevailing theory is that by consuming, people gain the means for further consumption, since when goods are consumed labor is needed to restock the shelves, and commodities are purchased with the wages of labor. The economy of abundance thus introduces new incentives to the spread of commercialization. Promotional activities increase beyond all measure, and perhaps more important, a proliferation of commodities sets in. Products become available for doing all sorts of things the individual had previously done with his own hands and mind: we acquire commodities to mix our drinks, shuffle cards, compose music, and solve problems.

To minimize commercialization, however, it is not necessary to slow down deliberately the rate at which commodities are produced, nor to eliminate or even minimize promotional activities. What is needed is a redirecting of these affairs, so that the object of production, distribution, and promotion becomes culturally significant. The needs of the city itself should be served, not the need for profits or for maintaining a maximum flow of commodities. There can be no objection to production, distribution, and promotion if their object is to create and maintain a good city, that is, to enhance its moral power, freedom, and community.

The social critics who emphasize the materialism of urban life ordinarily object to conformity on the ground that it interferes with the formation of genuinely autonomous persons. But in opposing conformity to autonomy, they invariably fail to notice the equally important contrast between conformity and community. Preoccupation with commodities does not draw people together, as the term "conformity" suggests, but divides them. This occurs when the commodities are dissociated from the public life of the city. The things with which the conformist is "saddled" are designed for personal consumption, generally within the circle of the family. In a sense the life of such a person is family-centered. By focusing his attention on personal consumption within the circle of the family, he locates there most of the intrinsic values of his life. In so doing, he is led to regard the life of the city beyond his family—the artistic, scientific, economic, educational, and religious institutions of the city —as means and instruments having value only in the contribution they make to his enterprise as a consumer. As a result of his inability to find these institutions valuable for their own sakes, he does not and cannot internalize them. Thus, for the city at large, the conformist-consumer is an enemy of community.

One might expect from this that what is lost in one sector of urban life is gained in another, that if consumer-orientation focuses attention on the family then there at least people are drawn together into genuine community. It is clear that community is more prevalent in family affairs than elsewhere in the city. But there is good reason to question whether preoccupation with commodities helps community in the family. Community does not mean the kind of togetherness the audience in a theater exhibits, when the spectators merely react collectively to a common object. Yet much of the impact of commodities on family life is of that sort: by taking over from the individual the necessity to act, so that in his use of it he is largely passive, the commodity tends to convert the family into an audience. Instead of acting, their function becomes that of reacting. No matter how much they do this together, their community is not enhanced. Worse, since community requires above all that people act, and more specifically, communicate, insofar as they are an audience the family members cease to form a community.

In opposing conformity to community, I do not wish to dispute the opposition of conformity to autonomy. The latter term has been used to designate independence of judgment, not failure to accept one's responsibilities, and a community whose members lack the ability to think for themselves is not and cannot be free. The city needs autonomous citizens fully as much as it needs community. But the critics of conformity and commercialization have weakened their case by unduly stressing the opposition between these and autonomy while ignoring other and equally distressing aspects of the situation. The consumer-conformist is often sharp and calculating, a good and independent shopper. If there is an appearance of conformity in his behavior, this is compatible with his independence of judgment. Consequently, having been encouraged by the critics themselves to evaluate the matter solely from the standpoint of autonomy, one rightly questions whether present conditions are as objectionable as they are said to be. The dangers of conformity can be fully assessed only when its impact on community is recognized. For no amount of independence of judgment can transform the consumer-oriented individual into a being capable of restoring community to the city, as long as the commodities that occupy him draw his attention away from the public life.

IV

The second reason often given for modern man's failure to internalize his institutions is the aridity and aseptic quality of life in the city. The city, it is said, is not built to a human scale; it swamps the inhabitants. This is partially an architectural criticism. Frequently the design of individual buildings and of entire residential and commercial districts inhibits the free exchange of ideas. Newly constructed housing projects, in particular, often lack even the physical facilities conducive to communication among the inhabitants, and their size and sheen have the same effect as a "no loitering" sign. Single-family dwellings in suburban developments as well as downtown high-rise developments deliberately exclude the physical equipment that a residential *community* requires. Not surprsingly, the developments are, as a result, lifeless. Their major deficiency is meeting places: facilities that afford an opportunity for the inhabitants to interact and, one would hope, communicate. The absence of halls specifically designed for public meetings is a minor aspect of the problem. Physical provision for informal and casual exchanges is much more important. Without such provision, communication, instead of becoming a pervasive feature of daily life, will remain a separate and specialized event for which specific times and places are allocated. Informal and casual exchanges should arise where people carry on their everyday affairs—along the streets of the city, on the sidewalks and in the shops and parks that border the streets. Unless the design of an area provides for sidewalks and pedestrian paths, shops and open spaces, and in such a form that people are encouraged to use them and linger there, the bare physical prerequisites of community will not be met.[4]

High-rise housing projects, which ordinarily exclude these physical facilities, characteristically lack most of the signs of life. Though the density of population in such projects is extreme, few of the inhabitants appear, for there is nothing to draw them out. By contrast, in the slums from which the inhabitants of the projects generally come there are numerous places where casual and informal exchanges can occur. The liveliness and excitement on slum streets compensate the inhabitants for the squalor of their living quarters. It would be too much to say that people are worse off in a housing project, but considering the cost of construction, their lot is not improved nearly as much as one should expect.[5]

But much of the emptiness of city life is traceable to shortcomings in the city's social structure that are unrelated to its architecture. Excessive mechanization renders patterns of urban action lifeless and vacuous. Routine and repetitive tasks in factories and offices have a deadening effect. When employees are not challenged by their jobs, they do not bring their minds and hearts to them and the institution itself reflects this withdrawal. Such conditions undermine community, because the workers are so far from finding a common purpose in their work that they find there no purpose whatever.

The vapid character of urban patterns of action, particularly in economic affairs, is symptomatic of deficiencies in moral power and freedom. Office and factory jobs become repetitive and mechanical because of lack of flexibility, and their dullness and deadening quality signify lack of richness. The restoration of moral power and freedom will vitalize the city, and this vitalization is the crucial first step toward the recovery of community.

V

There is a certain ambiguity in the formula that community exists in the city when the inhabitants' reasons for participating in its various institutions are identical with the actual purposes those institutions serve. Community in the city at large and community in a specific institution are not necessarily the same thing. One might legitimately argue that when the participants in urban institutions make the purposes of these institutions their own, it is assured only that the institutions will become communities, not that the city itself will. Instead of converting the settlement into a community, we seem to be in danger of converting it into a plurality of communities, one for each family, factory, church, school, and shop whose participants achieve the necessary identification of personal with institutional purpose.

In earlier forms of human settlement, when life was not as specialized and dispersed as it is in the modern city, this difficulty seldom arose. Institutional affairs merged together quite naturally; the demarcations between them were blurred and often nonexistent. Religion, for example, was not delegated to a special and separate observance but was introduced into almost every phase of settlement life; life in a city-state exemplified this fully as much as life in a village community. Because of the relative absence of structural differentiation, much the same life was lived by all the settlement's inhabitants, and there were few obstacles to the spread of community until it encompassed the entire settlement. There was insufficient separation of institutions to support a plurality of communities within the whole. The situation is obviously very different in the modern city. The highly specialized purposes of urban institutions give them a new discreteness. Their boundary lines are frequently so deeply etched as to form chasms that the spirit of community cannot easily bridge.

What we are speaking of here are obstacles to the establishment of community in the city at large, not conditions that absolutely preclude it. Much depends on whether or not the purposes of urban institutions exclude one another, or whether they are compatible. If all the activities in a city serve a common purpose, then the participants form one community by taking this inclusive purpose as their own and expressing the resulting unity of intent in all their affairs. The point is that purposes are not necessarily exclusive. It is possible and even, under ordinary circumstances, natural for a person to have more than one purpose in doing a particular thing. This does not mean merely that his action serves two separate ends; that, for example, he works for the sake of what his work produces as well as for the money he earns. He may regard his immediate purpose as a means for some more remote purpose, so that in effect the purposes that activate him are nested inside of one another. If he works in a shoe factory, his immediate purpose is to operate his machine properly. To act in this way is not in itself to make shoes, but it is a means to that end. But his purpose may be to make shoes as well. Shoes, in turn, have a use, and his purpose may even encompass that. If it does, his devotion to the immediate purpose of operating the machine properly need not be impaired.

Whether this nest should be regarded as three purposes or as one inclusive purpose is an open question. If we regard it as one inclusive purpose, however, we acknowledge the possibility that a person participating in a particular activity can enlarge his purpose until it includes the broadest ramifications of that activity. Community need not be destroyed or even weakened when a group of people hold purposes that refer to events far beyond the bounds of their immediate activity. Broadened aims are, in fact, basic to the expansion of community. Expansion of community presupposes an expansion of the purposes that activate the community's members.

Two conditions must be met before a plurality of communities in the city can, at the same time, be one community. The activities of the separate communities must be related so that they cooperate in producing a common object; and the inhabitants of the city must find common cause in pursuing that object: it must become their objective. And the only objective that could adequately serve as a common focus for the lives of the inhabitants of a city is that of creating and maintaining a good city. When the institutions of the city are rightly ordered, their overall effect is to intensify moral power and freedom, and we have already discovered that it would not be reasonable to expect the inhabitants to internalize their institutions unless they were thus ordered. But if the formation of a good city is the proper collective *effect* of the various urban institutions, then the internalization of urban life requires that the inhabitants adopt this effect as their enlarged purpose. *The common cause that unifies the inhabitants of a city should be, simply, the city—as it is, so far as it is good; as it might be, so far as it falls short of the ideal.*

VI

The city is not, however, an ultimate form of social organization. We cannot rest content with community in the city unless it extends beyond the city to form a national and ultimately a world community. If building community in the city meant minimizing the likelihood of a community of mankind, we should be wise to renounce our interest in a good city. Fortunately, the sacrifice is unnecessary. In principle, the same compatibility that exists between institutional community and community in the city at large exists between the city and the national and world community.

The ideal of a "continuous community" that circles the globe is at present dishearteningly remote, and the practical obstacles to its construction are immense. But we must understand the conditions for its realization so that if we succeed in restoring community to the city, it will be of a sort that can extend indefinitely beyond the city's limits. For a continuous community to be realized, the patterns of action that distinguish the city as an institution should not conflict with but should support the patterns of action that occur outside the city.

The human virtue that is uniquely appropriate to a continuous community is objectivity, a virtue better understood and more appreciated during the Middle Ages than now. Then the injunction was not to be a respector of persons; as we would say, not to show bias. But failure of objectivity consists in respecting organizations as well as persons. We make exceptions not only of ourselves and other persons, but also of the groups and organizations to which we belong and in which we are interested. Objectivity means successfully resisting such impulses. It means replacing interest, in the sense of showing partiality because of an emotional attachment, with disinterestedness or impartiality. Interest, bias, partiality, respecting persons all imply the drawing of a line between what is mine or ours and what is his or theirs. The line marks a limit beyond which values are not shared, not held in common. Interest promotes "in-groups" and "out-groups," and as a result makes for discontinuous communities.

To be objective, on the other hand, is to evaluate actions and objects by referring them not to oneself or one's group but to the whole. It is to live with an eye to that whole and to be moved by a sense of the need for its perfection. Consequently, objectivity, as a trait of character, is a force for continuity. A community formed by persons who exemplify this virtue is unified by a common devotion to values that are inclusive. Such a community is, therefore, susceptible of indefinite expansion.

In view of the ultimate value of world community, objectivity is the virtue most to be desired. Sensitivity, creativity, productivity, and autonomy—the virtues generally espoused by psychologically oriented critics of urban culture—are all less important than objectivity. The penalty we shall pay if we fail to construct a world community may be proportional in severity to the destructive power of the world's ballistic missiles at the time the final holocaust breaks out. The prospect makes the need for objectivity all the more immediate and intense; and the present endorsement of self-interest, as a principle of both social organization and the organization of human personality, becomes a pathetic symptom of people's all-too-human inability to realize wherein their best interests lie.

IV

Global Community

THE historic encyclical of Pope John XXIII holds out the promise of world community, asserting the rights and duties of man upon which such an order is founded. We are increasingly sensitive to the contraction of space in the world, to the growing interdependence of economic and scientific communities and to the dependence of all national states on peaceful solutions to their differences if the world is to escape massive destruction. We are likewise sensitive to the amassing of armaments and to the increasing divisions of rich and poor countries. In this context, the encyclical furnishes an important corrective to peace movements which have preoccupied themselves with peace and overlooked the conditions of peace in a technological world. The encyclical focuses attention, as Tillich notes, on justice and the dignity of persons, spelling out in considerable detail pathways to a just world in which peace might prevail.

In an essay quite representative of much of the thinking in the World Council of Churches, Richard Shaull voices concerns very similar to *Pacem in Terris* but from a radically different theological perspective. Where the papal encyclical takes its departure in natural law founded upon divine order (with all the problems which this entails as noted in the Introduction), Richard Shaull proposes a dynamic, contextual approach to decision-making in a revolutionary world, affirming that "when technical insight is set in the context of the humanizing activity of God, it makes sense to affirm that once the full facts are known, the appropriate action will follow."

The rights and duties in the encyclical express the consensus of Western religious and democratic development, as Tillich has underlined. The contextual ethic which Shaull is proposing, drawing on the work of Paul Lehmann, furnishes no criteria for distinguishing just and unjust uses of coercion, righteous and demonic revolutionary forces, etc. Richard Shaull speaks for a youthful revolt throughout the world—perhaps impatient with rational structures which have reflected the status quo; many who have lived through the Nazi period and its revolutionary fervor, not to speak of recent purges in the Maoist revolutionary thrusts of the Red Guard, look for rational criteria in assessing the rightness and wrongness of coercive activities.

Pacem in Terris and the revolutionary credo of Richard Shaull point to a fundamental ethical task of the emerging era— constituting movements and ethical structures through which peoples and nations may find their way to dignity and truth in a just order. Paul Tillich's reservations about the encyclical may be applied to both of these documents, for they both draw on the consensus of a Western religious tradition and furnish little grounding for other faiths and cultures, not to speak of the secularized and pluralistic world in which men are striving for world community and peace. What we call natural law or perceive as God's action in history is screened through our cultural traditions; this moral consensus needs to be shared with other cultures and faiths in order to lift up the universal elements. This can be the significant role of ethical reflection in shaping a new order in the world.

by Pope John XXIII

PEACE ON EARTH
(*Pacem in Terris*)

ORDER BETWEEN MEN

Every man is a person with rights and duties

FIRST of all, it is necessary to speak of the order which should exist between men. Any human society, if it is to be well-ordered and productive, must lay down as a foundation this principle, namely, that every human being is a person, that is, his nature is endowed with intelligence and free-will. By virtue of this, he has rights and duties of his own, flowing directly and simultaneously from his very nature, which are therefore universal, inviolable and inalienable.[1]

If we look upon the dignity of the human person in the light of divinely revealed truth, we cannot help but esteem it far more highly; for men are redeemed by the blood of Jesus Christ, they are by grace the children and friends of God and heirs of eternal glory.

RIGHTS

The right to life and a worthy standard of living. Beginning our discussion of the rights of man, we see that every man has the

Reprinted from the Encyclical Letter, *Pacem in Terris,* of His Holiness POPE JOHN XXIII, 1963, translated by the Vatican Polyglot Press and published by the Catholic Truth Society, London. Part I (pp. 9-20), and Parts III and IV (pp. 32-52). By permission of the translator.

right to life, to bodily integrity, and to the means which are necessary and suitable for the proper development of life; these are primarily food, clothing, shelter, rest, medical care, and finally the necessary social services. Therefore a human being also has the right to security in cases of sickness, inability to work, widowhood, old age, unemployment, or in any other case in which he is deprived of the means of subsistence through no fault of his own.[2]

Rights pertaining to moral and cultural values. By the natural law every human being has the right to respect for his person, to his good reputation; the right to freedom in searching for truth and in expressing and communicating his opinions, and in pursuit of art, within the limits laid down by the moral order and the common good; and he has the right to be informed truthfully about public events.

The natural law also gives man the right to share in the benefits of culture, and therefore the right to a basic education and to technical and professional training in keeping with the stage of educational development in the country to which he belongs. Every effort should be made to ensure that persons be enabled, on the basis of merit, to go on to higher studies, so that, as far as possible, they may occupy posts and take on responsibilities in human society in accordance with their natural gifts and the skills they have acquired.[3]

The right to worship God according to one's conscience. Every human being has the right to honour God according to the dictates of an upright conscience, and therefore the right to worship God privately and publicly. For, as Lactantius so clearly taught: *"We were created for the purpose of showing to the God who bore us the submission we owe Him, of recognizing Him alone, and of serving Him. We are obliged and bound by this duty to God; from this religion itself receives its name."*[4] And on this point Our Predecessor of immortal memory, Leo XIII, declared: *"This genuine, this honourable freedom of the sons of God, which most nobly protects the dignity of the human person, is greater than any violence or injustice; it has always* been sought by the Church, and always been most dear to her. This was the freedom which the Apostles claimed with intrepid constancy, which the Apostles defended with their writings, and which the Martyrs in such numbers consecrated with their blood."[5]

The right to choose freely one's state of life. Human beings have the right to choose the state of life which they prefer and therefore the right to set up a family, with equal rights and duties for man and woman, and also the right to follow a vocation to the priesthood or the religious life.[6]

The family, grounded on marriage freely contracted, monogamous and indissoluble, is and must be considered the first and essential cell of human society. To it must be given every consideration of an economic, social, cultural and moral nature which will strengthen its stability and facilitate the fulfillment of its specific mission.

Parents, however, have a prior right in the support and education of their children.[7]

Economic rights. Human beings have the natural right to free initiative in the economic field, and the right to work.[8]

Indissolubly linked with those rights is the right to working conditions in which physical health is not endangered, morals are safeguarded, and young people's normal development is not impaired. Women have the right to working conditions in accordance with their requirements and their duties as wives and mothers.[9]

From the dignity of the human person, there also arises the right to carry on economic activities according to the degree of responsibility of which one is capable.[10] Furthermore—and this must be specially emphasized—there is the right to a working wage, determined according to criterions of justice, and sufficient, therefore, in proportion to the available resources, to give the worker and his family a standard of living in keeping with the dignity of the human person. In this regard, Our Predecessor Pius XII said: *"To the personal duty to work imposed by nature, there corresponds and follows the natural right of each individual to make of his work the means to provide for his own life and the lives of his children; so profoundly is the empire of nature ordained for the preservation of man.*"[11] The right to private property, even of productive goods, also derives from the nature of man. This right, as We have elsewhere declared, " *is a suitable means for safeguarding the dignity of the human person and for the exercise of responsibility in all fields; it strengthens and gives serenity to family life, thereby increasing the peace and prosperity of the State.*"[12]

However, it is opportune to point out that there is a social duty essentially inherent in the right of private property.[13]

The right of meeting and association. From the fact that human beings are by nature social, there arises the right of assembly and association. They have also the right to give the societies of which they are members the form they consider most suitable for the aim they have in view, and to act within such societies on their own initiative and on their own responsibility in order to achieve their desired objectives.[14]

We Ourselves stated in the Encyclical *Mater et Magistra* that, for the achievement of ends which individual human beings cannot attain except by association, it is necessary and indispensable to set up a great variety of such intermediate groups and societies in order to guarantee for the human person a sufficient sphere of freedom and responsibility.[15]

The right to emigrate and immigrate. Every human being has the right to freedom of movement and of residence within the confines of his own country; and, when there are just reasons for it, the right to emigrate to other countries and take up residence there.[16] The fact that one is a citizen of a particular State does not detract in any way from his membership of the human family as a whole, nor from his citizenship of the world community.

Political rights. The dignity of the human person involves the rights to take an active part in public affairs and to contribute one's part to the common good of the citizens. For, as Our Predecessor of happy memory, Pius XII, pointed out: *"The human individual, far from being an object and, as it were, a merely passive element in the social order, is in fact, must be and must continue to be, its subject, its foundation and its end."*[17]

The human person is also entitled to a juridical protection of his rights, a protection that should be efficacious, impartial and inspired by the true norms of justice.

As Our Predessor Pius XII teaches: *"That perpetual privilege proper to man, by which every individual has a claim to the protection of his rights, and by which there is assigned to each a definite and particular sphere of rights, immune from all arbitrary attacks, is the logical consequence of the order of justice willed by God."*[18]

DUTIES

Rights and duties necessarily linked in the one person. The natural rights with which We have been dealing are, however, inseparably connected, in the very person who is their subject, with just as many respective duties; and rights as well as duties find their source, their sustenance and their inviolability in the natural law which grants or enjoins them.

For example, the right of every man to life is correlative with the duty to preserve it; his right to a decent standard of living with the duty of living it becomingly; and his right to investigate the truth freely, with the duty of seeking it and of possessing it ever more completely and profoundly.

Reciprocity of rights and duties between persons. Once this is admitted, it is also clear that in human society to one man's right there corresponds a duty in all other persons: the duty, namely, of acknowledging and respecting the right in question. For every fundamental human right draws its indestructible moral force from the natural law, which in granting it imposes a corresponding obligation. Those, therefore, who claim their own rights, yet altogether forget or neglect to carry out their respective duties, are people who build with one hand and destroy with the other.

Mutual collaboration. Since men are social by nature they are meant to live with others and to work for one another's welfare. A well-ordered human society requires that men recognize and observe their mutual rights and duties. It also demands that each contribute generously to the establishment of a civic order in which rights and duties are progressively more sincerely and effectively acknowledged and fulfilled.

It is not enough, for example, to acknowledge and respect every man's right to the means of subsistence: one must also strive to obtain that he actually has enough in the way of food and nourishment.

The society of men must not only be organized but must also provide them with abundant resources. This certainly requires that they observe and recognize their mutual rights and duties; it also requires that they collaborate together in the many enterprises that modern civilization either allows or encourages or even demands.

An attitude of responsibility. The dignity of the human person also requires that every man enjoy the right to act freely and responsibly. For this reason, therefore, in social relations man should exercise his rights, fulfill his obligations and, in the countless forms of collaboration with others, act chiefly on his own responsibility and initiative. This is to be done in such a way that each one acts on his own decision, of set purpose and from a consciousness of his obligation, without being moved by force or pressure brought to bear on him externally. For any human society that is established on relations of force must be regarded as inhuman, inasmuch as the personality of its members is repressed or restricted, when in fact they should be provided with appropriate incentives and means for developing and perfecting themselves.

Social life in truth, justice, charity and freedom. A political society is to be considered well-ordered, beneficial and in keeping with human dignity if it is grounded on truth. As the Apostle Paul exhorts us: *"Away with falsehood then; let everyone speak out the truth to his neighbour; membership of the body binds us to one another."*[19] This demands that reciprocal rights and duties be sincerely recognized. Furthermore, human society will be such as We have just described it, if the citizens, guided by justice, apply themselves seriously to respecting the rights of others and discharging their own duties; if they are moved by such fervour of charity as to make their own the needs of others and share with others their own goods: if, finally, they work for a progressively closer fellowship in the world of spiritual values. Human society is realized in freedom, that is to say, in ways and means in keeping with the dignity of its citizens, who accept the responsibility of their actions, precisely because they are by nature rational beings.

Human society, venerable brothers and beloved children, ought to be regarded above all as a spiritual reality: in which men communicate knowledge to each other in the light of truth; in which they can enjoy their rights and fulfill their duties, and are inspired to strive for moral good. Society should enable men to share in and enjoy every legitimate expression of beauty, and encourage them constantly to pass on to others all that is best in themselves, while they strive to make their own the spiritual achievements of others. These are the spiritual values which continually give life and basic orientation to cultural expressions, economic and social institutions, political movements and forms, laws, and all other structures by which society is outwardly established and constantly developed.

God and the moral order. The order which prevails in society is by nature moral. Grounded as it is in truth, it must function according to the norms of justice, it should be inspired and perfected by mutual love, and finally it should be brought to an ever more refined and human balance in freedom.

Now an order of this kind, whose principles are universal, absolute and unchangeable, has its ultimate source in the one true God, who is personal and transcends human nature. Inasmuch as God is the first truth and the highest good, He alone is that deepest source from which human society can draw its vitality, if that society is to be well ordered, beneficial, and in keeping with human dignity.[20] As St. Thomas Aquinas says: *"Human reason is the norm of the human will, according to which its goodness is measured, because reason derives from the eternal law which is the divine reason itself. It is evident then that the goodness of the human will depends much more on the eternal law than on human reason."*[21]

Characteristics of the present day. Our age has three distinctive characteristics.

First of all, the working classes have gradually gained ground in economic and public affairs. They began by claiming their rights in the socio-economic sphere; they extended their action then to claims on the political level; and finally applied themselves to the acquisition of the benefits of a more refined culture. Today, therefore, workers all over the world refuse to be treated as if they were irrational objects without freedom, to be used at the arbitrary disposition of others. They insist that they be always regarded as men with a share in every sector of human society: in the social and economic sphere, in the fields of learning and culture, and in public life.

Secondly, it is obvious to everyone that women are now taking a part in public life. This is happening more rapidly perhaps in nations of Christian civilization, and, more slowly but broadly, among peoples who have inherited other traditions or cultures. Since women are becoming ever more conscious of their human dignity, they will not tolerate being treated as mere material instruments, but demand rights befitting a human person both in domestic and public life.

Finally, the modern world, as compared with the recent past, has taken on an entirely new appearance in the field of social and political life. For since all nations have either achieved or are on the way to achieving independence, there will soon no longer exist a world divided into nations that rule others and nations that are subject to others.

Men all over the world have today—or will soon have—the

rank of citizens in independent nations. No one wants to feel subject to political powers located outside his own country or ethnical group. Thus in very many human beings the inferiority complex which endured for hundreds and thousands of years is disappearing, while in others there is an attenuation and gradual fading of the corresponding superiority complex which had its roots in social-economic privileges, sex or political standing.

On the contrary, the conviction that all men are equal by reason of their natural dignity has been generally accepted. Hence racial discrimination can in no way be justified, at least doctrinally or in theory. And this is of fundamental importance and significance for the formation of human society according to those principles which We have outlined above. For, if a man becomes conscious of his rights, he must become equally aware of his duties. Thus he who possesses certain rights has likewise the duty to claim those rights as marks of his dignity, while all others have the obligation to acknowledge those rights and respect them.

When the relations of human society are expressed in terms of rights and duties, men become conscious of spiritual values, understand the meaning and significance of truth, justice, charity and freedom, and become deeply aware that they belong to this world of values. Moreover, when moved by such concerns, they are brought to a better knowledge of the true God who is personal and transcendent, and thus they make the ties that bind them to God the solid foundations and supreme criterion of their lives, both of that life which they live interiorly in the depths of their own souls and of that in which they are united to other men in society.

. . . .

RELATIONS BETWEEN STATES

Subjects of rights and duties. Our Predecessors have constantly maintained, and We join them in reasserting, that political communities are reciprocally subjects of rights and duties. This means that their relationships also must be harmonized in truth, in justice, in a working solidarity, and in liberty. The same moral law, which governs relations between individual human beings, serves also to regulate the relations of political communities with one another.

This will be readily understood when one reflects that the individual representatives of political communities cannot put aside their personal dignity while they are acting in the name and interest of their countries; and that they cannot therefore violate the very law of their being, which is the moral law.

It would be absurd, moreover, even to imagine that men could surrender their own human attributes, or be compelled to do so, by the very fact of their appointment to public office, whereas they have been given that noble assignment precisely because the wealth of their human endowments has earned them their reputation as outstanding members of the body politic. Furthermore, authority is a necessary requirement of the moral order in human society. It may not therefore be used against that order; and the very instant such an attempt were made, it would cease to be authority, as the Lord has warned us: *"A word, then, for kings' ears to hear, kings' hearts to heed; a message for you, rulers, wherever you be! Listen well, all you that have multitudes at your command, foreign hordes to do your bidding. Power is none but comes to you from the Lord, nor any royalty but from One who is above all. He it is that will call you to account for your doings with a scrutiny that reads your inmost thoughts."*[22]

Lastly it is to be borne in mind that also in the regulating of relations between political communities, authority is to be exercised for the achievement of the common good, which constitutes the reason for its existence.

But a fundamental factor of the common good is acknowledgement of the moral order and respect for its prescriptions. *"Order between the political communities must be built upon the unshakable and unchangeable rock of the moral law, made manifest in the order of nature by the Creator Himself and by Him engraved on the hearts of men with letters that may never be effaced. . . . Like the rays of a gleaming beacon, its prin-*

ciples must guide the plans and policies of men and nations. These are the signals—of warning, safety and smooth sailing— they will have to heed, if they would not see all their laborious efforts to establish a new order condemned to tempest and ship- wreck."[23]

In truth. First among the rules governing the relations between States is that of truth. This calls, above all, for the elimination of every trace of racialism, and the consequent recognition of the principle that all States are by nature equal in dignity. Each of them accordingly is vested with the right to existence, to self-development, to the means fitting to its good name, and to the respect which is its due. Very often, experience has taught us, individuals will be found to differ considerably, in knowl- edge, virtue, talent and wealth. Yet these inequalities must never be held to excuse any man's attempt to lord it over his neigh- bours unjustly. They constitute rather a source of greater re- sponsibility in the contribution which each and everyone must make towards mutual improvement.

Similarly, political communities may have reached different levels of culture, civilization or economic development. Neither is that a sufficient reason for some to take unjust advantage of their superiority over others; rather should they see in it an added motive for more serious commitment to the common cause of social progress.

It is not true that some human beings are by nature superior, and others inferior. All men are equal in their natural dignity. Consequently there are no political communities which are superior by nature and none which are inferior by nature. All political communities are of equal natural dignity, since they are bodies whose membership is made up of these same human beings. Nor must it be forgotten, in this connection, that peoples can be highly sensitive, and with good reason, in matters touch- ing their dignity and honour.

Truth further demands that the various media of social com- munications made available by modern progress, which enable the nations to know each other better, should be used with serene objectivity. That need not, of course, rule out any legitimate emphasis on the positive aspects of their way of life. But methods of information which fall short of the truth, and by the same token impair the reputation of this people or that, must be discarded.[24]

In justice. Relations between political communities are to be further regulated by justice. This implies, over and above recognition of their mutual rights, the fulfillment of their respective duties.

Political communities have the right to existence, to self-development and to the means necessary for this. They have the right to play the leading part in the process of their own development and the right to their good name and due honours. From which it follows as a simultaneous consequence that they have also the corresponding duty of respecting these rights in others and of avoiding any act of violation. Just as an individual man may not pursue his own interests to the detriment of other men, so, on the international level, one State may not develop itself by restricting or oppressing other States. St. Augustine rightly says: *"What are kingdoms without justice but bands of robbers?"*[25]

Not only can it happen, but it actually does happen that the advantages and conveniences which nations strive to acquire for themselves become objects of contention; nevertheless, the resulting disagreements must be settled, not by force, nor by deceit or trickery, but rather in the only manner which is worthy of the dignity of man, i.e., by a mutual assessment of the reasons on both sides of the dispute, by a mature and objective investigation of the situation, and by an equitable reconciliation of differences of opinion.

The treatment of minorities. Since the nineteenth century there has been a rather widespread tendency in historical evolution for political communities to equate themselves with national communities. However, for various reasons, it has not always been possible to make geographical boundaries coincide with ethnic ones; this gives rise to the phenomenon of minorities and to the relative complex problems.

In the first place, it must be made clear that justice is seriously violated by whatever is done to limit the strength and numerical increase of these minority peoples; the injustice is even more serious if such sinful projects are aimed at the very extinction of these groups.

On the other hand, the demands of justice are admirably observed by those civil authorities who promote the natural betterment of those citizens belonging to a smaller ethnic group, particularly when that better concerns their language, the development of their natural gifts, their ancestral customs, and their accomplishments and endeavours in the economic order.[26]

It should be noted, however, that these minority groups, either because of a reaction to their present situation or because of their historical difficulties, are often inclined to exalt beyond due measure anything proper to their own people, so as to place them even above human values, as if that which is proper to humanity were to be at the service of that which is proper to the nation. Reason rather demands that these very people recognize also the advantages that accrue to them from their peculiar circumstances; for instance, no small contribution is made toward the development of their particular talents and spirit by their daily dealings with people who have grown up in a different culture. This, however, will be true only if they will know how to act as a bridge, which facilitates the circulation of life in its various expressions among different traditions or civilizations, and not a zone of discord which can cause great damage and choke natural development.

Active solidarity. Certainly relations between States must be regulated by the norms of truth and justice, but they also derive great benefits from active solidarity, through mutual co-operation on various levels, such as, in our own times, has already taken place with laudable results in the economic, social, political, educational, health and sport spheres. We must remember that, of its very nature, civil authority exists, not to confine its people within the boundaries of their nation, but rather to protect, above all else, the common good of that particular civil society, which certainly cannot be divorced from the common good of the entire human family.

This entails not only that civil societies should pursue their particular interests without hurting others, but also that they should join forces and plans whenever the efforts of an individual government cannot achieve its desired goals; but, in the execution of such common efforts, great care must be taken lest what helps some nations should injure others.

Furthermore, the universal common good requires that in every nation friendly relations be fostered in all fields between the citizens and their intermediate societies.

There are groupings of people of more or less different racial backgrounds. However, the elements which characterize an ethnic group must not be transformed into a watertight compartment in which human beings are prevented from communicating with their fellowmen belonging to different ethnic groups. That would contrast with our contemporary situation, in which the distances separating peoples have been almost wiped out. Nor can one overlook the fact that, even though human beings differ from one another by virtue of their ethnic peculiarities, they all possess certain essential common elements, and are inclined by nature to meet each other in the world of spiritual values, whose progressive assimilation opens to them the possibility of perfection without limits. They have the right and duty therefore to live in communion with one another.

The proper balance between population, land and capital. As everybody knows, there are countries with an abundance of arable land and a scarcity of man-power, while in other countries there is no proportion between natural resources and the capital available. This demands that peoples should set up relationships of mutual collaboration, facilitating the circulation from one to the other of capital, goods, and man-power.[27]

Here we deem it opportune to remark that, whenever possible, the work to be done should be taken to the workers, not vice versa.

In this way a possibility of a better future is offered to many persons without being forced to leave their own environment in order to seek residence elsewhere, which almost always entails the heart-ache of separation and difficult periods of adjustment and social integration.

The problem of political refugees. The sentiment of universal fatherhood which the Lord has placed in Our heart makes Us feel profound sadness in considering the phenomenon of political refugees: a phenomenon which has assumed large proportions and which always hides numberless and acute sufferings.

Such expatriations show that there are some political regimes which do not guarantee for individual citizens a sufficient sphere of freedom within which their souls are allowed to breathe humanly; in fact, under those regimes even the lawful existence of such a sphere of freedom is either called into question or denied. This undoubtedly is a radical inversion of the order of human society, because the reason for the existence of public authority is to promote the common good, a fundamental element of which is the recognition of that sphere of freedom and the safeguarding of it.

At this point it will not be superfluous to recall that such exiles are persons, and that all their rights as persons must be recognized, since they do not lose those rights on losing the citizenship of the States of which they are former members.

Now among the rights of a human person there must be included that by which a man may enter a political community where he hopes he can more fittingly provide a future for himself and his dependents. Wherefore, as far as the common good rightly understood permits, it is the duty of that State to accept such immigrants and to help to integrate them into itself as new members.

Wherefore, on this occasion, We publicly approve and commend every undertaking, founded on the principles of human solidarity and Christian charity, which aims at making migration of persons from one country to another less painful.

And We will be permitted to signal for the attention and gratitude of all right-minded persons the manifold work which specialized international agencies are carrying out in this very delicate field.

Disarmament. On the other hand, it is with deep sorrow that We note the enormous stocks of armaments that have been and still are being made in more economically developed countries, with a vast outlay of intellectual and economic resources. And so it happens that, while the people of these countries are loaded with heavy burdens, other countries as a result are deprived of the collaboration they need in order to make economic and social progress.

The production of arms is allegedly justified on the grounds that in present-day conditions peace cannot be preserved without an equal balance of armaments. And so, if one country increases its armaments, others feel the need to do the same; and if one country is equipped with nuclear weapons, other countries must produce their own, equally destructive.

Consequently, people live in constant fear lest the storm that every moment threatens should break upon them with dreadful violence. And with good reason, for the arms of war are ready at hand. Even though it is difficult to believe that anyone would deliberately take the responsibility for the appalling destruction and sorrow that war would bring in its train, it cannot be denied that the conflagration may be set off by some incontrollable and unexpected chance. And one must bear in mind that, even though the monstrous power of modern weapons acts as a deterrent, it is to be feared that the mere continuance of nuclear tests, undertaken with war in mind, will have fatal consequences for life on the earth.

Justice, then, right reason and humanity urgently demand that the arms race should cease; that the stockpiles which exist in various countries should be reduced equally and simultaneously by the parties concerned; that nuclear weapons should be banned; and that a general agreement should eventually be reached about progressive disarmament and an effective method of control. In the words of Pius XII, Our Predecessor of happy memory: *"The calamity of a world war, with the economic and*

social ruin and the moral excesses and dissolution that ac-
company it, must not be permitted to envelop the human race
for a third time."[28]

All must realize that there is no hope of putting an end to
the building up of armaments, nor of reducing the present
stocks, nor, still less, of abolishing them altogether, unless the
process is complete and thorough and unless it proceeds from
inner conviction: unless, that is, everyone sincerely co-operates
to banish the fear and anxious expectation of war with which
men are oppressed. If this is to come about, the fundamental
principle on which our present peace depends must be replaced
by another, which declares that the true and solid peace of
nations consist not in equality of arms but in mutual trust alone.
We believe that this can be brought to pass, and We consider
that it is something which reason requires, that it is eminently
desirable in itself and that it will prove to be the source of
many benefits.

In the first place, it is an objective demanded by reason.
There can be, or at least there should be, no doubt that relations
between States, as between individuals, should be regulated not
by the force of arms but by the light of reason, by the rule, that
is, of truth, of justice and of active and sincere co-operation.

Secondly, We say that it is an objective earnestly to be desired in itself. Is there anyone who does not ardently yearn to
see war banished, to see peace preserved and daily more firmly
established?

And finally, it is an objective which will be a fruitful source
of many benefits, for its advantages will be felt everywhere, by
individuals, by families, by nations, by the whole human family.
The warning of Pius XII still rings in our ears: *"Nothing is lost*
by peace; everything may be lost by war."[29]

Since this is so, We, the Vicar on earth of Jesus Christ,
Saviour of the World and Author of Peace, and as interpreter
of the very profound longing of the entire human family, following the impulse of Our heart, seized by anxiety for the good of
all, We feel it Our duty to beseech men, especially those who
have the responsibility of public affairs, to spare no labour in

order to ensure that world events follow a reasonable and human course.

In the highest and most authoritative assemblies, let men give serious thought to the problem of a peaceful adjustment of relations between political communities on a world level: an adjustment founded on mutual trust, on sincerity in negotiations, on faithful fulfillment of obligations assumed. Let them study the problem until they find that point of agreement from which it will be possible to commence to go forward towards accords that will be sincere, lasting and fruitful.

We, for Our part, will not cease to pray God to bless these labours so that they may lead to fruitful results.

In liberty. It has also to be borne in mind that relations be- tween States should be based on freedom, that is to say, that no country may unjustly oppress others or unduly meddle in their affairs. On the contrary, all should help to develop in others a sense of responsibility, a spirit of enterprise, and an earnest desire to be the first to promote their own advancement in every field.

The evolution of economically under-developed countries. Be- cause all men are joined together by reason of their common origin, their redemption by Christ, and their supernatural destiny, and are called to form one single family, We appealed in the Encyclical *Mater et Magistra* to economically developed nations to come to the aid of those which were in the process of development.[30]

We are greatly consoled to see how widely that appeal has been favourably received; and We are confident that even more so in the future it will contribute to the end that the poorer countries, in as short a time as possible, will arrive at that degree of economic development which will enable every citizen to live in conditions in keeping with his human dignity.

But it is never sufficiently repeated that the co-operation, to which reference has been made, should be effected with the greatest respect for the liberty of the countries being developed, for these must realise that they are primarily responsible, and that they are the principal artisans in the promotion of their own economic development and social progress.

Our Predecessor Pius XII already proclaimed that *"in the field of a new order founded on moral principles, there is no room for violation of freedom, integrity and security of other nations, no matter what may be their territorial extension or their capacity for defence. It is inevitable that the powerful States, by reason of their greater potential and their power, should pave the way in the establishment of economic groups comprising not only themselves but also smaller and weaker States as well. It is nevertheless indispensable that in the interests of the common good they, as all others, should respect the rights of these smaller states to political freedom, to economic development and to the adequate protection, in the case of conflicts between nations, of that neutrality which is theirs according to the natural, as well as international, law. In this way, and in this way only, will they be able to obtain a fitting share of the common good, and assure the material and spiritual welfare of their people."*[31]

It is vitally important, therefore, that the wealthier States, in providing varied forms of assistance to the poorer, should respect the moral values and ethnic characteristics peculiar to each, and also that they should avoid any intention of political domination. If this is done, *"a precious contribution will be made towards the formation of a world community, a community in which each member, whilst conscious of its own individual right and duties, will work in a relationship of equality towards the attainment of the universal common good."*[32]

Signs of the times. Men are becoming more and more convinced that disputes which arise between States should not be resolved by recourse to arms, but rather by negotiation.

It is true that on historical grounds this conviction is based chiefly on the terrible destructive force of modern arms; and it is nourished by the horror aroused in the mind by the very thought of the cruel destruction and the immense suffering which the use of those armaments would bring to the human family; and for this reason it is hardly possible to imagine that in the atomic era war could be used as an instrument of justice.

Nevertheless, unfortunately, the law of fear still reigns among peoples, and it forces them to spend fabulous sums for armaments: not for aggression, they affirm—and there is no reason for not believing them—but to dissuade others from aggression.

There is reason to hope, however, that by meeting and negotiating, men may come to discover better the bonds that unite them together, deriving from the human nature which they have in common; and that they may also come to discover that one of the most profound requirements of their common nature is this: that between them and their respective peoples it is not fear which should reign but love, a love which tends to express itself in a collaboration that is loyal, manifold in form and productive of many benefits.

RELATIONSHIP OF MEN AND OF POLITICAL COMMUNITIES WITH THE WORLD COMMUNITY

Interdependence between political communities. Recent progress in science and technology has profoundly affected human beings and influenced men to work together and live as one family. There has been a great increase in the circulation of ideas, of persons and of goods from one country to another, so that relations have become closer between individuals, families and intermediate associations belonging to different political communities, and between the public authorities of those communities. At the same time the interdependence of national economies has grown deeper, one becoming progressively more closely related to the other, so that they become, as it were, integral parts of the one world economy. Likewise the social progress, order, security and peace of each country are necessarily connected with the social progress, order, security and peace of all other countries.

At the present day no political community is able to pursue its own interests and develop itself in isolation, because the degree of its prosperity and development is a reflection and a component part of the degree of prosperity and development of all the other political communities.

Insufficiency of modern States to ensure the universal common good. The unity of the human family has always existed, because its members were human beings all equal by virtue of their natural dignity. Hence there will always exist the objective need to promote, in sufficient measure, the universal common good, that is, the common good of the entire human family.

In times past, one would be justified in feeling that the public authorities of the different political communities might be in a position to provide for the universal common good, either through normal diplomatic channels or through top-level meetings, by making use of juridical instruments such as conventions and treaties, for example: juridical instruments suggested by the natural law and regulated by the law of nations and international law.

As a result of the far-reaching changes which have taken place in the relations between the human family, the universal common good gives rise to problems which are complex, very grave and extremely urgent, especially as regards security and world peace. On the other hand, the public authorities of the individual political communities—placed as they are on a footing of equality one with the other—no matter how much they multiply their meeting or sharpen their wits in efforts to draw up new juridical instruments, they are no longer capable of facing the task of finding an adequate solution to the problems mentioned above. And this is not due to a lack of goodwill or of a spirit of enterprise, but because of a structural defect which hinders them.

It can be said, therefore, that at this historical moment the present system of organization and the way its principle of authority operates on a world basis no longer correspond to the objective requirements of the universal common good.

Connection between the common good and political authority. There exists an intrinsic connection between the common good on the one hand and the structure and function of public authority on the other. The moral order, which needs public authority in order to promote the common good in human society, requires also that the authority should be effective in attaining that end. This demands that the organs through which the authority is formed, becomes operative and pursues its ends, must be composed and act in such a manner as to be capable of bringing to realization the new meaning which the common good is taking on in the historical evolution of the human family.

Today the universal common good poses problems of world-wide dimensions, which cannot be adequately tackled or solved except by the efforts of public authorities endowed with a breadth of powers, structure and means of the same proportions: that is, of public authorities which are in a position to operate in an effective manner on a world-wide basis. The moral order itself, therefore, demands that such a form of public authority be established.

Public authority instituted by common consent and not imposed by force. A public authority, having world-wide power and endowed with the proper means for the efficacious pursuit of its objective, which is the universal common good in concrete form, must be set up by common accord and not imposed by force. The reason is that such an authority must be in a position to operate effectively; yet, at the same time, its actions must be inspired by sincere and real impartiality: in other words, it must be an action aimed at satisfying the objective requirements of the universal common good. The difficulty is that there would be reason to fear that a super-national or world-wide public authority, imposed by force by the more powerful political communities, might be or might become an instrument of one-sided interests; and even should this not happen, it would be difficult for it to avoid all suspicion of partiality in its actions, and this would take away from the efficaciousness of its activity.

Even though there may be pronounced differences between political communities as regards the degree of their economic development and their military power, they are all very sensitive as regards this juridical equality and their moral dignity. For that reason, they are right in not easily yielding in obedience to an authority imposed by force, or to an authority in whose creation they had no part, or to which they themselves did not decide to submit by conscious and free choice.

The universal common good and personal rights. Like the common good of individual political communities, so too the universal common good cannot be determined except by having regard to the human person. Therefore, the public authority of the world community, too, must have as its fundamental objective the recognition, respect, safeguarding and promotion of the rights of the human person; this can be done by direct action when required, or by creating on a world scale an environment in which the public authorities of the individual political communities can more easily carry out their specific functions.

The principle of subsidiarity. Just as within each political community the relations between individuals, families, intermediate associations and public authority are governed by the principle of subsidiarity, so too the relations between the public authority of each political community and the public authority of the world community must be regulated by the light of the same principle. This means that the public authority of the world community must tackle and solve problems of an economic, social, political or cultural character which are posed by the universal common good. For, because of the vastness, complexity and urgency of those problems, the public authorities of the individual States are not in a position to tackle them with any hope of a positive solution.

The public authority of the world community is not intended to limit the sphere of action of the public authority of the individual political community, must less to take its place. On the contrary, its purpose is to create, on a world basis, an environment in which the public authorities of each political community, its citizens and intermediate associations, can carry out their tasks, fulfil their duties and exercise their rights with greater security.[33]

Modern developments. As is known, the United Nations Organization (U.N.O.) was established on June 26, 1945, and to it there were subsequently added Intergovernmental Agencies with extensive international tasks in the economic, social, cultural, educational and health fields. The United Nations Organization had as its essential purpose the maintenance and consolidation of peace between peoples, fostering between them friendly relations, based on the principles of equality, mutual respect, and varied forms of co-operation in every sector of human society.

An act of the highest importance performed by the United Nations Organization was the Universal Declaration of Human Rights, approved in the General Assembly of December 10, 1948. In the preamble of that Declaration, the recognition and respect of those rights and respective liberties is proclaimed as an ideal to be pursued by all peoples and all countries.

Some objections and reservations were raised regarding certain points in the Declaration. There is no doubt, however, that the Document represents an important step on the path towards the juridical-political organization of the world community. For in it, in most solemn form, the dignity of a person is acknowledged to all human beings; and as a consequence there is proclaimed, as a fundamental right, the right of free movement in the search for truth and in the attainment of moral good and of justice, and also the right to a dignified life, while other rights connected with those mentioned are likewise proclaimed.

It is Our earnest wish that the United Nations Organization— in its structure and in its means—may become ever more equal to the magnitude and nobility of its tasks, and that the day may come when every human being will find therein an effective safeguard for the rights which derive directly from his dignity as a person, and which are therefore universal, inviolable and inalienable rights. This is all the more to be hoped for since all human beings, as they take an ever more active part in the public life of their own political communities, are showing an increasing interest in the affairs of all peoples, and are becoming more consciously aware that they are living members of a world community.

by Paul Tillich

On PEACE ON EARTH

IT is my task to express some thoughts about the subject of this Convocation and its basic document, the encyclical *Pacem in Terris,* by Pope John XXIII, as a theologian who comes from both a Protestant and a Humanist tradition and has tried for many decades to show their ultimate unity.

My first reaction to the encyclical is the general one that its appearance is an important event in the history of religious and political thought and may have practical consequences for man's historical existence. Most valuable seems to me the way in which is emphasized throughout the document the ultimate principle of justice, the acknowledgment of the dignity of every man as a person, from which follow his rights and his obligations in the manifold encounters of man with man. There is no difference in this point of view among Jews, Protestants, and Humanists: Jews in whose prophetic tradition this principle has arisen and has been reformulated up to Martin Buber's description of the ego— the thou encounter between person and person; Protestants who should never forget that the backbone of love is justice and that without the solid structure of justice, love becomes sentimentality; Humanists who have in Immanuel Kant's unconditional im-

Reprinted by permission from *To Live as Men: An Anatomy of Peace* (Santa Barbara, Calif.: Center for the Study of Democratic Institutions, 1965), pp. 12-23. For a personal note on PAUL TILLICH see p. 120.

perative to respect every person as person the highest criterion of *humanitas*. All three agree with the basic principle of the papal encyclical.

On this foundation, questions arise, some of which are rooted in other traditions and may serve as a transition to the practical work of this Convocation.

My first question stems from the fact that the agreement as to the determining principle of the encyclical reaches only as far as the Western, Christian-Humanist culture, but not essentially beyond it. Therefore, if we envisage "peace on earth," we must remain aware of the fact that there are large cultural groups, some of them shaped by thousands of years of different religious traditions, in which the principle of the dignity of the individual man is not ultimate. Only a prolonged mutual interpenetration, in which the West must take as well as give, can change the situation. This should restrain those who adhere to the spirit of the encyclical from attempts to force some of its consequences, e.g., particular ideas of freedom and equal rights, upon people with other principles. Such attempts are hopeless even if they lead to external victory.

The second problem concerning the encyclical refers to the question of resistance against those who violate the dignity of the individual. Such resistance unquestionably belongs to the rights of the person as well as of the group which has accepted and is willing to defend the dignity of the person and the principles following from it. But such resistance can become rebellion, and rebellion can become revolution, and revolution can become war; and history leaves no doubt that the wars over contrasting ideas of justice are the most cruel, most insistent, and most devastating ones. So it was in the religious wars when the rights of man were identical with the truth about man. So it is now in the ideological wars when the rights of man are identical with the social organization which guarantees these rights. And there is hardly a situation in which the dignity of the person is more deeply violated than in the struggles for the establishment of conditions under which this dignity shall be guaranteed.

This is true of person-to-person relationships as well as of the relation of individuals to groups and of groups to groups. There are situations in which resistance without armed violence is possible; but even then, destructive consequences are hardly avoidable, be it through psychological, through economic, or through sociological forms of compulsion. And there are situations in which nothing short of war can defend or establish the dignity of the person. Nothing is more indicative of the tragic aspect of life than the unavoidable injustice in the struggle for justice.

A third problem which must be considered to create a transition from the encyclical to the political thought of the Convocation is the role of power in relation to force and the principles of justice. Power can be identified neither with force nor with authority. In several statements of the encyclical this has been done, and a direct discussion of the ambiguities of power is lacking. But without it, a realistic approach to the peace problem is impossible.

There is no effective authority without a structure of power behind it; and, under the conditions of existence, no power can become effective without coercion applied against those who try to undercut it. For power is something positive; it is a basic quality of being. It is the power to resist what tries to distort and to annihilate the structures of being. I remind the theologians of the fact that they open the majority of their prayers with words like "all-mighty or all-powerful God," thus consecrating power in itself. And I remind the philosophers that potentiality means "power of being." In every individual and in every group is some power of being and the affirmation of this power and the drive to defend and to increase it. In the encounters of power with power, union as well as conflict arises and the conflicts lead to the use of force for the sake of coercion. Then the great question arises: when is coercion a just expression of power, when an unjust one? We acknowledge just coercion in the enforcement of the law. Is there a just enforcement in the relation of power-groups? This question has been answered for many centuries by the concept of the just war. But this concept has lost its validity through the fact that in a serious atomic conflagration there is no victor and there is no vanquished; in other words, neither a coercer nor a coerced will be left.

Only in minor conflicts the old concept has meaning and may lead to a kind of world police. But a conflict between those who give power and authority to such a police force could not be solved in this way. The problem is neither power nor coercion, but the use of coercion with or without justice in the necessary exercise of power.

In this connection, a fourth problem arises: the question to what degree a political group, for instance a social group with a center of power, able to act politically, can be judged in the way in which one judges human individuals. Such analogy, if taken seriously, has dangerous consequences. It considers a contingent government as the deciding and responsible center of the group. This makes it possible that the government is asked to follow moral laws like the Ten Commandments or the Sermon on the Mount or the Natural Moral Law for individuals—as is often demanded by a legalistic pacifism. But no government can make a total sacrifice of its nation, such as an individual can and sometimes ought to make of himself. However, this does not and should not prevent a government from inducing its nation to bring the sacrifice of self-restriction for the common good of a group of nations, including itself, even if some loss of the questionable and pernicious possession called prestige is involved.

There is another consequence which the personification of a group can have. If the government is considered as the deciding center of the social body, no individual has the right to resist it. And this is the surest and most frequently used road to despotism. The group lies in another dimension of being than the individual; and the moral laws valid for the latter can be applied to the former only indirectly and with essential qualifications. A direct application of the rights and duties of the individual to the rights and duties of a group is impossible. This fact, together in unity with the three other problems we have mentioned, shows the limits of any realistic hope for "peace on earth."

This statement forces me to lead into a more universal and more basic consideration of the question of "peace on earth."

We must ask: which are the predispositions for the fulfillment of this aim in human nature and in the character of history? Most differences about the problems of peace are rooted ultimately in different interpretations of human nature and consequently of the meaning of history. At this point I must speak both as a Protestant theologian and as an existentialist philosopher. I see human nature determined by the conflict between the goodness of man's essential being and the ambiguity of his actual being, his life, under the conditions of existence. The goodness of his essential nature gives him his greatness, his dignity, the demand, embodied in him, to be acknowledged as a person. On the other hand, the predicament in which he finds himself, the estrangement from his true being, drives him into the opposite direction, preventing him from fulfilling in actual life what he essentially is. It makes all his doings, and all that which is done by him, ambiguous, bad as well as good. For his will is ambiguous, good as well as bad. And one should not appeal to "all men of good will" as the encyclical does. One should appeal to all men knowing that in the best will there is an element of bad will and that in the worst will there is an element of good will. This view of the ambiguity of man's moral nature has direct consequences for the way a peace conference should look at the chance for a future state of peace.

It should distinguish genuine hope from utopian expectations. The bearers of hope in past and present had and have to learn this, mostly the hard way. The classical book of hope, the Old Testament, is a history of broken and revived hope. Its foundation was in the first place the belief in divine acting, in the second, the confidence in man's right response to it. In both respects it was disappointed. "My ways are not your ways," says God through the prophet to the disappointed; and nothing is more often expressed in the prophets than the unreliable character of the people, who turn away from the covenant which justified this hope. Nevertheless, a genuine hope remained in Israel up to today and kept the nation alive.

There is a profound analogy between the history of the religious hope in Israel and the history of the secular hope in the

Western world from the great Utopias of the Renaissance up to our day. In the movements which were striving for a state of peace and justice in modern times, hope was based partly on the belief in man's growing reasonableness.

Both hopes were disappointed, perhaps most profoundly in the first half of our century. We cannot close our eyes any longer to the fact that every gain produced—for example, by scientific and technical progress—implies a loss; and that every good achieved in history is accompanied by a shadow, an evil which uses the good and distorts it. And we know just through our better understanding of man's personal and social life that human reason is not only determined by the natural laws of reason but also by the dark elements in his total being which struggle against reason. In view of the two main examples for this predicament of man, the ambiguity of blessing and curse in the scientific penetration into the atomic structure of the universe, and the well-reasoned outbreak of destructive anti-rationality in Hitlerism and Stalinism, it is understandable that hopelessness has grasped large masses in the Western nations, especially in the younger generations. And it is understandable that a conference like this meets a widespread skepticism, perhaps by some in the conference itself.

But there are not only utopian expectations, there is also genuine hope in our time and in what we are trying to do—here and now—just as in the men of the Old Testament. A realistic view of man and history need not lead to cynicism. But it may often ask for hope against hope, and certainly it demands the courage to risk, even if failure is more probable than success.

Where then lies the difference between utopian expectations and genuine hope? The basis for genuine hope is that there is something present of that which is hoped for, as in the seed something of the coming plant is present while utopian expectations have no ground in the present. So we must ask: which are the seeds out of which a future state of peace can develop?

The first basis for genuine hope is something negative, which, however, can have and partly has had positive effects: the atomic threat and the fear of mutual destruction. The limited peace forced upon us by the threat is in itself merely negative. But it does something which is somehow positive: it makes the conflicting groups of mankind feel that there is mankind with a common destiny. This experience of a "community of fear" is still weak and easily overwhelmed by a stronger feeling of national and ideological conflict. But it does exist as a small seed.

A second basis of genuine hope for peace is the technical union of mankind by the conquest of space. Of course, nearness can intensify hostility; and the fact that the first manifestation of the technical oneness of our world was two world wars proves this possibility. But nearness can also have the opposite effect. It can change the image of the other as strange and dangerous; it can reduce self-affirmation and effect openness for other possibilities of human existence and, particularly as in the encounter of the religions, other possibilities of genuine faith.

A third basis of genuine hope for peace is the increasing number of cross-national and cross-ideological fields of cooperation, some of them desirable, as, for example, collaboration in the sciences, some of them necessary for the future of mankind, as, for example, the problems of food, medicine, overpopulation, conservation of nature.

A fourth basis of genuine hope is the existence and effectiveness, however limited, of a legal roof for all these types of limited groups. Man can extend the realm of hope, which nature cannot. He can establish a legal structure which guarantees peace among those who are subject to it, not absolutely but to a certain degree, not absolutely, for everyone subjected to the legal structure can break through it for his own interest or his conviction.

Therefore, something more than the legal structure for peace is needed. One has called it "consensus." But it is not something as intellectual as this word indicates. It is communal *eros,* that kind of love which is not directed to an individual but to a group. It is said that one cannot love another nation. This may be true in relation to a national state; but it is not true with respect to the people of the other nation. One can have *eros* toward them in their uniqueness, their virtues, their contributions, in spite of their shortcomings and vices. It seems that no world community is possible without this *eros* which trespasses interest as well as law. Every expression of such *eros* is a basis of hope for peace, every rejection of it reduces the chances of peace.

And now a last word about what we as a peace conference can hope for. First of all: we can only *hope*. We cannot calculate, we cannot know. The uncertainty remains. All the seeds of hope mentioned can be destroyed before they come to fulfillment. And further: there is no hope for a final stage of history in which peace and justice rule. History is not fulfilled at its empirical end; but history is fulfilled in the great moments in which something new is created, or, as one could express it religiously, in which the Kingdom of God breaks into history conquering destructive structures of existence, one of the greatest of which is war. This means that we cannot hope for a final stage of justice and peace within history; but we can hope for partial victories over the forces of evil in a particular moment of time.

With this hope, without utopian expectations, this conference should begin its work.

by Richard Shaull

REVOLUTIONARY CHANGE IN THEOLOGICAL PERSPECTIVE

AS we have become increasingly aware of the dynamic nature of society today, ecumenical social thinking has focused on *rapid social change*. Technology has emerged as the central factor, in a close and unusual relationship with other elements. The technological revolution developed in the West as a consequence of a fundamental change in man's understanding of reality and of the social order. At the same time, the spread of technology seems to accelerate this shift to a functional and secular attitude and to make imperative the development of new and more flexible forms of institutional life. In *Christianity in World History,*[1] Professor A. Van Leeuwen insists that this is part of an irresistible historical process in which traditional "ontocratic"[2] patterns of life are being shattered. All orders of society are losing their sacral character and are now open toward the future, to be shaped as man wills. At the same time, the author discerns a growing tendency toward the emergence of messianic movements dedicated to the liberation of man from all that enslaves and dehumanizes him.

Reprinted from *Christian Social Ethics in a Changing World,* John C. Bennett, ed. (New York: Association Press and Geneva: World Council of Churches, both 1966), pp. 23-43. By permission. RICHARD SHAULL is Professor of Ecumenics, Princeton Theological Seminary. He has been a pioneer in Church and society studies in Latin America, and is the author of *Encounter with Revolution*.

Given the fluidity of a dynamic society, we should now be witnessing gradual progress toward the shaping of new social structures, which would offer a greater degree of justice and well-being to the depressed classes of the world. Thus far, however, this has not happend to any significant extent. Over against the discovery that society can be changed stands the fact that those who most benefit from the present situation have tremendous economic and political power and are willing to go to almost any length to preserve it. Entire classes and races of people have discovered that their suffering is not inevitable and have thus awakened to a new hope for a better life. But this hope has not been fulfilled. Institutions structured for a stable society have failed to adjust to the new order and are in crisis. Economic development, industrialization and the rapid growth of large cities, the population explosion and other factors have raised new problems, which they are unable to meet creatively; especially in the developing nations, this technological progress has often tended to increase the misery and insecurity of the poor, provide even greater opportunities for the few to profit, and leave the masses in greater insecurity than before. The process of secularization has undercut traditional concepts of authority, but new patterns of relationships have not yet evolved. In the midst of rapid social change, the uprooted masses discover the extent to which society has deprived them of their selfhood and left them in a state of alienation. In these circumstances, mass movements become the way by which they acquire a new identity as they participate in a struggle to shape a new society.[3]

We are thus confronted by a new and unprecedented polarization between those who have enjoyed the benefits of the status quo and those who are most anxious to change it. Our world is divided sharply between the rich and the poor nations; and in each country, a struggle is taking shape between those groups, races and classes who have awakened to their inferior position and those who are reluctant to make way for a new order. Consequently, it would seem that *social revolution* is the primary fact with which our generation will have to come to terms.

Except in Latin America, the anticolonial struggle has now

passed its peak; but the struggle of the poor and weak nations for an opportunity to participate more fully in international life and to have a more equitable share of the wealth of an interdependent world has only just begun. In developing and developed nations, the revolution of the dispossessed is still in its early stages. The Negro revolution in the United States now occupies the center of attention; it may well trigger similar upheavals among other underprivileged racial and economic groups, especially in large urban centers. The tremendous concentration of economic and political power in a few hands, which has occurred in our modern technological society, will sooner or later lead to revolutionary demands for greater participation on the part of many groups of people. There are signs that this is already taking place in some of the communist countries; it may not long delay in western Europe and America. All around the world, a sort of revolution is brewing among young people, which may take on increasing significance in the years ahead.

If the analysis above is correct, it will be on the frontiers of revolution that many of the major issues of humanization and dehumanization will be decided in our modern world; it will be on these frontiers that those most concerned for the well-being and for the future of man will find themselves involved. This will be true not only for those young people—from both the privileged and underpriviledged classes—who discover that their responsibility for their fellowmen leads them to participation in revolution, but it will also be true for those in positions of power in the established order who understand the world in which they are living and feel compelled to work for change. If we hope to preserve the most important elements of our cultural, moral and religious heritage and to contribute to the shaping of the future, we cannot remain outside the revolutionary struggle or withdraw from it. The only path of responsibility is the one that passes through it toward whatever may lie ahead.

For most of us, this will not be easy. Our past experience and training have not prepared us for this type of struggle. Many of us are too closely identified with the status quo to understand or participate freely in a revolution against it. Moreover, we are surrounded by evidences that revolution is a highly ambiguous phenomenon. It represents a passion for the liberation of the oppressed, but it also releases great forces of destruction and leads to new forms of injustice. Vast numbers of men and women have struggled and sacrificed their lives for the sake of a new society; all too often, the order that is established after the revolution has spent itself is not very different from the previous one. Movements that succeed in awakening the masses and invite them to participate in the use of public power often lead to destructive fanaticism and end up by depriving them of power. New centers of power are indispensable if change is to be brought about, but, in a revolutionary situation, it is impossible to predict how this power will eventually be used. The unselfish commitment of the young revolutionary to the service of his people is one of the most hopeful developments in the modern world, but this very attitude may lead him to exaggerate the rightness of his cause, as well as the injustices on the other side, and to close his eyes to aspects of reality that must be taken into account if the revolution is to achieve its goals.

If revolution is to be our destiny, we are challenged to find new categories of thought about social and political questions, and a new perspective on the relationship between stability and change. We are confronted by the need to develop communities of thought and action, on both sides of the major revolutionary struggles, that will search for solutions and work for reconciliation in the midst of tension and conflict.

Our major political movements do not offer much ground for hope. Conservative ideologies cannot understand the problem, much less meet its challenge; liberal ways of thinking do not seem to fare much better. The liberal, who works for *orderly* change in a world in which he can perceive signs of continued progress toward a better society, may be quite at a loss when confronted with the reality of a revolutionary upheaval. Marxism stands alone in its attempt to understand revolution as essential to the creation of a more stable and just society, and, in some parts of the world, it is the supreme symbol of hope for those who long for a new day. Yet after it comes to power, alters the structures of society and institutionalizes a new order, the situation changes. Then, the very ideology that provided the dynamic for revolution gets in the way of a creative response to the problem of order and change.

In this situation, has Christianity any contribution to make? Religion has traditionally given a sacral character to the institutions of the status quo and has thus been a major factor in preserving them against the forces of revolution. In the West, Christianity has been so closely identified with the established order of Christendom that it has tended to play the same role. In the face of revolutionary upheavals, the great temptation for the church is to become the rallying point of all who fear change.

At the same time, the breakdown of Christendom and the process of secularization have undercut the authority of the church, transferred this task of saving the status quo to new secular ideologies and movements and thus set the church free to be once again a revolutionary force.[4]

Moreover, as small groups of Christians become involved in revolutionary struggles, they discover in the Christian heritage resources for thought and action of which they were not previously aware. If these resources are available, we should give a certain priority to the type of study and research that will work them out and put them at the disposal of those who are now moving toward involvement in these areas. We indicate below some lines which may deserve further investigation.

Toward a Theological Perspective on Revolution

If we look at our history in the light of biblical history, we may feel quite at home in the midst of revolution. There are several strands of biblical thought that may justify such an affirmation:

1. *The fact that God is both the Creator and Ruler of all spheres of nature and of society.* These are temporal realities existing to serve God's purpose for *man;* therefore, they can and must be used and changed in line with the purpose. Throughout the Bible, there is a strong eschatological emphasis, which stresses

the dynamic nature of God and the fact that his action in history is moving toward a goal. It is this which has led Professor Van Leeuwen to conclude that the biblical attitude toward the world has made our modern revolution both possible and inevitable. It has desacralized all institutions and awakened a concern for the reshaping of human life.

2. *The revolutionary character of biblical messianism.* From the first pages of the Old Testament, it is evident that God's rule over the nations and over Israel constantly runs into difficulties. His redemptive action means judgment, which is, at the same time, a new beginning. The scattering of the nations of Babel (Genesis 11) is followed by the calling of Abraham (Genesis 12), who will be the instrument for their restoration. In Israel, those most sensitive to the divine activity are convinced that he is tearing down in order to build up (Jeremiah 1:10), that he breaks the power of the oppressor in order to establish his justice.[5] As H. Berkhof puts it, "The Gospel introduced . . . a revolutionary God, whose 'righteousness,' according to the Psalms and the prophets, means that he lifts up those who are bowed down and humiliates the oppressors."[6]

In this atmosphere of revolution, the Messiah is the central figure. He arises after the house of David has been destroyed, as a shoot out of an apparently dead trunk. In Isaiah especially, central attention is given to his role as a political revolutionary, an emphasis that breaks forth in the New Testament in the Magnificat (Luke 1:50-53). In the life, death and resurrection of Jesus, the messianic theme of destruction and restoration finds new meaning and focus.

3. *The dynamic historical character of God's action.* Israel meets and knows God in the midst of her history, in her involvements in political crises and complex social and cultural problems. In the Incarnation, this God relates himself once and for all to man within a dynamic process. As God's action in the world aims at its transformation, the coming of Christ and the work of the Holy Spirit release new and disturbing forces in history that affect the process itself. As the influence of Christ grows, old stabilities are swept away, and the struggle for hu-

manization moves to new frontiers; at the same time, new threats appear, and the forces that resist Christ become stronger and more manifest. Along this road, there can be no turning back; those who would participate in God's work cannot seek refuge in old ways nor draw back from the front lines because the situation is becoming increasingly dangerous. For it is in this struggle that the battle for the future of man is being waged; it is in the midst of apocalyptic events that we perceive signs of imminent victory (Luke 21:28).

THE AUGUSTINIAN VIEW OF SOCIAL CHANGE

The history of Christian thought does not provide us with many theologians of revolution. Augustine stands out across the centuries. Living as he did at the time of the collapse of the Roman Empire, much of his thought, especially in *The City of God,* deals with questions similar to those which face us today. As Professor Charles Cochrane has shown, the trinitarian dogma provided him with a foundation for thought and action precisely at those points where classical culture had failed.[7] Taking as his starting point a "principle" *beyond* nature and history, which was nevertheless at work *in* nature and history and which was capable of being apprehended there, he was able to take account of "being and movement in the universe" in a new way.[8] Trusting in a divine sovereignty at work in and through an "order of causes," Augustine was able to admit the impossibility of finding a satisfactory rational relationship of these causes to each other. And, at the same time, he sought new clues to an order, which, though not fully perceived, was nonetheless present. Convinced that the Logos of Christ, revealed in Scripture, was the ultimate reality in human life and history, he could think and act on the conviction that "each and every occurrence in the manifold of events bears witness to the activity of God."[9] It was this "principle of intelligibility," according to Professor Cochrane, which was capable of "saving the reason as well as the will,"[10] for, in the working out of it, the rich diversity of human experience was pulled together in a meaningful configuration, and the historical process was seen as full of meaning and purpose.

Those who looked at the world in the perspective of the Logos of Christ as its "creating and moving principle," perceived that personality was as central in the historical process; crisis and change became meaningful. Historical events were seen as occurring along a line set by the dynamic reality of God's Providence, his bringing in of his Kingdom, the work of the Holy Spirit in the world and the movement of history toward its final goal. Along this road, two cities coexist. In constant conflict with each other, they are also "inextricably intermingled . . . in the concrete reality of history."[11] Both these cities are striving after one thing only, *peace,* which Augustine defined as "the tranquility of order."[12] The peace of the eternal city, which is constantly permeating and transforming the city of man, is that of a "perfectly ordered and harmonious communion of those who find their joy in God and in one another in God."[13] But the peace of the earthly city, which is an attempt to develop some sort of order among men motivated by self-love, is a temporary, partial and unstable peace. It is an order that is always being established in the midst of conflict, in which men must often wage war for the sake of peace, and in which the divine judgment upon human pride and self-centeredness means that, from time to time, certain structures of society must be reformed and, in some cases, must collapse.[14]

This Augustinian perspective, with its wealth of insight into the meaning of events and the nature of responsible action in a revolutionary world, provides a basis for political realism that recognizes both the importance and the ambiguity of political action. The political struggle forms an essential part of the life of the earthly city and contributes to the renovation and reconstruction of human life in community, but not to its regeneration. For the Christian, the vortex of the social struggle has a very definite attraction. It is there, at the heart of the commingling of the two cities, that both the inevitable destructiveness of human self-love and new possibilities for social reform and for new structures of human relationships are exposed. Thus, the decline and collapse of the old order is not necessarily a disaster; it may well be the one way by which the divine purpose for a more just human order can move forward.

Among the theologians, Professor Paul L. Lehmann seems to have gone furthest in exploring Augustine's thought about the action of the triune God in history and has provided a number of theological categories for dealing with revolution; and, not surprisingly, there is, among those who are involved in revolutionary struggles, a certain interest in his thought. Professor Lehmann contends that it is only in Christianity that history is understood as a compound of stability and change, decay and fulfillment, in such a way that change is seen as the prelude to authentic stability, and decay as the occasion for fulfillment. This unusual perspective is the result of God's revelation of himself as "I will be who I will be," the God whose "moving strength" is at the heart of events and whose action must be understood by looking to the future, more than to the past.[15] But, for Professor Lehmann, it is primarily the messianic tradition and imagery of the Bible that provide the real clue to what is going on in the world. Here the focus is on the "political character" of God's activity, by which he is creating the conditions for human fulfillment in interrelatedness in the world.[16] The Messiah is the bearer of God's new deliverance where all human possibilities are played out; his purpose goes forward as he tears down in order to rebuild (Jeremiah 1:10; Luke 1:46-55). He is the Incarnate Son of God, "the humanization of God for the sake of the humanization of man."[17]

The Messiah was also crucified: It is only God's program, not man's that offers the road to human fulfillment, a fulfillment that comes through judgment and reconciliation. The church is a sign and foretaste of this possibility present in the midst of life. When it is faithful to its Lord, the church incarnates this "passion for and vision of human deliverance and fulfillment";[18] its disobedience contributes to the creation of a messianic vacuum, such as is evident today.

For Lehmann, revolution must be understood theologically, for it is set firmly in the context of God's humanizing activity in history. As a political form of change, revolution represents the cutting edge of humanization. We must therefore look to the revolutionary process if we hope to understand the dynamics and direction of change. But, in this context, revolution is the bearer both of signs of fulfillment and of symptoms of decay. The Christian looks for stability on the other side of change; he is therefore free to be fully involved in the revolution. At the same time, his understanding of what is going on there obliges him to work constantly for reconciliation.

The Role of the Christian Koinonia in the Revolutionary Process

As a consequence of the self-invalidation of Christianity and the increasing dominance of a secular mentality, especially among revolutionaries, Christians cannot speak to the revolution by means of systematic theological treatises on the nature of the divine activity. What is now called for is rather the presence on the frontiers of revolution of communities dynamically involved in the struggle for humanization and engaged in a constant running conversation with their biblical and theological heritage. Such *koinonias* will find it easier to raise questions than to provide answers, and their voice may sound weak over against that of political ideologies. To the degree that they are faithful to their heritage, they will live in sharp tension with the revolutionary movements in which they participate or with the established order of which they are a part. And yet it is precisely this type of existence that may contribute something to the deepening of insight, the recovery of purpose, the rebirth of courage and the work of reconciliation among Christians and non-Christians alike. Certain concrete issues reveal that the possibilities are these:

1. *The dynamics of the revolutionary process.* Christians, and many others, especially of the middle class, are upset and confused when confronted with the reality of revolution. Although identified with the status quo, they see certain injustices around them and want to work for reasonable and gradual changes in

society. They may even be enthusiastic about revolution in its early stages. But they find themselves confronted by a dynamic process which they cannot understand, and which leads those on each side to assume more radical positions. As attitudes become more extreme and actions more excessive, the Christian may find himself attempting to expose the exaggerations of both groups but unable to identify with either of them. Thus he soon finds himself far from the front lines of the struggle and ignored by all.

At this point, a radical theological reorientation would seem to be called for. The God who is tearing down old structures in order to create the conditions for a more human existence is himself in the midst of the struggle. It is his presence in the world and his pressure upon those structures which stand in his way that constitute the dynamics of this process. God has taken human form in the concreteness of historical life and has called us to follow this path if we are to be the salt of the earth and the light of the world (Matthew 5:13-14). In this context, the Christian is called to be fully involved in the revolution as it develops. It is only at its center that we can perceive what God is doing, understand how the struggle for humanization is being defined and serve as agents of reconciliation. From within this struggle we discover that we do not bear witness in revolution by preserving our purity in line with certain moral principles, but rather by freedom to be *for man* at every moment. It is also in the midst of this situation that we who have been silent and inactive in the face of suffering and injustice are made to see our guilt and accept the judgment that has come upon us. If our failure to act in the past is responsible for this radicalization of the revolutionary process, we can accept our guilt and work for reconciliation only as we are free to participate in movements in which we have lost the right to be heard and in which our sincerity may now be called into question.

Here we also face *the nature of the revolutionary process itself.* The forces of reaction often tend to ignore or underestimate the dynamics of this process; the revolutionaries consider it as an inevitable law of historic necessity. Especially since the time of the French Revolution, revolution has been understood as a series of tremendous events following a destined course beyond human control. Hegel's philosophy of history may well have been greatly influenced by his reflection upon these events, and Marx gave definitive formulation to this deterministic view.

In a Christian perspective, the revolutionary process is a reality that we dare not ignore, but it loses its character of determinism and inevitability. As Augustine interpreted history in the light of God's sovereignty over an order of causes, so the Christian understands events in a revolutionary situation. He is free to attempt to understand what is happening by analyzing the concrete social, economic and political realities, while remaining sensitive to the direction in which things seem to be moving. The dynamics of the process is determined not by some inevitable law of history, but by the interworking of God's pressure for change and man's response to it—by trying to stop it, or by absolutizing the revolutionary struggle or by taking concrete steps toward a more just society. The development of the revolution will thus be determined by the way in which those on each side of the struggle respond to the pressures for a more human society, as it takes shape in the "providence of God and the confusion of men."

2. *Stability and change.* In the Christian perspective, order is the order of humanization as it is made visible in the *koinonia;* it can be established only in and through the renewal and transformation of structures, even though such changes bring with them also new possibilities of dehumanization. A crisis in any social structure does not necessarily endanger the well-being of those who live in it; it is more likely to be a new opportunity for a richer life, especially for those groups whose well-being has been ignored. In a world that operates this way, the past can be preserved only as it is constantly being transformed. Efforts to save our heritage by enclosing it in rigid institutional forms of a former era can lead only to its repudiation.

In this context, men and women discover new possibilities for creative thought and action in the midst of revolution. Those who are closely identified with the established order may be free to recognize the judgment upon their way of life, accept the loss of privileges in the interest of their neighbor and look for new opportunities of fulfillment, even for themselves, as the new order takes shape around them. They may be able to take initiatives in bringing about changes in their society, thus opening the way to a more gradual and less violent transition.

Likewise, the revolutionary may discover that he should not make an idol of revolution. The overthrow of the old order will not automatically bring about a more just society. That can come only as the result of an intensive effort that works toward the shaping of the new out of the concrete material given in a specific situation. Moreover, in the long run, the new order will be an instrument of humanization only if it, too, is open to change. A revolution will be able to move toward an approximate realization of its objectives only if it develops a type of institution in which self-criticism and sensitivity to dissatisfaction are built into its very structures. It is this fact that modern revolutionaries, dominated as they have been by a mistaken understanding of the historical process, seem singularly unable to comprehend. It is hard to find examples that match Thomas Jefferson's reaction to the news of Shays' uprising: "God forbid that we should ever be twenty years without such a rebellion."

Moreover, in the Christian community, we have certain clues to the type of structure that is most clearly in line with God's work of humanization. Revolutions today are basically struggles for justice. But, in God's world, justice and reconciliation belong together. The enemy must be taken seriously. This does not necessarily imply that a two-party political system must be preserved in all circumstances nor does it imply that the nerve of revolutionary action must be cut by endless and fruitless search for an agreement on a program that satisfies all groups in society. It does mean openness toward those whose criticism exposes our rationalizations and our mistakes, and constant efforts toward reconciliation of conflicting interests and restoration of broken relationships. In the *koinonia,* human fulfillment comes through growth to maturity in interrelatedness. Thus, only as a person has the opportunity to participate in the life of his community and in the decisions that shape his destiny, can he be fully human.

3. *The new revolutionary order and the Kingdom of God.* The conservative of the established order may be aware of its limitations, and even of its injustices; what he tends to ignore is the dynamics of history. The revolutionary, on the other hand, is sensitive to the dynamics of the historical process; his temptation is to trust in the power of man to build a completely new order and to solve all problems that may arise.

The Kingdom of God always stands over against every social and political order, thus exposing its dehumanizing elements and judging it. At the same time, the Kingdom is a dynamic reality; it is "coming" through the work of him who is restoring the nations (II Isaiah) and in whose good time the kingdom of this world shall become the Kingdom of our Lord and of his Christ (Revelations 11:15). Thus, a particular crisis of structures may be the result of God's relentless pressure; and the Christian may perceive, in certain situations, a relative coincidence of direction of the revolutionary struggle with God's humanizing action in the world.

When this occurs, we are confronted with forces that will shape the future, and in relation to which our obedience must be defined. Guidance for such discernment cannot come from a philosophy of history or a political ideology, but only from participation in a community that, orientated by God's revelation, is also involved in the world where he is at work. For those who have eyes to see, this coincidence of direction will be found not only in the crisis of structures of a feudal or bourgeois society but also in the struggle for humanization in those orders established by revolutions today. In the perspective of the Kingdom, involvement in revolution means living in a state of tension that can become a creative force. The new order of society is a "gift." It comes in the midst of, and in spite of, our limitations and failures. What is of ultimate significance is the fulfillment of human life in a new context of relationships. For this new order, a change of structures in society is essential, but it is only one element in a larger process of humanization. Thus, we can participate fully in the political struggle at the same time as we recognize its limitations. We can be open to unexpected possibilities of meaning and fulfillment, which may come at any moment, even when our most strenuous political efforts seem to suffer complete defeat. Each new experience of community points to the Kingdom toward which we are moving, but in which, even now, we participate in a partial way.

4. *Thought and action orientated toward the future.* In our dynamic society, the categories of thought on which we rely for understanding are soon outmoded, the shape of the problems we confront is constantly changing, and our methods of dealing with them can become inadequate almost overnight. Those who are bound to the past become victims of fear and frustration, and men who have offered creative leadership at one moment may discover that they are suddenly unable to meet the new challenge before them. Even those who contribute to the establishment of a new society may betray their cause because they are not free to think and act in the new situation, which their own revolution has created.

In spite of our traditional ways of thinking, Christian faith does look at the present in the light of the future; and the future, brought into the present, provides a unique perspective of understanding and becomes an explosive force. As we respond to the God who is moving ahead, we find ourselves directed toward "the shape of things to come." This action of God is hidden to a certain extent, but we need not, for this reason, formulate a world view that affirms the absence of God or the absurdity of history. Trusting that every moment of history is shaped by the divine activity, we can await the manifestations of God's action along the road toward the future. This understanding of reality saves the reason by freeing it from the tendency to absolutize its systems of thought and from the pretension to omniscience and infallibility. At the same time, it grounds our efforts at understanding upon an order of truth which is not necessarily logical, but which is determined by the providential ordering of God, partially apprehended by faith in the midst of concrete historical reality. Along this road, reason is free to seek new patterns of society not according to some social dogma or utopian dream, but by a realistic apprehension of the possibilities of change and development that open up as we move from one stage to another in the revolutionary struggle. What matters at each stage is not the success or failure of a specific project, but the way in which, in success or failure, the struggle for humanization moves to a new level.[19] To the degree that we participate in a community that is present on the frontier and lives by this hope, we shall be able to meet the breakdown of present structures without fear and act in a way that points to the shape of things to come.

ORIENTATION FOR ETHICAL DECISIONS

The Christian in a revolutionary movement finds himself surrounded by a variety of groups and ideologies, each of which has specific proposals for the creation of a new society. Has Christian faith anything to say about the shape of the new structures that are to be established after the collapse of the old? This question, central in all Christian ethical reflection today, takes on new importance in a revolutionary situation for at least two reasons:

1. The revolutionary finds himself caught up in an accelerated process in which he is confronted, at every moment, with a new configuration of facts and events. All schematic definitions of ethical responsibility tend to hinder him from dealing with concrete reality. In fact, it is in the revolutionary struggle that the attempt of modern secular man to formulate a new conception of reality and find a new basis for ethical decisions has a special appeal.

2. In the midst of revolution, life is insecure, the shape of the future is unclear. The struggle for a new order takes place in the midst of opposition, repeated failures and the constant appearance of new threats of dehumanization. For the revolutionary, the ethical question is not merely that of a logical definition of a

new order; what he most needs is an understanding of the revolutionary process that orientates his struggle for change in the direction of the future and provides a context of hope and trust in which he can make wise decisions.

In the face of these demands, it is not surprising that the natural-law tradition, with its rational definition of cosmic order and its attempt to formulate general principles for an ideal society, breaks down. What may not yet be so evident is that our ecumenical studies, to the degree that they depend upon this tradition, may prove irrelevant. To speak only of the situation I know most directly, in Brazil, the rapid social change studies were widely used until we confronted a revolutionary situation. Then we discovered that those most involved were turning elsewhere for orientation.

Professor Hendrik Van Oyen, in his paper on "Fundamental Problems of Evangelical Social Ethics," suggests why this was so.[20] He finds that our ecumenical studies have preserved the unresolved tension in Anglo-Saxon Christian social thought between "the Calvinistic ideal of the rule of the Kingdom of God over the whole creation" and "the claim of natural law as a cosmic order of life, in other words, the ideal of reason."[21] Many of our more specifically theological statements have followed the first line; our definitions of structure, the second. Useful as the latter has been, it is questionable whether this logical enterprise can deal effectively with the concreteness of the revolutionary process or with the increasing demands to give sufficient attention to the knowledge of the specialist in the formulation of ethical goals.[22]

Where, then, can we seek answer to the question regarding the shaping of structures in a revolutionary situation? In Brazil, among certain groups, there has been a decisive shift toward a contextual ethic, the starting point of which is a "theology of messianism" rather than a theological anthropology together with a modified natural-law theory. As Professor Lehmann describes it, a theology of messianism focuses on what God is doing in the world to make and keep human life human. This divine action follows a line indicated by the doctrines of Providence, the Kingdom of God and eschatology, as well as by the third article of the Creed, regarding the activity of the Holy Spirit in the church and in the world. Along this road, every situation in which the Christian finds himself called upon to live and act is an expression of the commingling of the two cities, which continues throughout history. In this process, the pressures of the redemptive God upon the earthly city and the constant encounter and conflict between the two constitute the context in which men strive for order and peace in the world. In Lehmann's words: "The complexity of the actual human situation . . . is always compounded of an intricate network of circumstances and human interrelationships bracketed by the dynamics of God's political activity on the one hand and God's forgiveness on the other."[23]

If this is the nature of the reality with which we are dealing, the proximate good for which Christians or non-Christians strive cannot be defined in terms of principles and precepts; it is, rather, a question of relationships and acts that point to the opportunities for human fulfillment, which God opens up at a particular time and place, on the road to the future. Guidance for the shaping of structures cannot be provided primarily by any general, rational set of values, but by participation in the *koinonia,* where —through word, sacrament and interrelatedness—the concrete shape of God's humanizing work in the world is becoming visible.

The basic issue is not whether the Christian can formulate certain values with which the non-Christian can agree as a basis for common action. It is, rather, whether or not the Christian is able to perceive and respond to fundamental dimensions of reality, which Christian and non-Christian alike should take into account in making ethical decisions. In every situation, there are certain aspects of worldly reality that can be understood and analyzed only by the sociologist, the political scientist or the economist. But none of these disciplines is able to capture the full dimensions of this reality. This real world, in its concreteness, has been accepted, is judged and is being reconciled to God. In the midst of the full complexity of this situation, God is creating the conditions for the fulfillment of human life. Only as these elements of reality receive attention, alongside the technical, can proximate goals be realistically defined; only in the light of the ultimate toward which it is moving can the penultimate be properly understood.

THE CHRISTIAN CONTRIBUTION TO REVOLUTIONARY GOALS

What, specifically, are the elements at the center of God's humanizing activity in the world? One of them is the fact of forgiveness, which sets us free to act for our neighbor; free to see the ambiguities of the situation, as well as of our own motivation, and still move ahead; free to participate fully in a struggle involving conflict and the risk of violence, injustice and the power of self-interest, and there know that the power of sin is broken; free to perceive that when the human situation is falling apart, God is picking up the pieces and putting them together again. Another basic element is justice, the recognition that God's order is being established on the other side of change, as structures are shaped that defend those classes and groups in society that have no power and can count on no one to defend them. A third is reconciliation, which occurs in the midst of struggle and hostility as all perspectives are transformed through the encounter and reconciliation of differences.

If Christians are able to deal competently with reality in full openness to these dimensions, their presence could make a significant difference in the definition of proximate goals. Their participation will be a constant reminder that, at every point, the crucial issue is what is happening and what is likely to happen in human relationships. They will recognize that revolutionary structures can contribute to this goal only as they provide all classes and groups in society with an opportunity for increasing participation in the shaping of the life of the community, the economic order and the nation. They will make evident that the most adequate goals are those which are worked out in dialogue with the widest variety of ideologies and with those technically competent in many different aspects of the problem. They will recognize that only those structures open to change and renewal can serve the well-being of man in a dynamic society such as ours today. Most important of all, they should bring into the situation a basic attitude of trust and hope and a creative imagination for handling the facts, which are manifest because the absoluteness of the technical has been broken and each situation is seen in the light of the goal toward which it is moving.

In the revolution confronting us, the real test of any theological and ethical perspective will be its ability to recognize fully the importance of the insights of the expert and to contribute something in the dialogue with him. Recent writings of Professor Denys Munby provide a basis for further reflection on this question. In his book, *The Idea of a Secular Society*,[24] and in an essay, "The Importance of Technical Competence,"[25] he contends that the size of our society, the wide variety of situations in it and the fact of rapid social change make it impossible to find much help in any set of principles or values. We live in a world in which there is no longer any image that reflects generally accepted common ideals. If we want to get anywhere in solving our problems, we must study the diverse aspects of reality with the tools provided by the various scientific disciplines: "It is only possible to discover the truth about men in society by the patient application of complicated techniques to the empirical facts."[26]

Has a Christian ethic, then, anything to contribute to the definition of goals? Professor Munby would urge caution at this point: "Men do not always act according to facts, but it remains, nevertheless, surprisingly true that, in a large number of cases, once the facts have been elucidated, the appropriate action almost inevitably follows."[27] This may be true as far as it goes. But the technical mind all too easily acquires a very restricted idea of just what the "facts" are and forgets that the technical is ethically ambiguous. As a phenomenon of the commingling of the two cities, it points toward the ethical and contributes to the dehumanization of man. The technical is concerned with knowledge and power, and power is both "gracious" and demonic. Unless the technical analysis of reality is confronted constantly with a witness to the dimensions of that reality, which may escape the technician, we face a very dangerous situation in the society.

Professor Munby is always dealing with the technical in the context of Christian faith. His deep concern for the well-being of man, his relative optimism about the human enterprise and his confidence in the redemptive activity of God in the world all have a decisive influence. He is an economist, but he looks upon worldly reality in terms of an Anglican sacramental theology.[28] But, if a creative dialogue is to develop between the expert and the theologian, our reflection on these problems in ecumenical circles must give more attention to the terms of the dicussion and explore further the lines suggested both directly and indirectly by Professor Munby.

It is our contention that a contextual theology and ethic offer creative possibilities at this point. When technical insight is set in the context of the humanizing activity of God, it makes sense to affirm that once the full facts are known, the appropriate action will follow. Along this road, it may be possible for theology to move into the center of the current struggle—rather than being, as is so often the case, a burden or an irrelevant factor for those who are involved in the secular world—and thus "assume its servant-critical function through which all the sciences may be summoned once again to their authentic humanistic occasion and promise."[29]

NOTES

Introduction: Religion, Ethics, and Society

1. For discussions of the general field of social ethics, see Walter G. Muelder, *Moral Law in Christian Social Ethics* (Richmond, Va.: John Knox Press, 1966); also Gibson Winter, *Elements for a Social Ethic* (New York: The Macmillan Co., 1966).

2. For an historical analysis of problems of social order, see the studies by Eric Voegelin which are summarized, at least in broad perspectives, in his volume, *The New Science of Politics* (Chicago: University of Chicago Press, 1952).

3. An extensive literature has emerged through the work on ethics by language analysts. These problems are taken up in another volume of this series of source books; however, a few suggestions for reading may be helpful to the reader, since problems of moral justification are an essential task within social ethics. See Henry David Aiken, *Reason and Conduct* (New York: Alfred A. Knopf, 1962); R. M. Hare, *The Language of Morals* (New York: Oxford University Press, Galaxy Book, 1965); William K. Frankena, *Ethics* (Englewood Cliffs, N.J.: Prentice-Hall, 1963).

4. For an analysis of the literature on this topic, see Gordon Allport, *The Nature of Prejudice* (Cambridge, Mass.: Addison-Wesley Pubs., 1954).

5. This approach to an understanding of culture and processes of reflection owes much to the work of Alfred Schutz; see references to this perspective in Winter, *op. cit.* The principal writings of Alfred Schutz are now available in three volumes of *Collected Essays* (The Hague: Martinus Nijhoff, 1962, 1964, 1966).

6. The term "societal identity" or "conditions" is developed in Winter, *op. cit.,* esp. Chap. 8.

7. Max Weber, "Politics as a Vocation" in *From Max Weber's Essays in Sociology,* Hans Gerth and C. Wright Mills, eds. (Fair Lawn, N.J.: Oxford University Press, 1946).

8. Cited by Walter Muelder, *op. cit.,* p. 19.

9. "Radical" is used here to mean cutting the roots of the ethical order by invoking a transcendent will which gives the power to discern the right decision without reference to rules, thus obviating any rational or ethical structures; for this view, see the writings of Joseph Fletcher, Paul Lehman, and Joseph Sittler.

I. ASSOCIATIONAL COMMUNITY

Towards a Quaker View of Sex,

by a Group of Friends

1. This was never suggested by Jesus, but seems to have come from Paul; see Rom. 5:12-14.

2. John Macmurray, *Reason and Emotion* (London: Faber & Faber, 1935), p. 132.

"On Taking Sexual Responsibility Seriously Enough,"

by Paul Ramsey

1. Friends Book Store, 302 Arch Street, Philadelphia 4, Pa., 75¢.
2. P. 45.
3. *Ibid.*
4. *Ibid.*
5. *Ibid.*
6. P. 39.
7. *Ibid.*
8. April 20, 1963.
9. P. 41.
10. "Taking Sex Seriously," Oct. 14, 1963.
11. William K. Frankena, *Ethics* (Englewood Cliffs, N. J.: 1963), pp. 43-44.
12. P. 40.

The Racial Problem in Christian Perspective,

by Kyle Haselden

1. Benjamin E. Mays, "The Moral Aspects of Segregation," published by the Southern Regional Council, republished by "Christian Community."

2. Reprinted by permission from the June 1956 issue of *Pastoral Psychology.* Copyright 1956 by Pastoral Psychology Press, Great Neck, N. Y.

3. Dred Scott v. Sanford (1857), 19 How. 393, 15 L.Ed. 691. For

this reference I am indebted to Judge Edward F. Waite, who "opened his eyes upon a torn and distracted country when the fires from the *Dred Scott* eruption were kindling civil war" and who died in 1958, dean of all men of good will in the upper Midwest. See: "The Negro in the Supreme Court" by him. 30 *Minnesota Law Review* 219-304, Minneapolis, 1946.

4. Erich Fromm, *The Art of Loving* (New York: Harper & Brothers, 1956), p. 18.

5. William Temple, *Christianity and the Social Order* (Harmondsworth, Middlesex, Eng.: Penguin Books, Pelican reprint, 1956), p. 20.

"Justice and Love,"
by E. Clinton Gardner

1. See *Southern School News,* Vol. 111, No. 3 (September, 1956) p. 5; Vol. 111, No. 4 (October, 1956), p. 10.

2. J. H. Oldham, ed., *The Oxford Conference: Official Report* (New York: Willett, Clark & Co., 1937), p. 78. Cf. "Churches and Segregation," an editorial in *Life,* Vol. 41, No. 14 (Oct. 1, 1956), p. 46.

3. *Basic Christian Ethics* (New York: Charles Scribner's Sons, 1950), p. 4 ff.

4. R. L. Kahn, "Kodesh, Mishpat, and Chesed," *Religion in Life,* Vol. XXV, No. 4 (Autumn, 1956), p. 581.

5. Ramsey *op. cit.,* p. 9.

6. Waldo Beach and H. Richard Niebuhr, *Christian Ethics* (New York: Ronald Press Co., 1955), p. 33.

7. *Ibid.,* p. 34.

8. *Love, Power, and Justice* (New York: Oxford University Press, 1954), p. 66.

9. Emil Brunner, following the Lutheran antimony between the social and personal spheres of ethics, falls into the same error as those who relegate love to personal relationships alone when he declares that "love knows naught of systems" (*Justice and the Social Order* [New York and London: Harper & Brothers, 1945], p. 116). See the criticisms of Brunner's position in Daniel Day Williams' *God's Grace and Man's Hope* (New York: Harper & Brothers, 1949), pp. 94 ff.; Paul Ramsey, *op. cit.,* pp. 2 ff.; and Reinhold Niebuhr, *The Nature and Destiny of Man,* Vol. II (New York: Charles Scribner's Sons, 1943), p. 251. Brunner is right, however, in seeing that the Aristotelian formula for distributive justice must be converted from the consideration of the contribution or merit of each to consideration of the need of each.

10. *Ibid.,* p. 248.

11. *Christian Ethics and Moral Philosophy* (New York: 1955), p. 254.

12. Cambridge, Mass: (Harvard University Press, 1954), p. 477.

13. *Op. cit.,* p. 102.

14. See Albert T. Rasmussen, *Christian Social Ethics* (Englewood Cliffs, N. J.: Prentice-Hall, 1956), p. 6.

15. *A Theological Conception of Goals for Economic Life,* A. Dudley Ward, ed. (New York: Harper & Brothers, 1953), p. 418; cf. Paul Tillich, *The Protestant Era* (Chicago: University of Chicago Press, 1948), p. xviii.

16. *Nature and Destiny of Man,* II, p. 246.

17. Reinhold Niebuhr, "The Christian Faith and the Economic Life" in *Goals for Economic Life, op. cit.,* p. 451.

18. Compare the incisive comment of Alexander Miller (*The Renewal of Man* [New York: Doubleday & Co., 1956], p. 126): "To give men bread is not to affirm that they live by bread alone, but to witness that we do not."

19. John A. Hutchison, ed., *Christian Faith and Social Action* (New York: Charles Scribner's Sons, 1953), p. 241.

II. ECONOMIC COMMUNITY

"Toward a Theory of Normative Economics,"

by Clark Kucheman

1. Paul Tillich, *Gesammelte Werke,* Vol. I: *Frühe Hauptwerke* (Stuttgart: Evangelishches Verlagswerk, 1959), p. 121.

2. Paul Tillich, *Systematic Theology,* Vol. III (Chicago: University of Chicago Press, 1963), pp. 27-28.

3. Paul Tillich, "Man and Society in Religious Socialism," *Christianity and Society* (Fall, 1943), p. 17.

4. While it will not be possible here to go into the problem in detail, it should be pointed out that this contention touches also upon the question of the defeasibility of prescriptive rules. According to the view I have taken, any particular rule of rightness or wrongness can be defeased—suspended—by an appeal to the principle of the common end. For example, lying is generally or *prima facie* wrong, or unfair, for the reason that it cannot be generalized. But if it should be necessary to lie, say, in order to save the life of someone being pursued by a madman, then it is clear that it is *better* to save the life of the person involved than to tell the truth. In such a case the rule against lying is defeased; in this instance it is wrong *not* to lie.

5. Paul Tillich, "Freedom in the Period of Transformation," in *Freedom: Its Meaning,* Ruth Nanda Anshen, ed. (New York: Harcourt, Brace & Co., 1940), p. 124.

6. Paul Tillich, "Man and Society in Religious Socialism," *op. cit.,* p. 17.

7. *Ibid.*

8. Paul Tillich, *Systematic Theology,* Vol. III, *op. cit.,* p. 40.

9. Paul Tillich, *Systematic Theology,* Vol. I (Chicago: University of Chicago Press, 1951), pp. 176-77.

10. Cf. Frank H. Knight, *The Economic Organization* (Chicago: University of Chicago Press, 1933), pp. 6-13.

11. This distinction is not the same as the distinction between socialism and capitalism. The latter distinction has to do with how productive property is owned rather than with who makes the economic decisions. In practice, however, the market does require, for the most part, private ownership of production property, although some degree of social ownership is not incompatible with it.

12. It should be pointed out, however, that much criticism of the market system in its "capitalist" form has to do with whether or not it *does* work. It is frequently argued, for example, that the system has defects such as cycles of prosperity and depression and a trend toward monopoly concentration. Although it is not feasible to discuss these issues here, I do not think criticisms such as these are correct. For it is possible to deal with cycles as well as with monopoly power within the framework of the market system; they do not amount to fundamental "contradictions" within market capitalism.

13. It is unnecessary to quibble about numbers here. One need only take a ride through the slums of Chicago, or through the rural South, to confirm the fact that poverty exists. However, it must be conceded that what is regarded as poverty is relative to circumstances. What is poverty in the United States is extreme wealth in, say, India.

14. Robert J. Lampman, "Income Distribution and Poverty," *Poverty in America,* Margaret S. Gordon, ed. (San Francisco: Chandler Publishing Co., 1965), p. 103.

15. Emanuel T. Weiler, "The Distribution of Income in the United States, 1959," *Economic Policy,* William D. Grampp and Emanuel T. Weiler, eds. (Homewood, Ill.: Richard D. Irwin, 1961), p. 187.

16. Milton Freidman, *Capitalism and Freedom* (Chicago: University of Chicago Press, 1962), pp. 190-95.

On The Development of Peoples,
by Pope Paul VI

1. Cf. *Acta Leonis* XIII, t. XI (1892), pp. 97-148.
2. Cf. AAS 23 (1931), pp. 177-228.
3. Cf. AAS 53 (1961), pp. 401–64.
4. Cf. AAS 55 (1963), pp. 257-304.
5. Cf. in particular the Radio Message of June 1, 1941, for the 50th anniversary of *Rerum Novarum,* in AAS 33 (1941), pp. 195-205; Christmas Radio Message of 1942, in AAS 35 (1943), pp. 9-24; Address to a group of workers on the anniversary of *Rerum Novarum,* May 14, 1953, in AAS 45 (1953), pp. 402-8.
6. Cf. Encyclical *Mater et Magistra,* May 15, 1961: AAS 53 (1961), p. 440.
7. *Gaudium et Spes,* nn. 63-72: AAS 58 (1966), pp. 1084-94.
8. *Motu Proprio Catholicam Christi Ecclesiam,* Jan. 6, 1967. AAS 59 (1967), p. 27.
9. Encyclical *Rerum Novarum,* May 15, 1891: *Acta Leonis* XIII, t. XI (1892), p. 98.

10. *Gaudium et Spes,* n. 63, § 3.
11. Cf. Lk 7: 22.
12. *Gaudium et Spes,* n. 3, § 2.
13. Cf. Encyclical *Immortale Dei,* Nov. 1, 1885: *Acta Leonis* XIII, t. V (1885), p. 127.
14. *Gaudium et Spes,* n. 4, § 1.
15. L.-J. Lebret, O.P., *Dynamique concrète du développement* (Paris: Économie et Humanisme, Les Éditions Ouvrières. 1961), p. 28.
16. 2 Thes 3: 10.
17. Cf., for example, J. Maritain, *Les conditions spirituelles du progrès et de la paix,* in *Rencontre des cultures à l'UNESCO sous le signe du Concile oecuménique Vatican II* (Paris: Mame, 1966), p. 66.
18. Cf. Mt. 5:3.
19. Address to the Representatives of non-Christian Religions, Dec. 3, 1964, AAS 57 (1965), p. 132.
20. Jas 2: 15-16.
21. Cf. *Mater et Magistra,* AAS 53 (1961), pp. 440 f.
22. Cf. AAS 56 (1964), pp. 57-58.
23. Cf. *Encicliche e Discorsi di Paolo VI,* Vol. IX, Roma, ed. Paoline, 1966, pp. 132-36, *Documentation catholique,* t. 43, Paris, 1966, col. 403-6.
24. Cf. Lk 16: 19-31.
25. *Gaudium et Spes,* n. 86, § 3.
26. Lk 12:20.
27. Message to the world, entrusted to Journalists on Dec. 4, 1964. Cf. AAS 57 (1965), p. 135.
28. Cf. AAS 56 (1964), pp. 639 f.
29. Cf. *Acta Leonis* XIII, t. XI (1892), p. 131.
30. AAS 57 (1965), p. 896.
31. Cf. Encyclical *Pacem in terris,* April 11, 1963, AAS 55 (1963), p. 301.
32. AAS 57 (1965), p. 880.

III. POLITICAL COMMUNITY

The Children of Light and the Children of Darkness,
by Reinhold Niebuhr

1. The success of Nazi diplomacy and propaganda in claiming the poor in democratic civilization as their allies against the "plutocrats" in one moment, and in the next seeking to ally the privileged classes in their battle against "communism," is a nice indication of the part which the civil war in democratic civilization played in allowing barbarism to come so near to a triumph over civilization.

2. John of Salisbury expresses a quite perfect rationalization of clerical political authority in his *Policraticus* in the twelfth century. He

writes: "Those who preside over the practice of religion should be looked up to and venerated as the soul of the body. . . . Furthermore since the soul is, as it were, the prince of the body and has a rule over the whole thereof, so those whom our author calls the prefects of religion preside over the entire body." Book V, Chap. ii.

A modern Catholic historian accepts this justification of clerical rule at its face value as he speaks of Machiavelli's politics as a "total assault upon the principles of men like John of Salisbury, preferring to the goodness of Christ, the stamina of Caesar." (Emmet John Hughes, *The Church and the Liberal Society* [Princeton, N.J.: Princeton University Press; London, H. Milford, Oxford University Press, 1944], p. 33.)

John of Salisbury's political principles were undoubtedly more moral than Machiavelli's. But the simple identification of his justification of clericalism with the "goodness of Christ" is a nice illustration of the blindness of the children of light, whether Christian or secular.

3. Matt. 10:39.

4. Thus vast collective forms of "free enterprise," embodied in monopolistic and large-scale financial and industrial institutions, still rationalize their desire for freedom from political control in terms of a social philosophy which Adam Smith elaborated for individuals. Smith was highly critical of the budding large-scale enterprise of his day and thought it ought to be restricted to insurance companies and banks.

5. *Wealth of Nations*, Book IV, Chap. 7.

6. *Ibid.*, Book V, Chap. 1, part 3.

7. John Locke, *Two Treatises on Government*, Book II, Chap. 2, part 6.

8. *Dissertations on Government, the Affairs of the Bank, and Paper-Money* (1786).

9. The peril of inflation which faces nations in wartime is a case in point. Each group seeks to secure a larger income, and if all groups succeeded, the gap between increased income and limited consumer goods available to satisfy consumer demand would be widened to the point at which all groups would suffer from higher prices. But this does not deter shortsighted groups from seeking special advantages which threaten the commonweal. Nor would such special advantage threaten the welfare of the whole, if it could be confined to a single group which desires the advantage. The problem is further complicated by the fact that an inflationary peril never develops in a "just" social situation. Some groups therefore have a moral right to demand that their share of the common social fund be increased before the total situation is "frozen." But who is to determine just how much "injustice" can be redressed by a better distribution of the common fund in wartime, before the procedure threatens the whole community?

10. William Godwin, *Political Justice*, Book VIII, Chap. ix.

11. Lenin, *Toward the Seizure of Power*, Vol. II, p. 214.

12. "Your first duty," wrote Mazzini, "first as regards importance, is toward humanity. You are men before you are citizens and fathers. If you do not embrace the whole human family in your affections, if you do not bear witness to the unity of that family, if—you are not ready, if

able, to aid the unhappy,—you violate your law of life and you comprehend not that religion which will be the guide and blessing of the future."

Mazzini held kings responsible for national egotism: "The first priests of the fatal worship [of self-interest] were the kings, princes and evil governments. They invented the horrible formula: every one for himself. They knew that they would thus create egoism and that between the egoist and the slave there is but one step." *The Duties of Man,* Chap. xii.

13. G. W. F. Hegel, *Philosophy of Mind,* sec. II, par. 539.

14. J. G. Fichte, "Patriotische Dialoge," in *Nachegelassene Werker,* Vol. III, p. 226.

15. G. W. F. Hegel, *Saemmtliche Werker,* Vol. III, p. 74.

16. Hegel, *Philosophy of Right,* par. 33.

17. *Philosophy of Mind,* sec. II, par. 552.

The Good City,
by Lawrence Haworth

1. Le Corbusier, *The Home of Man,* Clive Entwistle trans. (London: Architectural Press, 1948), p. 62.

2. The conception of community developed here is in a tradition that extends from Hegel's *Philosophy of Right* to Dewey's *Individualism Old and New.* Community, as I have defined it, is approximately the same condition as that which Hegel identifies as "Ethical Life," a synthesis of "Abstract Right" and "Morality." The English Hegelians, especially Bradley and Bosanquet, work with a similar ideal, and Bosanquet, in the concluding chapter of *The Philosophical Theory of the State,* uses the notion to identify the ethical significance of the neighborhood in urban life. In *Individualism Old and New,* Dewey restates the Hegelian triad by describing modern urban life as essentially "corporate." However, the corporateness is external, that is, it is a mechanical system of interdependent activity, and the problem is to internalize it. External corporateness replaces Hegel's "Abstract Right," and internal corporateness, which replaces "Ethical Life," arises, as in the case of Hegel, when individual volition converts the necessities of the corporate order into opportunities. The essential difference between Dewey and Hegel is that Dewey regards this process of internalization as one which reshapes the external order, so that it signifies democratic control, whereas Hegel regards the process more nearly as one of accommodation to fixed arrangements. On this score, the position adopted here, is of course, in agreement with that of Dewey.

3. The literature, running the gamut from Erich Fromm to Vance Packard, is well known. Probably no one book, with the possible exception of Riesman's *The Lonely Crowd,* draws together all the strands. As a result, the account in the text is a montage.

4. See Jane Jacobs, "Downtown Is for People," in *The Exploding Metropolis,* the Editors of *Fortune,* eds. (New York: Doubleday & Co., 1958), pp. 157-84, for a brief statement of her view of the importance

of the street and a criticism of superblocks and similar projects that deaden urban life by denuding the street. There is a danger that a view such as this, though basically sound, will be overstated, as would be the case if it were used to criticize the concept of a superblock project instead of to suggest alterations that would make the project area a lively and exciting place. The principal alteration needed is the inclusion of a wide range of community facilities, so that the project becomes something more than a dormitory. These remarks are particularly applicable to the neighborhood unit plan discussed in the following chapter.

5. "The tenants usually pay only enough to cover maintenance costs. Capital charges in big projects run to more than $13,000 per unit and are sometimes as high as $20,000." Daniel Seligman, "The Enduring Slums," in *The Exploding Metropolis, op. cit.,* p. 126.

IV. GLOBAL COMMUNITY

Peace on Earth,

by Pope John XXIII

1. Cf. Pius XII Broadcast Message, Christmas 1942, AAS 35 (1943), pp. 9-24; and John XXIII Sermon, Jan. 4, 1963, AAS 55 (1963), pp. 89-91.

2. Cf. Pius XI Encyclical *Divini Redemptoris,* AAS 29 (1937), p. 78; and Pius XII Broadcast Message, Whitsun June 1, 1941, AAS 33 (1941), pp. 195-205.

3. Cf. Pius XII Broadcast Message, Christmas 1942, AAS 35 (1943), pp. 9-24.

4. *Divinae Institutiones,* lib. IV, c. 28, 2; PL. 6, 535.

5. Encyclical *Libertas Praestantissimum. Acta Leonis* XIII, VIII, 1888, pp. 237-38.

6. Cf. Pius XII Broadcast Message, Christmas 1942, AAS 35 (1943), pp. 9-24.

7. Cf. Pius XI Encyclical *Casti Connubii,* AAS 22 (1930), pp. 539-592; and Pius XII Broadcast Message, Christmas 1942, AAS 35 (1943), pp. 9-24.

8. Cf. Pius XII Broadcast Message, Whitsun, June 1, 1941, AAS 33 (1941), p. 201.

9. Cf. Leo XIII Encyclical *Rerum Novarum, Acta Leonis* XIII, XI, 1891, pp. 128-29.

10. Cf. John XXIII Encyclical *Mater et Magistra,* AAS 53 (1961), p. 422.

11. Cf. Pius XII Broadcast Message, Whitsun, June 1, 1941, AAS 33 (1941), p. 201.

12. John XXIII Encyclical *Mater et Magistra,* AAS 53 (1961), p. 428.

13. Cf. *ibid.,* p. 430.

14. Cf. Leo XIII Encyclical *Rerum Novarum, Acta Leonis* XIII, XI, 1891, pp. 134-42; Pius XI Encyclical *Quadragesimo Anno,* AAS 23

(1931), pp. 199-200; and Pius XII Encyclical *Sertum Laetitiae,* AAS 31 (1939), pp. 635-44.

15. Cf. AAS 53 (1961), p. 430.

16. Cf. Pius XII Broadcast Message, Christmas 1952, AAS 45 (1953), pp. 33-46.

17. Cf. Pius XII Broadcast Message, Christmas 1944, AAS 37 (1945), p. 12.

18. Cf. Pius XII Broadcast Message, Christmas 1942, AAS 35 (1943), p. 21.

19. *Eph.* 4:25.

20. Cf. Pius XII Broadcast Message, Christmas 1942, AAS 35 (1943), p. 14.

21. *Summa Theol.,* Ia-IIae, q. 19, a. 4; cf. a. 9.

22. *Wis.* 6:2-4.

23. Cf. Pius XII Broadcast Message, Christmas 1941, AAS 34 (1942), p. 16.

24. Cf. Pius XII Broadcast Message, Christmas 1940, AAS 33 (1941), pp. 5-14.

25. *De civitate Dei,* lib. IV, c. 4; PL. 41, 115; Cf. Pius XII Broadcast Message, Christmas 1939, AAS 32 (1940), pp. 5-13.

26. Cf. Pius XII Broadcast Message, Christmas 1941, AAS 34 (1942), pp. 10-21.

27. Cf. John XXIII Encyclical *Mater et Magistra,* AAS 53 (1961), p. 439.

28. Cf. Pius XII Broadcast Message, Christmas 1941, AAS 34 (1942), p. 17; and Benedict XV exhortation to the Rulers of the belligerent Powers, Aug. 1, 1917, AAS 9 (1917), p. 418.

29. Cf. Pius XII Broadcast Message, Aug. 24, 1939, AAS 31 (1939), p. 334.

30. AAS 53 (1961), pp. 440-41.

31. Cf. Pius XII Broadcast Message, Christmas 1941, AAS 34 (1942), pp. 16-17.

32. John XXIII Encyclical *Mater et Magistra,* AAS 53 (1961), p. 443.

33. Cf. Pius XII Allocution to Young Members of Italian Catholic Action, Rome, Sept. 12, 1948, AAS 40 (1948), p. 412.

"Revolutionary Change in Theological Perspective,"
by Richard Shaull

1. London; Edinburgh House Press, 1964.

2. By "ontocratic," Professor Van Leeuwen means having an understanding of reality in terms of a total order of harmony between the eternal and the temporal, the divine and the human. The divine order is identified with nature and society, especially with the state conceived of as the "embodiment of cosmic totality." All structures of society are given a sacred character; they dare not be tampered with or changed.

3. Eric Hoffer, commenting on the Negro revolution in the United States, writes: "Mass movements are often the means by which a popula-

tion undergoing drastic change acquires a sense of rebirth and a new identity." *New York Times Magazine,* Nov. 29, 1964, p. 109.

4. For an interesting discussion of this thesis, see the paper by B. Morel: "L'Avenir du ministère de l' Eglise dans un monde en voie de sécularisation," *Bulletin du Centre Protestant d'Études,* Geneva Vol. XIV, No. 4 (June 1962). Taking as his starting point a recent discussion, in anthropology, of the role of *interdit* and *transgression* in the social sphere, he suggests that the task of preserving certain *interdits,* formerly exercised by the church, has now passed to secular institutions, and that the church is now called to be a force of *transgression* against the limitations imposed by such restrictions.

5. See I Sam. 2:1-10; Ps. 9, 72, 146.

6. *The Doctrine of the Holy Spirit* (Richmond, Va.: John Knox Press, 1964), p. 102.

7. Christianity and Classical Culture (New York: Oxford University Press, 1940).

8. *Ibid.,* p. 456.

9. *Ibid.,* p. 480.

10. *Ibid.,* p. 384.

11. *The City of God,* X, 2.

12. *Ibid.,* XIX, 13.

13. *Ibid.*

14. Speaking of the Romans who were upset by the crisis of the empire, Augustine says, "If they only had sense, they would see that the hardships and cruelties they suffered from the enemy came from that Divine Providence who makes use of war to reform the corrupt lives of men." *The City of God,* I, 1.

15. See his development of this theme in "The Dynamics of Reformation Ethics," *Princeton Seminary Bulletin,* Vol. XLIII, No. 4 (Spring, 1950), pp. 17-22.

16. See his *Ethics in a Christian Context* (New York: Harper & Row, 1963), esp. Chap. 3.

17. Paul L. Lehmann, *Ideology and Incarnation* (Geneva: John Knox House, 1962), p. 24.

18. *Ibid.*

19. Interesting examples of this are provided by the civil rights struggle in the United States. A small group of Negro and white students organizes a sit-in at a few lunch counters in an Alabama city. They do not accomplish their immediate objective, yet they spark off a movement that affects the entire country. Other similar efforts fail, but they do lead to the adoption of civil rights legislation by Congress, which changes the pattern of race relations at many points.

20. *Background Information,* World Council of Churches, No. 32 (February, 1964), pp. 1-9.

21. *Ibid.,* p. 3.

22. This unresolved tension, with its consequences, is evident especially in the Evanston Report. The introductory statement ends thus: "Our hope in Christ does not offer technical answers of specific solutions which statesmen and experts have not found. But in the context

of Christian faith, we gain new insights into our dilemmas and ways to overcome them." Rather than pursuing this line, the report then moves into anthropology and natural law, defining a responsible society, which provides "a criterion by which we judge all existing orders and at the same time a standard to guide us in the specific choices we have to make."

23. *Ethics in a Christian Context, op. cit.*, p. 141.

24. London: Oxford University Press, 1963.

25. In *Essays in Anglican Self-Criticism*, D. M. Paton, ed. (London: SCM Press, 1958).

26. *Ibid.*, p. 47.

27. *The Idea of a Secular Society, op. cit.*, p. 26.

28. *Ibid.*, pp. 89-91.

29. Paul L. Lehmann, "The Formative Power of Particularity," *Union Seminary Quarterly Review*, Vol. XVIII, No. 3, ii (March 1963), p. 318.